291.42
So 4   Solomon, Victor.
a   A handbook on conversions
       to the religions of the world.

Temple Israel
Library
Minneapolis, Minn.

Please sign your full name on the above
card.

Return books promptly to the Library or
Temple Office.

Fines will be charged for overdue books
or for damage or loss of same.

A HANDBOOK ON
CONVERSIONS
TO THE RELIGIONS
OF THE WORLD

a handbook on
CONVERSIONS
to the religions of the world

VICTOR SOLOMON, B.A., M.A., S.T.D.

stravon educational press

©

Copyright MCMLXV

by

STRAVON PUBLISHERS

Library of Congress Catalog Card Number: 65-22701

Manufactured in the United States of America

To my beloved wife
Marcia
This book is affectionately dedicated

She openeth her mouth with wisdom;
And in her tongue is the law of kindness.

(Proverbs 31:26)

Preface

MILTON'S OBSERVATION THAT "Heav'ns high behest no Preface needs" does not fit this volume, which touches on spiritual and heavenly matters. A few prefatory remarks are in order to bring into focus certain considerations essential to a full understanding of this book.

Religion continues to be one of the most potent factors influencing the lives of millions throughout the world, despite the jeremiads of yesterday's prophets of gloom. Religious institutions continue to be built. People still pattern their lives according to religious creeds, suffer persecution for their religious beliefs, and accept martyrdom in the name of religion in awakening areas of the world.

Every year, uncounted men and women, for a variety of reasons, elect to "convert" or change their religious affiliation. Some do so in response to a call of conscience, a new insight, an inner spiritual need. Others have more "practical" considerations, such as marriage or social convenience. Many are unable to explain their reasons for changing faiths. Among the legions of people in search of a new faith can be found vast numbers who wander aimlessly for want of direction and guidance.

The purpose of this book is *not* to encourage conversion. On the contrary, it is hoped that many a reader will be helped to find the road *back to his own faith!* This book can serve as an effective antidote to prevent impulsive, reckless, superficial conversions by providing a sobering study of the facts.

Young people on the threshhold of an interfaith marriage may, through it, be influenced to think carefully before dashing impetuously into the maze of commitments, implications, and religious changes involved in such a marriage.

What makes this book unique is that it is the first serious attempt at a presentation of data on conversion to most world religions, with straightforward descriptive introductions explaining the basic tenets of each faith. As for the omission of a number of independent Protestant church groups, this was deemed essential to avoid unnecessary repetition. I gratefully acknowledge my indebtedness to the publisher and the editors for their invaluable guidance and suggestions, which resulted in editorial surgery performed with anesthesia and skill. My appreciation also goes out to the many church leaders, rabbis, scholars, lay dignitaries and clergymen of every persuasion who, with faith in the positive value of this work, were exceedingly helpful in providing facts and figures.

And at the top of my "thank you" list, is my beloved Marcia, the "woman of valor" who gave unselfishly of her time, and paid for neglect—the fate of many a writer's wife—with the currency of cheerful inspiration and sage advice.

Finally, a prayer of thanksgiving to the Father of all, whose love and mercy endure forever. To Him I turn with the plea of David: *Who can understand his errors? Cleanse Thou me from secret faults* (Psalm 19:12).

Victor Solomon
Fairfield, Conn.
February 24, 1965

Publisher's Note

THE AUTHOR has included in this work most of the major as well as the less familiar religions and quasi-religious groups here and abroad. Several religious bodies were purposely omitted because the conversion data relevant to these groups is similar to information the reader can glean from chapters presented herein.

Conversion procedures for the various divisions of Christianity are discussed under three general headings: Roman Catholicism, Eastern Orthodox Church, and Protestantism. Those Christian movements that do not consider themselves as a part of any of these three are to be found in the section OTHER DENOMINATIONS, BELIEFS, AND PHILOSOPHIES.

In the interest of simplifying matters for the reader, the publisher has transposed all dates—of whatever calendars—to the nearest date in the Gregorian calendar, the one now in general use. The responsibility for this arrangement is exclusively that of the publisher and does not in any way reflect the theological thinking of the author.

Acknowledgments

Grateful acknowledgment is made to the following for permission to quote copyright material listed below:

The Macmillan Company, New York, from *The Spirit of Catholicism* by Karl Adam, and from *A Catholic Dictionary* by Attwater.

Hebrew Publishing Co., New York, from *The Reverend's Handbook* edited by S. Druckerman.

Pardes Publishing House, Inc., New York, from *Jewish Religion* by Dr. Michael Friedlander.

Bloch Publishing Co., Inc., New York, from *The Hertz Daily Prayer Book* edited by Dr. Joseph Hertz.

Central Conference of American Rabbis, New York, from *Rabbi's Manual*, from *Judaism*, and from the *C.C.A.R. Year Book*, 1957.

Philadelphia Yearly Meeting of Friends, Philadelphia, from *How To Become a Member of the Religious Society of Friends*, and from *Quaker Worship—An Invitation*.

Joint Department of Evangelism of the National Council of Churches, New York, from "Protestantism Affirms" by Winfred E. Garrison in *World Call*.

Mennonite Publishing House, Scottsdale, Pa., from *Confession of Faith* and from *Minister's Manual* by J. F. Funk.

The Rabbinical Assembly, New York, from the *Rabbinical Assembly Manual* edited by Rabbi Isadore Singer.

New York Federation of Reform Synagogues, New York (An Agency of the Union of American Hebrew Congregations), from *How To Become a Jew* by Rabbi Daniel L. Davis.

Sherwood Presbyterian Church, Washington, D.C., from *So You Are Going To Be a Presbyterian* by Dr. Carl G. Howie.

American Lutheran Publicity Bureau, St. Louis, Mo., from *How To Join the Lutheran Church*.

Sivananda Yoga Vedanta Centre, Montreal, Canada, from *What Is Yoga?*

The Russian Orthodox Year Book, New York, from the "Introduction" by Reverend Alexander Schmemann.

Publication Data of the Chicago Rabbinical Council, from *Thy People Shall Be My People* by Rabbi Aaron M. Rine.

Union Theological Seminary, New York, from *A Guide to the Religions of America* by Dr. Henry D. Van Dusen.

Buddhist Churches of America, San Francisco, from *Membership Data*.

The Judson Press, Valley Forge, Pa., from *Why I Am a Baptist* by J. Sherman Wallace.

National Council of Churches, New York, from *The Yearbook of American Churches* (1963) edited by Benson Y. Landis.

World Council of Churches, Geneva, Switzerland, from *Ye Are Baptized* by Dr. Lucas Vischer.

United Presbyterian Church in the United States of America, Division of Evangelism, New York, from *My Certificate of Church Membership.*

Knights of Columbus, St. Louis, Mo., from Data on Conversion.

Central Offices of the Society of Friends, London, England, from *Christian Discipline in the Religious Society of Friends in Great Britain.*

Watchtower Bible and Tract Society of New York, Inc., from *Which Is the Right Religion?*

Macmillan & Co. Ltd., London, England, from *Truth in Religion and Other Sermons* by Claude G. Montefiore.

Reformed Church in America, New York, from *The Liturgy of the Reformed Church in America.*

United Church of Christ, Division of Publication, New York, from their Evangelism forms.

The Church of Jesus Christ of Latter-day Saints, Salt Lake City, from *About Mormonism* by Stephen L. Richards, and from *After Baptism What?* by Mark E. Petersen.

National Spiritual Assembly of the Baha'is of the United States, Wilmette, Ill., from *Baha'i Answers.*

Trustees Under the Will of Mary Baker Eddy, Boston, Mass., from *The Church Manual.*

The Mercier Press Ltd., Cork, Ireland, from *A Handbook for Converts* by Reverend A. Bullen.

Rosicrucian Order (A.M.O.R.C.), San Jose, Calif., from their membership literature.

The American Ethical Union, New York, from *What is an Ethical Culture Society?*

American Unitarian Association, Boston, from *Meet the Unitarians* by Reverend Jack Mendelsohn.

General Brotherhood Board, Church of the Brethren, The Brethren Press, Elgin, Ill., from *What Does Church Membership Mean* by Rufus D. Bowman.

Lutheran Church in America, The Commission on Evangelism, New York, from *An Invitation* and from *Do You Know the Answer?*

Founding Church of Scientology, L. Ron Hubbard, Washington, D.C., from *What Is Scientology?*

I wish to express my sincere appreciation to the following individuals for their counsel and cooperation:

Father Gregory Adakr, Reverend Hampton Adams, Shahid M. Amin, Dr. Reginald C. Armor, George J. Bacoulos, Dr. Jesse M. Bader, Dr. Andrew Bagley, Dr. Ralph G. Calder, Rabbi Hershel Cohen, Father Christopher Condeleon, Dastur Khurshed S. Dabu, Reverend Max F. Daskam, Dr. Daniel L. Davis, Reverend Dale De Witt, Father Divine, Arthur Dore, Monsignor Francis X. Duffy, Dr. David Max Einhorn, Dr. Ira Eisenstein, Dr. Willis E. Elliott, Monsignor Emilianos Bishop of Meloa, The Very Reverend Alexander J. Federenko, Martha Feldstein, Kenneth W. Finlay, Reverend John Fudge, Reverend K. Fujinaya, Dr. Ora W. Garber, Reverend Garen Gdanian, Colonel John Grace, Mustapha Hashim, Reverend David M. Henkelmann, Dr. Horatio S. Hill, Dr. Mahmoud Hoballah, Reverend Donald W. Hoffman, Dr. Gerald J. Jud, Consul Z. L. Kaul, Dr. Peter L. Kjeseth, Suk Tal Limb, Dr. Sheldon E. Mackey, Reverend Jack Mendelsohn, Reverend Lewis S. Mudge, Dr. Paul Myers, Swami Nikhilananda, Reverend William A. Norgren, Dr. Hugo L. Odhner, Dr. H. Talbot Pearson, Arthur C. Piepenbrink, Dr. Dan M. Potter, Dr. Sidney L. Regner, Reverend Cecil Rhoades, Sophia A. Rieger, Rabbi Aaron M. Rine, Reverend Vincent M. Ross, Dr. Ermanno Rostan, Ruth F. Sasaki, Reverend Alexander Schmemann, Reverend Milton Cox Sealey, Akil Serdaroglu, Blanche W. Shaffer, Dr. Mahmoud Youssef Shawarbi, Dr. Franklin I. Sheeden, Bishop Fulton J. Sheen, Dr. N. Shoreibah, Reverend Leon A. Smith, Reverend Neophytos Spyros, Reverend J. Sabin Swenson, Reverend Richard H. Tafel, Reverend Takashi Tsuji, Dr. Henry D. Van Dusen, Dr. Ernest A. Villas, Dr. Lukas Vischer, Dr. Leroy H. Walker, Dr. Robert S. Wilson, Reverend Theodore Wittrock, Dr. Morris Wolf, Reverend Melvin C. de Workeen, Reverend Nelson Ying, Jr., Dr. Mohammed Zarmegar, Dr. Ellrose D. Zook.

PICTURE ACKNOWLEDGMENTS

Air France, 80; Baha'i Publications, 366; B.O.A.C., 260, 345; China News Service, 270; Congregation Emanu-El of the City of New York, 63; Consulate General of Japan, N.Y., 269; Ewing Galloway, 140; Information Service of India, 281, 285, 308, 313; Israel Information Services, 30, 44, 54, 57, 65, 363; Japan Air Lines, 277, 279, 297, 301; Japan Information Service, 276; Jordan Tourist Department, 106, 250; Religious News Service, 28, 68, 70, 73, 76, 86, 100, 104, 109, 110, 114, 118, 147, 151, 156, 160, 164, 174, 177, 191, 197, 201, 207, 212, 225, 230, 242, 244, 246, 256, 289, 311, 326, 336, 339, 341, 352; Rhode Island Development Council, 34; UNESCO/Cart, 293; United Nations, 266; United Press International, 272, 317; Utah Tourist & Publicity Council, 332

Contents

Islam

Indian and Far Eastern Religions

Other Denominations, Beliefs, and Philosophies

Glossary

List of Illustrations

Judaism

A Torah scroll

Introduction—Judaism

THE JEWISH RELIGION MAY be described as a system of faith and action bounded by ritual and ethics. In many ways, Judaism defies definition. It is the oldest of the important monotheistic religions; yet, there is no biblical Hebrew word for "religion." It is a way of life; yet, it concerns the mysteries of another world. Judaism preaches a universal message, but also cultivates ethnic and national values.

Judaism is dedicated to the sanctification of time, through the Sabbath and Holy Seasons, and the sanctification of space, through the Holy Land, the Temple, and other concrete instruments of spiritual abstractions used in the fulfillment of *mitzvoth* or "Divine Commandments."

To a Jew, Judaism represents a commitment to a sacred vocation. He is a member of a divinely ordained Kingdom of Priests, a Holy Nation charged with the unceasing task of witnessing for God.

Judaism is basically a non-proselytizing religion. However, several Jewish organizations have recently been founded for conducting missionary activities. One of these groups, the Jewish Information Society,[1] hopes

1. The Jewish Information Society lists several prominent rabbis on its roster. Headquarters are located at 127 Dearborn St., Chicago, Ill.

to convert the great body of uncommitted Gentiles to the Jewish faith. The constitution of the Jewish Information Society clearly defines its aims:

> The purposes of the *Jewish Information Society* are the propagation and dissemination by means of lectures, pamphlets, books and by such other means as may be deemed suitable, of the views of God, Man and the World as set forth in the basic tenets of Judaism, and expounded and explained in the Hebrew Bible and in the Jewish Tradition, and to unite all the people of the world in a commitment to the One Universal God and the Brotherhood of Man.

Some Jewish leaders have advocated a concerted effort on the part of the leadership of Jewish organizations to launch a missionary program among the unaffiliated Gentile population in the Western world and Japan.

Dr. Morris Goodblatt, director of the Academy of Judaism, an information center for prospective converts established by the Conservative movement within Judaism in Philadelphia, Pennsylvania, suggests:

> Jews ought to steer clear of any form of aggressive missionizing since it is both undignified and often futile. There is but one way to deal with this problem, namely, to follow the indirect approach. The Jew of today can win respect for his faith and impress non-Jews with the great worth and effectiveness of Judaism by demonstrating that adherence to it makes a substantial difference in his personal life and his moral conduct. He can show that living as a Jew has molded him into an attractive and ethical personality, that the name "Jew" symbolizes affiliation with a

spiritual aristocracy and dignified way of winning converts to Judaism.[2]

The mildness of Dr. Goodblatt's position should not devaluate the significant fact that a Conservative group has seen fit to create an institution for purposes of preparing prospective converts.

An attitude similar to that of Dr. Goodblatt is discernible in a view expressed by a prominent Orthodox spokesman, a former Chief Rabbi of Great Britain, in a sermon entitled "Is Judaism A Missionary Faith?":

> Judaism has in very truth a missionary vocation to fulfill, in the highest and noblest sense of the term, a propagandism which does not rest on the imperfect agency of human words and human persuasion, but on the silent moral force of truth, truth which must and will prevail. The missionary labours of Judaism must be carried on in calm and dignified silence, by showing the world that adherence to our faith constitutes our life and our happiness, by helping to destroy prejudice and error, and by teaching the world the holy truths enshrined in the book of books.[3]

Spokesmen of Orthodox Judaism and of Israel have also expressed aversion to the use of overly vigorous techniques in winning adherents to the Jewish faith. Yaacov Shimoni, director-general of the Asian Division at the Israeli Ministry of Foreign Affairs, expressed his disapproval of the intention of "certain Israelis to create a missionary movement in Japan" in response to a wide interest shown in that country in

2. *The Jewish Exponent,* May 11, 1962.
3. As quoted in Claude G. Montefiore, *Truth in Religion and Other Sermons* (London: Macmillan and Co., Ltd., 1906), p. 26.

Judaism. He pointed out that the intellectual interest in Judaism current in Japan today should not be misinterpreted as a burning desire for conversion. "He then emphasized that Asian nations generally have a distaste for missionaries, and for any attempt by one religion to claim superiority over others." [4]

Before discussing the practical steps for conversion to Judaism, including the requirements for eligibility, the manner of application, the rituals and ceremonies involved, and the diverse attitudes of the groups within Judaism, it would be useful, as an aid to understanding, to explore the background of conversion in Jewish history.

Hebrew Scripture abounds in references to the universal message of Judaism: Israel is appointed to be "a light of the nations." (Isaiah 42: 1-8) Jonah is sent to preach to the Gentiles of Nineveh. The heroine of the Book of Ruth is a Moabitess who embraced Judaism; she was, nevertheless, deemed worthy to be the ancestress of David and the messianic line.

Many biblical statements regarding the *ger*, which is usually translated as "stranger," actually refer to the proselyte. In the Mosaic legislation, the convert is given status, rights, and protection. According to the lyrical words of Isaiah:

> Also the sons of the stranger, that join themselves unto the Lord, to serve Him, and to love the name of the Lord, to be unto Him as servants, every one that keepeth the Sabbath by not violating it, and those who take hold of My covenant. Even these will I bring to My holy mountains, and make them joyful in My house

4. *The Young Israel Viewpoint*, May 7, 1962 (from an item datelined Jerusalem).

of prayer; their burnt-offerings and their sacri-
fices shall be accepted upon My altar; for My
house shall be called a house of prayer for all
the nations. (Isaiah, 56: 6-7)

In spite of this universalistic spirit characteristic
of the Bible, one searches in vain for any systematic
procedure for conversion.

Occasionally, however, there were periods when
large numbers of people converted to Judaism. A ferment of proselytizing activities, facilitated by the dis-
persion of the Jews throughout the Mediterranean
world, occurred in the Hellenistic period. A vast body
of Gentiles who were dissatisfied with paganism came
into contact with Jews and adopted their religion. The
Maccabean victories, which tended to raise the prestige
of the Jews and their religion, encouraged additional
conversions. Josephus, the historian, records the inclina-
tion of a multitude of Gentiles to follow the religious
observances of Judaism. Abundant evidence testifying
to this fact can be found in the literature of Greece
and Rome.

Even in this period, however, the official spokesmen and teachers of Judaism refused to sanction an
aggressive missionary program. They were unalterably
opposed to the least use of violence or compulsion.
The only instance of coercive conversion occurred during the reign of John Hyrcanus and his successors, who
forcibly converted the Idumeans and other kindred
tribes. The rabbis frowned upon this deviation from
normal Jewish practice, and expressed their condemna-
tion by omitting from rabbinic literature any direct
reference to this improper act.

During this period one of the celebrated conversions took place when the royal family of Adiabene,
a Hellenistic state on the Tigris River, embraced the

Jewish religion. They remained constant in their devotion to their adopted faith through all the vicissitudes that followed.

The talmudic period which followed brought with it a renewed interest in Judaism throughout the Roman Empire. Large numbers of aristocrats and commoners embraced the Jewish faith. Many others joined circles of "semi-proselytes" who lived according to some of the tenets of Judaism. The Gospel writer's complaint that Pharisees "compass sea and land to make one proselyte" (Matthew 23: 15) may have been a hyperbolic reaction to the ferment current during that period. At this time much religious legislation pertaining to conversion was enacted.

When Christianity became the official religion of the Roman Empire, prohibitions against conversion to Judaism brought this chapter of missionary activity to a close. The Magian persecutions in Babylon and the rise of an active proselytizing program among the Muslims along the southern shores of the Mediterranean extended the area in which Judaism could not be propagated.

During the Middle Ages, proselytizing by Jews was extremely rare. The earlier enactments forbidding conversion were strictly enforced. An eminent Christian scholar has this to say: "For the proselyte-maker, the legislation went on to equate the crime to *laesa maiestas* (treason), and finally made it simply capital, whether the convert was freeman or slave. Against all such attempts of pagan or Christian rulers to shut up Judaism in itself and prevent its spread, the Jews persisted in their missionary efforts to make the religion God had revealed to their fathers the religion of all mankind." [5]

5. George Foote Moore, *Judaism* (Cambridge: Harvard University Press, 1927), I, 353.

One of the chief instruments used to halt conversions to Judaism in the Middle Ages was the ghetto, which simply prevented Jews and Christians from coming into contact with each other. Other prophylactic measures included a rule that a non-Jew might not reside in a Jewish home, and wholesale massacres or the expulsion of an entire community in which a conversion took place.

A more effective measure was adopted by the synagogue itself. From the ninth century onward, records show that rabbinical authorities forbade any form of proselytizing.

Nevertheless, this did not discourage many individuals from converting to Judaism. Some of them, like Rabbi Abraham the Proselyte, a French *Tosafist* (one who interprets the Talmud), attained great prominence in the Jewish community. Many of these proselytes, however, were destined for martyrdom.

Judah Halevi, the medieval Hebrew poet and philosopher, perpetuated one of the great conversion stories in his philosophic work, *Sefer ha-Kuzari*.[6] The book is the lyrical record of the conversion to Judaism of the royalty, nobility, and many of the common people of the Khazars, a proud and fierce people inhabiting what is now southeastern Russia. This was the last major conversion effort by Jews.

Modern times found quasi-Jewish sects (of former Christians) in Russia and Transylvania seeking admission into the Jewish fold. Many of them had never come in contact with Jews, so their interest in Judaism was certainly not the result of any Jewish effort.

The rise of Reform Judaism in the last century created a new interest in bringing the message of Juda-

6. *Kitab al-Khazari,* trans. Hartwig Hirschfeld (London: George Routledge and Sons, 1905).

The Wailing Wall, a holy place of the Jews, is the only extant piece of the western wall of the Temple of Solomon at Jerusalem

ism to the world. Conversion requirements were relaxed and simplified in order to encourage Gentiles to adopt the Jewish religion. In 1891, the Central Conference of American Rabbis, the organized Reform rabbinate in America, suspended the traditional requirement of circumcision. The conversion ceremony was greatly simplified and made less "frightening" to the newcomer.

Many American Jews today display a keen interest in increasing their ranks through conversion. Many leaders in the Reform and Conservative branches of Judaism support this interest. However, no clear-cut program has yet been devised to translate this idea into action.

The Orthodox view remains steadfast in its opposition to any missionary program. In the words of the Chicago Rabbinical Council: "The Jewish Community does not seek converts because in heaven there is room for the righteous of all nations." On the other hand, Orthodox Judaism does not shut the door to prospective converts who come of their own accord.

Judaism welcomes sincere converts. Although the less traditional quarters favor an active missionary effort, all groups share the traditional reluctance to engage in a militant program of missionary activities. They confine their work to the dissemination of appropriate literature and the practical preparation of agencies and institutions to facilitate such a program.

Orthodoxy, even though opposed to any form of active solicitation, welcomes any sincere candidate whose motives are beyond question and who is prepared to follow the Jewish way of life as outlined in the religious classics of Judaism. The ritual of conversion, as developed and defined in rabbinic literature, includes the requirements of preparatory instruction, circumcision, Ritual Immersion, and the acceptance of

Remains of Beth Shearim, the residence of Rabbi Judah, the redactor of the Mishna

all that is implied by Judaism.

Conservative Judaism does not deviate from the traditional requirements; however, individual officiating rabbis show wide latitude in the practical application of the requirements. The Reconstructionist wing of the Conservative movement is more flexible regarding the requirements of ritual immersion.

Reform Judaism, in keeping with its general philosophy, rejects the traditional rites of circumcision and Ritual Immersion. The candidate must agree to be loyal to the tenets of Reform Judaism, with emphasis on the ethical teachings of the faith.

All groups discourage mixed marriages. No rabbi, with the exception of a minority in the Reform rabbinate, will solemnize such marriages.

1
Orthodox Judaism

O RTHODOX JEWS HAVE SUBSCRIBED to a clearly defined conversion procedure since antiquity. The substance of the generally accepted steps is as follows. An applicant presents himself, of his own free will, before a *beth din* and requests admission. The *beth din* makes an exhaustive study of the motives which led the prospective convert to make his decision. Then the candidate is informed about the difficulties involved in the Jewish observances—the heavy burdens implied in the "Yoke of Torah" [1] that every Jew carries throughout life. The candidate is also enlightened about the many problems he must face as a Jew.

When the *beth din*, consisting of three scholarly men, is convinced that the applicant has come out of love of God, not merely Judaism or admiration of Jews, the candidate is welcomed into the fold. This course of action is suggested in the Book of Ruth: "When she (Naomi) thus saw that she (Ruth) was persisting to go with her, she left off speaking unto her" (Ruth 1: 18).

At a later date, when the social position of the Jew had deteriorated, a prospective convert was also required to answer the following questions:

1. "Yoke" in this sense means "direction." An animal is directed by means of the yoke.

32

"Why do you seek to convert? Do you not know that Israel in our time is persecuted and oppressed, and that misfortune is their lot? [And some add:] They bury their children and grandchildren [in their youth]; they are martyred because of their observance of the *mitzvah* of circumcision and on account of Ritual Immersion and other *mitzvoth,* and are unable to practice their religion like other peoples." [2]

If his answer is, "I am aware of these things and I am not worthy to offer up my life for the Creator," or "I am not worthy to partake in their woe—I wish I were!" he is accepted without delay. [3]

He is then given instruction in the observance of the *mitzvoth* of the Torah. The lesser ones are explained first, lest the candidate be overwhelmed in the very beginning. Instruction in the difficult *mitzvoth* follows. He is also taught the fundamentals of Judaism, with emphasis on the doctrine of the unity of God and the prohibitions regarding idolatrous practices. To avoid misconceptions, the candidate's instructions must include a candid explanation of the difficult observances and unique practices of Judaism.

If the applicant still wants to enter the Jewish religion, he is promptly introduced to the beautiful side of Judaism. He is told about the Jewish belief in divine reward for the observance of *mitzvoth;* he is told about the hereafter, in which the scales of justice are balanced and the righteous are recompensed. His attention is drawn to the survival of Israel throughout history.

Conversion Procedure

In this rabbinic system for conversion, there is no

2. *Tractate Gerim,* I, 1.
3. *Ibid.*

Touro Synagogue in Newport, Rhode Island, is the oldest Synagogue in the United States

room for reservations. Conversion must be complete and unconditional.[4]

The ancient conversion ritual consisted of three steps for men, according to the following sequence:

1. Circumcision, the Covenant of Abraham
2. Ritual Immersion in a *mikvah,* a pool of waters designed for ritual purification
3. The offering of a sacrifice

And it required two steps for women:
1. Ritual Immersion
2. The offering of a sacrifice

After the destruction of the Temple about 70 A.D., the requirement of a sacrifice for conversion was eliminated.

The *mohel* recites the traditional blessings at the time of circumcision, which must precede Immersion. During Immersion a *beth din* briefs the proselyte a second time on the subject of the *mitzvoth,* because the acceptance of the *Yoke of Mitzvoth* must take place anew during the act of Immersion. In the case of a female convert, the *beth din* remains outside while a religious woman attendant supervises the Immersion.

The proselyte recites two blessings at the time of Immersion:

1. Blessed art Thou, O Lord our God, King of the universe, Who hast sanctified us with Thy Commandments and hast commanded us regarding Immersion.
2. Blessed art Thou, O Lord, our God, King of the universe, Who hast kept us in life, and sustained us, and enabled us to reach this season.

4. Talmud, *Bechoros* 30b.

According to rabbinic law, the ritual of conversion may take place only in the daytime and not on the Sabbath.

After the requirements of conversion have been met, the proselyte is recognized as a full-fledged member of the Jewish faith. His status is protected by religious law and its validity is credited to the ancient Revelation on Mt. Sinai.[5] He is considered an integral part of the "seed of Abraham."[6] A proselyte is on a par with all Jews legally, socially, and religiously. He is counted as part of a *minyan,* and may lead a congregation in public worship.[7] Moreover, proselytes are destined to receive a portion in the Land of Israel.[8]

Upon conversion, a proselyte becomes one of the "chosen" people and may recite, in his devotions, with all Israel: "Blessed art Thou, O Lord our God, King of the universe, Who has *chosen us* from among the peoples . . ." (The doctrine that the Jews are the chosen people can only refer to Israel's vocation of service to God and man. It does not imply any pretention to superiority or racial preeminence.) He may use the expression: "*Our* God and God of *our* fathers . . ." in his prayers.

A convert is, in the eyes of the rabbis, equivalent to a newborn infant.[9] He is like the orphan who should be given an extra measure of love. Care should be exercised in all relationships with the proselyte. He should be given special consideration in the areas of business, social, and personal contact. He may not be wronged with words (nor should he be reminded of his former non-Jewish status). Conversion represents a washing

5 . Talmud, *Shebuoth* 39a based on Deuteronomy 29: 13-14.
6 . Talmud, *Nedarim* III, 11.
7 . *Shulcan Aruch* (Code of Law), Orach Chaim, 53; 19.
8 . Ezekiel 47: 21-23.
9 . Talmud, *Yebamoth* 48b (22a, 62a).

away of old relationships and the genesis of a new spiritual personality. Should persecution compel the proselyte to forsake his adopted faith against his will, his status as a Jew will, nevertheless, be respected.

A convert to Judaism enjoys all the rights, privileges, and responsibilities of a native Israelite. However, the female convert must be prepared for one limitation: she may not marry a *Kohen*, that is, a "priest."

The *Amidah*, the most important section of worship after the Confession of Faith, which dates back to early talmudic times, contains a benediction, number thirteen, which includes a prayer for proselytes. However, in keeping with the Orthodox attitude on conversion, *The Authorized Daily Prayer Book* does not include the steps of the conversion service.

The traditional Orthodox attitude toward conversion speaks in eloquent silence from the pages of this same Prayer Book. In spite of the cordial sentiments expressed in connection with the prayer for proselytes presented above, this Prayer Book, which is encyclopedic in its coverage of religious services, ceremonies, and a multiplicity of religious activities of various degrees of significance, does not provide a service or procedure of conversion. This is perfectly consistent with traditional thinking and is not peculiar to this Prayer Book alone. *Hamadrikh*,[10] a comprehensive Rabbi's Guide, also does not include anything pertaining to conversion. The same applies to the *Reverend's Handbook*[11] popular with Yiddish-speaking clergymen.

10. Hyman E. Goldin, *Hamadrikh* (New York: Hebrew Publishing Co., 1939).

11. S. Druckerman (ed.), *Reverend's Handbook* (New York: Hebrew Publishing Co.) 1929.

2
Conservative Judaism

THE JEWISH CONSERVATIVE MOVEMENT follows with reasonable fidelity the traditional laws and procedures of conversion prescribed by rabbinic usage. However, unlike Orthodox handbooks, the *Rabbinical Assembly Manual*,[1] the official handbook for Conservative rabbis, features a section on conversion with a procedural outline. The following information can be found in the section called "A Guide for the Admission of Proselytes": [2]

1. A rabbi, when approached by an applicant for conversion, should first attempt to become acquainted with the person's family background and ascertain the motives which led to his decision to convert.

2. Acknowledging the fact that most candidates for conversion are motivated by matrimonial reasons, it is still possible, through wise guidance, to make proselytes of them.

3. One need not be discouraged by an indifferent mate. A sincere proselyte can sometimes stimulate the Jewish partner to a higher level of religious observance.

4. The Jewish partner should be involved in the

1. Rabbi Isadore Singer (ed.), *Rabbinical Assembly Manual* (New York: The Rabbinical Assembly of America, 1952).
2. *Ibid.*, pp. 49ff.

preconversion instruction and should be made aware of the seriousness of the step about to be taken as well as the added responsibilities it implies.

5. The candidate should be informed at the outset that conversion to Judaism implies more than a mere change of religion. It involves a complete spiritual rebirth with serious implications—the casting of one's lot with a group in which he obtains membership. The traditional formula of discouragement should be employed, not to dampen the ardor of the applicant, but to make him aware of the profound significance of the step.

6. The program of preparation should be planned in detail, with emphasis on personal interviews.

7. Hasty conversions should be discouraged, except in cases of extreme urgency in which case the applicant agrees to follow a prescribed course of study after conversion.

8. Three months of preparation is the required minimum. The points which differentiate Judaism from other religions should be stressed.

9. The course of study should include:
   a. The Jewish idea of God and His attributes.
   b. The messianic belief in Judaism.
   c. Selected readings from the Bible (especially the Ten Commandments, Leviticus, Chapter 9, and important chapters from the Prophetic books used as illustrations for the lessons given the candidate).
   d. Ceremonies of Judaism
   e. The Jewish calendar
   f. Sabbath and holidays
   g. Synagogue and worship
   h. The dietary laws, especially when the applicant is a woman

    i. A general idea of the contents of the Bible

    j. The historical development of Judaism in biblical and post-biblical times, stressing personalities and movements

    k. A rudimentary knowledge of the Hebrew language to enable intelligent participation in Synagogue worship.

10. The candidate should be given a prayer book, a Bible, and an appropriate textbook on the Jewish religion. He should also be encouraged to read a Jewish newspaper and periodical.

11. He should be advised to attend Synagogue services as often as possible, visit Jewish homes, become oriented to a Jewish atmosphere, and get to know Jewish people during the period of preparation.

12. The process of instruction is determined by individual needs and considerations.

13. At the termination of the period of instruction, the rabbi should consult at least two colleagues or, when this is not possible, two religious, intelligent members of the community. They are to be briefed on all the details and invited to participate in the ceremony of formal admission.

14. "The essential legal requirements for admission are circumcision and Ritual Immersion in the case of a man, and Ritual Immersion in the case of a woman. The presence of witnesses is necessary according to tradition. In the case of a woman, the requirements of the law may be satisfied in one of the following ways:

    a. Two pious women should accompany the applicant to the *mikvah* and report to the *beth din* that all details of the law have been complied with.

    b. Two male witnesses stand in the vestibule

removed from the *mikvah* and listen as the applicant, prompted by a pious Jewish woman, recites the benedictions and *Kabbalat hamitzvot*." [3]

Conversion Procedure

The procedure for conversion as outlined in the *Rabbinical Assembly Manual* would be acceptable to most Orthodox authorities. However, there is a wide latitude of variations allowed by individual Conservative rabbis or rabbinic groups so that their procedures sometimes differ considerably from the Orthodox procedures. A case in point was the mass conversion conducted by the Conservative rabbinical group of Philadelphia, in which a swimming pool (that of Beth Sholom Congregation in Elkins Park) was substituted for a *mikvah*. This provoked a veritable avalanche of protests from Orthodox circles.

The Jewish reconstructionist group is to the left of the spectrum of Conservative Judaism. An understanding of Reconstructionist philosophy and theology can best be obtained from reading the books written by Dr. Mordecai Kaplan, founder of the movement.

Dr. Ira Eisenstein, president of the Jewish Reconstructionist Foundation, Inc., defines the position of his group on conversion:

. . . We have approached the problem of conversion in the usual, traditional manner. We have required several months of instruction, and we go through the regular initiation ceremonies at the close. The only innovation, if you want to call it that, which I have personally intro-

3. *Ibid.*, p. 52.

duced, is to make the visit to the *mikvah* optional.
Very often Christians prefer to go through the
ceremony and make no difficulties about it;
however, there are those who feel they would
not like to go through this and I do not insist
upon it . . .

Therefore, the conversion procedure required by
an officiating Reconstructionist rabbi would differ from
that prescribed by an Orthodox or Conservative rabbi
only in the matter of ritual immersion. Rabbinic law,
however, regards this rite as fundamental and indispensable to a bona fide conversion.

The Ritual Immersion in the *mikvah* is accompanied by the two traditional blessings:

1. Blessed art Thou, O Lord our God, King of the
universe, Who hast hallowed us with Thy commandments and commanded us concerning immersion.

2. Blessed art Thou, O Lord our God, King of the
universe Who hast kept us in life and sustained us and
enabled us to reach this significant moment.

The convert is then asked a number of questions
parallel to the ideas contained in the formal declaration, which the convert reads at the conclusion of the
ceremony and then signs.

Next the convert recites the declaration of desire
for conversion. Three copies are signed. One is taken
by the convert, a second copy is given to the head of
the *beth din,* and a third one is sent to the Bureau of
Records of the Jewish Theological Seminary.

The rabbi, or the convert if he is qualified, recites
in Hebrew from Deuteronomy 6: 5-9

And thou shalt love the Lord thy God with all
thine heart, and with all thy soul, and with all

thy might. And these words, which I command thee this day, shall be upon thine heart. And thou shalt teach them diligently unto thy children, and shalt talk of them when thou sittest in thine house, and when thou walkest by the way, and when thou liest down, and when thou risest up. And thou shalt bind them for a sign upon thine hand, and they shall be for frontlets between thine eyes. And thou shalt write them upon the door posts of thy house, and upon thy gates: that ye may remember and do all my commandments, and be holy unto your God.

For women converts, the rabbi may read from the Book of Ruth 1: 16-17:

And Ruth said: Entreat me not to leave thee, and to return from following after thee; for whither thou goest, I will go; and where thou lodgest, I will lodge; thy people shall be my people, and thy God my God; where thou diest, I will die, and there will I be buried; the Lord do so to me and more, if aught but death part thee from me.

At this point, the rabbi delivers a charge to the proselyte, leading up to the significance of acquiring a Hebrew name.

The rabbi, in bestowing the Hebrew name, says:

In token of your admission into the household of Israel, this Rabbinical Tribunal welcomes you by bestowing upon you the name of .... by which you will henceforth be called in Israel.[4]

A special prayer for the welfare of the proselyte is added:

May he who blessed our fathers, Abraham, Isaac and Jacob (mothers, Sarah, Rebecca, Rachel and

4. *Ibid.*, pp. 54-55.

Tomb of Rabbi Meir Baal Hanes at Tiberias, Israel

Leah) bless you our brother (sister) [state the name] on the occasion of your acceptance into the heritage of Israel and your becoming a true proselyte in the midst of the people of the God of Abraham. May you, under God, prosper in all your ways and may all the work of your hands be blessed. Amen.[5]

The rabbi then reads the Certificate of Admission signed by the *beth din* and hands it to the proselyte. Then he pronounces the priestly benediction with hands placed on the bowed head of the proselyte.

Summarizing the Conservative approach to conversion, it may be stated that the official attitude and procedure are predicated on the traditional forms and norms of Jewish law and usage. But this does not eliminate the prerogative of individual Conservative rabbis to follow a pattern based on their own interpretation.

5. *Ibid.*, p. 55.

Documents

(Reproduced with permission from the Rabbinical
Assembly of America)

PLEDGE OF FAITH
For the Proselyte

To the Children of Israel everywhere—
Greetings!

I HEREBY ATTEST that I have voluntarily
decided to adopt the Jewish religion as my own,
and to become a *ben yisrael lekhol davar, a full-*
fledged member of the Jewish people.

TO THIS END I have fulfilled the obliga-
tory rite of *milah* on ...., corresponding to
................., 19........, and thus entered into the
Covenant of our Father Abraham. On this day,
.... corresponding to ...., 19........, I
have performed the rite of *Tevilah* in the presence
of qualified witnesses.

MOREOVER in order to prepare myself for
active and intelligent participation in Jewish life,
I have engaged in the study of the fundamental
beliefs and practices of Judaism, and the history
of the Jewish people. In token of my Jewish
allegiance, my name shall henceforth be called
in Israel ....

I PLEDGE to cleave loyally to the principles of the Jewish religion, and do my best to
observe its commandments, cherishing the Synagogue and other holy institutions, and hallowing
the Sabbath and the Festivals. I pledge to do
my best to enrich my understanding of Judaism

and its culture through further study, reading and discussion.

I PLEDGE to marry within the fold of Israel, to raise my children as Jews, circumcising all male children that may be born to me. I shall give my children a Jewish education that they may carry on the name and heritage of Judaism.

IN SUM, I SINCERELY PLEDGE to regard the Jewish people as my very own, participating in its joys and sorrows, and to share its life and activities to the best of my ability.

IN WITNESS THEREOF I have set my name to this PLEDGE OF FAITH.

Name...

Date.............................

ATTESTATION

WE HEREBY TESTIFY that ....
has come before us voluntarily, performed the necessary rites preliminary to admission into the Jewish fold according to Jewish law, and adopted the faith of Judaism as his own.

WE ATTEST that on this day ....
we have admitted him into the Jewish fold as a *ben yisrael lekhol davar,* a full-fledged member of Israel, in token whereof he shall be called

....

Beth Din: ....

....

....

Date...........................57...........
...........................19...........

CERTIFICATE OF THE ADMISSION OF A
PROSELYTE

THIS IS TO CERTIFY

that on .... corresponding to ....,
19........., in .... there came before the under-
signed, constituted as a Rabbinical Tribunal,
Beth Din, *Mr., (Mrs.,) (Miss)* ....
and declared *his (her)* intention and desire to
enter the Covenant of Israel, as a righteous
proselyte. Upon questioning *him (her)* we found
him (her) to be sincere in *his (her)* intentions
and adequately conversant with the doctrines
and laws of our holy Faith. We have also
received testimony that *he (she)* has undergone
the required initiation ceremonies as prescribed
by Jewish law and tradition.

We have, therefore, declared *him (her)*
a true Israelite, a full member of the Jewish
people, and we give *him (her)* the name of
.... by which *he (she)* shall be known
in Israel.

May the God of our father, Abraham, bless
this proselyte, give *him (her)* the determination
to abide faithfully and loyally by the precepts
and doctrines of our holy Torah, so that *he (she)*
may become worthy of the great privilege conferred upon *him (her)* in being called to share
in the destiny of the people of Israel, bearing
testimony throughout the world to God's unity
and righteousness.

Signed by us in this City of ....
and State of ....

....
....
....

IN THE PRESENCE OF GOD
AND OF THIS RABBINICAL TRIBUNAL

I hereby declare my desire to accept the principles of Judaism, to adhere to its practices and ceremonies, and to become a member of the Jewish People.

I do this of my own free will and with a full realization of the true significance of the tenets and practices of Judaism.

I pray that my present determination guide me through life so that I may be worthy of the sacred fellowship which I am now privileged to join. I pray that I may ever remain conscious of the privileges and the corresponding duties that my affiliation with the House of Israel imposes upon me. I declare my firm determination to live a Jewish life and to conduct a Jewish home.

If I shall be blessed with male children, I promise to have them brought into the Covenant of Abraham. I further promise to bring up all the children with whom God shall bless me in loyalty to Jewish beliefs and practices and in faithfulness to Jewish hopes and the Jewish way of life.

Hear, O Israel, the Lord our God, the Lord is One!

Blessed is His glorious sovereign Name forever.

....

Witnesses to this Declaration:

....

....

....

Date...

(Certificate of Admission)

תעודה

מעידים אנו ח"מ בישיבת בית דין שבאה לפנינו
מרת..................................והביעה את רצונה להסתפח
בנחלת ישראל ולהמנות על גרי הצדק בתוך בני ישראל.
בדקנו אחריה וראינו שהיא ישרת-לב. דברנו אתה ומצאנו
שידועים לה עיקרי דתנו. גם מלאה את כל החובות
המוטלות על כל הבאה להתגייר וטבלה לשם גרות בפני
שלשה עדים כשרים כדת וכדין.
לכן מקבלים אנחנו אותה תחת כנפי השכינה
ואומרים לה אחותנו את. ומהיום והלאה יקרא שמה
בישראל..................................
יברכה יי אלהי אברהם אבינו ויחזק ויאמץ אותה
להיות תמימה עם אלהי ישראל ונאמנה לתורתנו הקדושה
ובת מסורה לעם ישראל. אמן:
בד"צ..................................
....
....

תעודה

אנו החתומים מטה באנו על החותם להעיד כי
מר..................................בא לפנינו והביע את רצונו
הכביר להסתפח בקהל ה' ולהחסות תחת כנפי השכינה.
לשם זה נמול כדת וכדין ביום..................................על ידי מוהל
כשר וטבל לשם גרות בפני עדים ומלא את כל אשר נדרש
ממנו באמת ובתמים והראה ידיעה בעיקרי אמונתנו
הקדושה ואהבה לעמנו ולתורתנו.
על כן מעידים אנו שנתקבל על ידינו ונכנס לקהל
ישראל ביום..................................והנהו ישראל לכל דבר
ישראל ביום..................................והנהו ישראל לכל דבר
שבקדושה ויקרא שמו בישראל אברהם בן אברהם. יהי ה'
עמו ויעל.
פה..................................
נאום..................................
נאום..................................
נאום..................................

3
Reform Judaism

R EFORM JUDAISM, FROM ITS very inception, has
sought to activate a major missionary program.
Reform rabbis, here and abroad, have pressed
for a return to the attitude on conversion that characterized Judaism in pre-Christian times. They have
searched for a program which would give the idea
sanction, method, and scope. [1]

They have spoken of the "mission of Israel," and
have been quite serious about the literal implications
of those words. But this missionary activity has not
been conceived as an aggressive militant program with
the machinery and personnel usually associated with a
missionary movement. In essence, its position differs
very little from that of the other groups cited. The point
of radical departure is in the practical implications
of that position.

Reform Judaism has activated its philosophy on
conversion by making informational literature widely
available, by welcoming those who sincerely wish to
convert, by publicizing the fact that converts are welcome, and by relaxing the restrictions on conversion.

Their philosophy is summarized in the *Manual for*

1. One example is the series of two sermons by Claude G.
Montefiore included in his *Truth in Religion and Other Sermons*
(London: Macmillan and Co., Ltd., 1906).

the Instruction of Proselytes published by the Reform movement in 1928:

> Judaism extends the hand of fellowship to all who come to it with sincerity of purpose. It is not militant in bringing people of other creeds, or of no beliefs, into its fold, but is hospitable to all who wish to join it to go up to the mountain of the Lord.
>
> Judaism is a world religion, not a tribal or racial religion. Its teachings are intended for all mankind. The supreme task of Israel has been first to receive and develop our faith and then to make it known to the peoples of the earth.[2]
> . . . Judaism says to all who would accept our faith: You are welcome to share with us every truth and every hope that has come to us from God.[3]

Those interested in the Reform approach to conversion can find some helpful information in the *Rabbi's Manual.* A resolution of the Central Conference of American Rabbis is included in the section called "Historical and Explanatory Notes" in the 1952 edition of the *Rabbi's Manual:*

> Resolved that the Central Conference of American Rabbis, assembled in this city of New York, considers it lawful and proper for any officiating rabbi, assisted by no less than two associates, and in the name and with the consent of his congregation, to accept into the sacred covenant of Israel, and declare fully affiliated with the congregation *L' chol Davar Shebikdushah*[4] any

2. *Judaism* (Cincinnati: Central Conference of American Rabbis, 1928), p. 5.
3. *Ibid.,* p. 10.
4. "In all sacred matters."

honorable and intelligent person who desires
affiliation, without any initiatory rite, ceremony
or observance whatever; provided such person
be sufficiently acquainted with the faith, doctrine
and religious usages of Israel; that nothing
derogatory to such person's moral and mental
character is suspected; that it is his or her free
will and choice to embrace the cause of Judaism
and that he or she declare verbally, and in a
document signed and sealed before such officiating rabbi and his associates, his or her intention
and firm resolve—

1. To worship the One Sole and Eternal
   God and none besides Him.
2. To be conscientiously governed in his or
   her doings and omissions in life by God's
   laws, ordained for the child and image
   of the Father and Maker of all, the sanctified son or daughter of the divine covenant.
3. To adhere in life and death, actively and
   faithfully, to the sacred cause and mission of Israel as marked out in Holy
   Writ.[5]

The corresponding section of the revised (1961)
edition of the *Rabbi's Manual* reaffirms this view:

Judaism welcomes all sincere converts without
regard to racial or national origin or to their
former religious faith. The biblical laws excluding
certain peoples from admission to the community
of Israel were declared obsolete early in the
talmudic period (*Yadayim* 4, 4). Tradition prescribed that a prospective convert must be

5. *Yearbook* (Cincinnati: Central Conference of American
Rabbis, 1891-92), Vol. I, 36.

warned in advance of the many religious responsibilities which a Jew must assume and of the
disabilities he may suffer; but it was further
ordained that the candidate should not be un-
duly discouraged (*Yevamoth* 47a). Jewish literature has much to say in praise of converts
and records the names of many illustrious and
pious proselytes.

The traditional *halacha* requires male converts to submit to circumcision and afterwards
to receive a ritual bath; women are converted
by the ritual immersion. But in 1893, the Central
Conference of American Rabbis declared that no
initiatory rite was necessary: the prospective
convert should simply declare orally and in
writing, in the presence of a rabbi and no less
than two associates, his acceptance of the Jewish
faith and his intention to live by it. At times this
formal admission of the proselyte took place during a Sabbath service, but the procedure outlined in this Manual is the more usual one.

It is understood that the formal conversion
is to be preceded by a suitable period of instruction by the rabbi or some other qualified person.
This will enable the rabbi to satisfy himself not
only that the candidate has sufficient knowledge,
but is a person of responsible character who is
sincerely desirous of living as a Jew.[6]

The Reform group, in keeping with its attitude on
conversions, has produced the largest volume of popular
literature on the subject. In a folder entitled *How to
Become a Jew*,[7] Rabbi Daniel L. Davis, Director of the
New York Federation of Reform Synagogues, an agency

6. *Rabbi's Manual* (Revised ed.; New York: Central Conference of American Rabbis, 1961), pp. 116-17. Reprinted with
permission.
7. *How to Become a Jew* (New York: The New York
Federation of Reform Synagogues, undated).

Ruins of a third-century Synagogue at Capernaum, the modern town of Tell Hum, Israel

of the Union of American Hebrew Congregations, presents an outline on conversion in the form of questions and answers which include the following:

Can Anyone Become A Jew?

The answer is yes—anyone who desires to learn the meaning of Judaism and to live according to the teachings of Judaism. Birth, nationality, economic condition, former belief or nonbelief bar none from entering the household of Israel.

How Do I Go About Becoming a Jew?

Seek out and confer with the rabbi of a Jewish congregation. The rabbi is a teacher of Judaism. As the spiritual leader of the congregation, his primary purpose is to teach the meaning of Judaism. In asking for information, no one will be obligated or committed to go beyond the search for knowledge and guidance. After having discussed your interest in Judaism with the rabbi, if you wish to acquire a fuller knowledge of Judaism, the rabbi will make it possible for you to pursue a course of studies. In New York City, under the auspices of the New York Federation of Reform Synagogues and the Association of Reform Rabbis of New York, there is a continuing course for the preparation of prospective converts to Judaism, to which the rabbi may refer you. There is a similar course in Chicago. In other communities, the rabbi will arrange for individual instruction.

What Will I Learn In My Course Of Study About Judaism?

You will learn something of the history of the Jews and Judaism, the basic concepts of Judaism concerning God, Israel, mankind, the Torah, the moral law and ethical ideals. You will be introduced to the literature, rituals, practices and prayers of Judaism. You will be given an understanding of the place and function of the Synagogue in Jewish life, of the present-day organizations within the Jewish community, and the cultural interests and philanthropic undertakings of Jews who seek actively to express their Judaism by contributing to the welfare of fellow Jews and the advancement of humanity. In your initial course of instruction, you will not learn all there is to know about the vast life and lore and teachings of Judaism. All Jews should continue their study of Judaism throughout their lifetime, for study is regarded not only as a means of increasing the knowledge and meaning of religion, but also as an incentive to apply its values in influencing the conduct of life.

How Will I Actually Be Converted To Judaism?

Upon completion of your initial course of study, the rabbi will plan a ceremony of conversion which usually takes place in the Synagogue (but not usually as part of public worship) in the presence of several witnesses, other rabbis and leaders of the congregation. In that ceremony you will be welcomed into the household of Israel. You will be asked to share in the faith and fate of the Jewish people, to promise that you will lead a Jewish life and to pledge that you will rear any children that may be yours as Jews. You will be given an additional biblical name as symbol and reminder of your acceptance of Judaism and a certificate as an official record of the event. A duplicate of the certificate will be placed in the archives of the congregation.

Will I As A Convert To Judaism Be The Same As Any Other Jew?

You will be in every way, having the same opportunities and the same responsibilities. You

The oldest known fragment of Deuteronomy, one of the Five Books of Moses, was found among the Dead Sea Scrolls

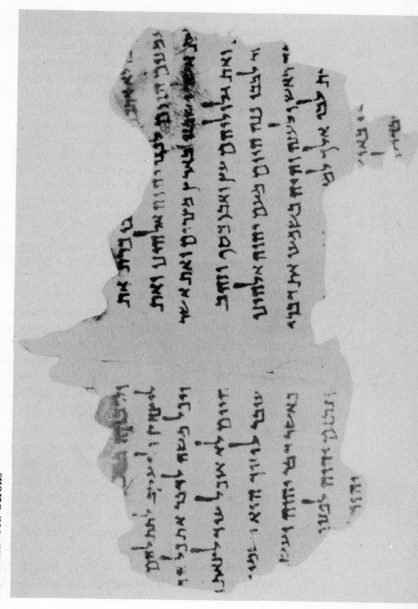

will be asked to affiliate with a Synagogue, make your home a Jewish home and a sanctuary of the Jewish spirit, teach your children the meaning and practice of Judaism, work with fellow Jews for the understanding and application of the ideals of Judaism, seek to advance the welfare of the community and the nation in which you live, practice philanthropy, aiding Jews and Jewish institutions everywhere, serving the cause of humanity and promoting the peace of the world. You may marry another Jew or Jewess without restrictions and in accordance with the usual practices of Judaism concerning marriage. Rabbi Solomon B. Freehof in his book on *Reform Jewish Practices* points out: "Both traditional and Reform Judaism consider the marriage between a Jew and a convert to Judaism as full Jewish marriage."

To reemphasize, the Reform group has dropped the requirements of circumcision and Ritual Immersion, whereas the Orthodox and Conservative groups still adhere to *halacha,* or traditional "Jewish law," which prescribes circumcision and Ritual Immersion as a *sine qua non* of conversion, without which a conversion is not considered valid. Even the left-wing Reconstructionists, while yielding on *mikvah,* do not recognize the conversion of a man who was not circumcised. However, while the 1952 edition of the *Rabbi's Manual*[8] requires the convert to agree to have all male children circumcised, the revised (1961) edition eliminates this requirement.

It is also important to note that the terms "Jewish home" and "Jewish life" have a radically different connotation for the various groups that comprise the House of Israel. Consequently, a person who is sincere in his

8. *Rabbi's Manual* (New York: Central Conference of American Rabbis, 1952), p. 31.

desire to become a convert to Judaism and truly means to build a "Jewish home" and live a "Jewish life" should endeavor to obtain a true understanding of what these terms mean and imply.

In reference to Dr. Freehof's remark, it should be stated that traditional Judaism does insist on the one restriction forbidding the marriage between a woman convert and a *Kohen* (priest).

Another important point is that, traditionally, Judaism has not sanctioned mixed marriage.[9] The status of the children is determined by the religious affiliation of the mother. Thus, the child of a Jewess married to a Gentile is considered *ipso facto* Jewish. The father's affiliation is of no consequence.

Even the leadership of the Reform group, with few exceptions, has regarded mixed marriage with alarm. The Central Conference of American Rabbis at its New York meeting (1909) passed the following resolution (which was reaffirmed in 1947):

> The C.C.A.R. declares that mixed marriages are contrary to the tradition of the Jewish religion and should therefore be discouraged by the American rabbinate.[10]

Leaders of the Reform group also discourage mixed marriage. Recent developments, however, indicate a possible change in this attitude. In 1957, Dr. David Max Eichhorn, well known for his research in the field of conversion, called for a bold reappraisal of the traditional Jewish position on mixed marriage. His primary

9. For a sobering appraisal of the threat to Jewish survival posed by intermarriage, see Thomas B. Morgan, "The Vanishing American Jew," *Look Magazine*, May 5, 1964, pp. 42ff.

10. *Yearbook* (New York: Central Conference of American Rabbis, 1909, 1947), Vol. XIX, p. 170 and discussion thereon on pp. 174-84, and Vol. LVII, p. 161.

concern is the welfare of the children resulting from the marriage.[11] This leads Dr. Eichhorn to the following position:

> After carefully discussing with the couple all the problems and possibilities involved (in a mixed marriage) and after assuring myself that, if I refuse to marry them, they will get married anyway, I agree to officiate at the marriage if the non-Jew gives me his or her word that he or she accepts the following marital stipulations: All children are to be reared as Jews in the manner that most nearly conforms to the family background of the Jewish partner in the marriage. All children are to receive an intensive Jewish education. The non-Jewish marriage partner is to attempt to the best of his or her ability to make the home atmosphere conform to the pattern of the teachings of the children's religious school. There are to be no non-Jewish religious symbols or celebrations of any kind in the home. Christmas trees, Easter eggs, and non-Jewish religious adornments are specifically proscribed. The non-Jewish marriage partner is to try to become familiar with the principles and practices of Judaism and is to attend Synagogue services, for a time at least, in an effort to determine whether or not he or she would accept Judaism without doing violence to his or her conscience. The advantages of religious homogeneity in the home are stressed.[12]

The official Reform conversion service, as it appears in the *Rabbi's Manual,* calls for a ceremony in the Synagogue, preferably before the open Ark and in

11. "A New Look at Conversion or Marriage," *Central Conference of American Rabbis Journal* (January, 1957), p. 12.
12. *Ibid.,* p. 16.

A menorah

the presence of the rabbi and two persons representative of the congregation. It is understood that the applicant has, by then, met the preparatory requirements.

The opening words of the ceremony are: "Blessed be you who come in the name of the Lord. We bless you from the House of the Lord." The rabbi continues with a prayer of thanksgiving in behalf of the proselyte:

> Our God and Father, with grateful hearts we thank Thee for many blessings. We thank Thee that Thou dost reveal Thy truth to mankind. Above all, we praise Thee for the gift of the Torah, which has ever been a lamp unto our feet and a light unto our path. We recall with reverence and gratitude all those of the seed of Abraham who have been faithful unto Thee, and those who of their own choice have sought to serve Thee in the faith and fellowship of Israel. Be near us in this solemn hour. Grant, O God, Thy loving favor to .... as in this holy place we welcome him (her) into Jewish life. Help him (her) to live in fidelity to the decision he (she) has made, and to the promise he (she) is about to utter. May he (she) always find joy in the fulfillment of Thy Torah and enduring satisfaction in the practice of Judaism. Vouchsafe unto him (her) many years of strength and happiness as a worthy son (daughter) of the Synagogue. Blessed art Thou O Lord, in Whose presence is fullness of joy. Amen. [13]

A brief charge is here delivered by the rabbi, who proceeds to ask the following questions, which the convert answers:

1. Do you of your own free will seek admittance into the Jewish faith?

13. *Rabbi's Manual, op. cit.* p. 17. Reprinted by permission of the Central Conference of American Rabbis.

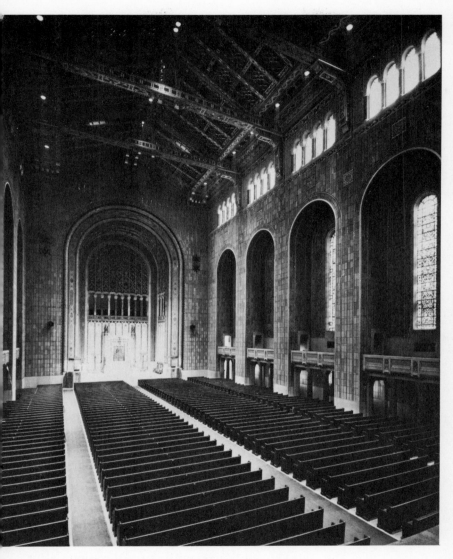

Interior of Temple Emanu-El, New York City

2. Have you given up your former faith and severed all other religious affiliations?
3. Do you pledge your loyalty to Judaism and to the Jewish people amid all circumstances and conditions?
4. Do you promise to establish a Jewish home and to participate actively in the life of the Synagogue and of the Jewish community?
5. If you should be blessed with children, do you promise to rear them in the Jewish faith? [14]

(The 1952 Edition of the *Rabbi's Manual* includes the additional question, "Do you also agree to have male children circumcised?" [page 31] as well as a pledge affirming the ideas embodied in the list of questions.)

After the convert affirms each of the questions, the rabbi makes the following declaration:

I summon you then to pronounce the affirmation by which the Jew lives, and which is on his lips even in his last moment on earth.[15]

The convert recites the Confession of Faith:

Shma Yisrael Ado-nay Elo-haynu Ado-nay Echad [Hear O Israel: the Lord our God, the Lord is One], Baruch Shem K'vod Malchuto L'olam Vaed [Praised be His name Whose glorious kingdom is for ever and ever].

Readings follow from Deuteronomy 6: 5-9, and, when the convert is a woman, readings from Ruth 1: 16-17 may be included.

The service continues with an Adoration, after which the rabbi takes the convert's hand and says:

14. *Ibid.*, p. 18.
15. *Ibid.*

King David's Tomb in Mt. Zion, Jerusalem

May God strengthen you in the solemn commitment you have made. As a rabbi in Israel, and with the consent of these witnesses, I welcome you warmly and joyously into our faith and fellowship; and I confer upon you the Hebrew name ....,[16]

He then places his hand on the convert's head and says:

May the Lord bless thee and keep thee. May the Lord cause His countenance to shine upon thee and be gracious unto thee. May the Lord lift up His countenance unto thee and give thee peace. Amen.

or:

The Lord recompense thy work, and be thy reward complete from the Lord, the God of Israel, under Whose wings thou art come to take refuge.

Documents

After the ceremony, the following certificate of conversion, properly signed by the rabbi and countersigned by the witnesses and by the convert, is read before it is handed to the convert. A duplicate of this certificate, properly signed and countersigned, is put into the archives of the congregation represented by the officiating rabbi.

16. *Ibid.*, p. 20.

Certificate of Conversion[17]

Hear O Israel: the Lord our God, the Lord is One.

This is to certify that .... of ....came before me ...., on the .... day of ...., 19........ corresponding to the Hebrew date .... expressing .... desire for conversion to the Jewish religion and giving satisfactory evidence that .... knows and understands the principles and practices of Judaism. Therefore, with the sanction of the two associates whose names are signed below, I received the said .... into the fellowship of the Jewish people and faith, giving .... the additional Hebrew name ....

On .... part, ... has solemnly declared .... intention to cast in .... lot with the Jewish people, to live in accordance with the Jewish religion, and if blessed with children, to rear them as Jews.

....

Rabbi of Congregation ....
City ....

....

....

Witnesses

....

Convert

Thy people shall be my people and
thy God my God.

17. *Ibid.*, p. 22.

Seventh-century icon of St. Peter is one of the Byzantine art treasures at the Monastery of St. Catherine on Mount Sinai, Egypt

Roman Catholicism

Fathers of the Second Vatican Council kneel in prayer along the nave of St. Peter's Basilica, Vatican City

Introduction—Roman Catholicism

PERHAPS THE BEST WAY to introduce Catholicism is to reproduce the following excerpt from *The Catholic Almanac.*[1]

> The main points of Catholic belief are stated in creeds, which are simplified summaries designed for use in professing the faith, in prayer and instruction. The one most widely known is the Apostles' Creed:
>
> I believe in God, the Father Almighty, Creator of heaven and earth; and in Jesus Christ, His only Son, Our Lord; Who was conceived by the Holy Ghost, born of the Virgin Mary, suffered under Pontius Pilate, was crucified, died, and was buried. He descended into hell; the third day He arose again from the dead; He ascended into heaven, sitteth on the right hand of God, the Father Almighty; from thence He shall come to judge the living and the dead. I believe in the Holy Ghost, the Holy Catholic Church, the communion of saints, the forgiveness of sins, the resurrection of the body, and life everlasting. Amen.

1. From *The Catholic Almanac,* pp. 234-35. Copyright © 1963 by St. Anthony's Guild. Reprinted by permission of Doubleday and Company, Inc.

GOD: There is one God, a pure spirit, Creator of heaven and earth, without beginning or end, all holy, all good, omnipresent, knowing and seeing all, omnipotent, infinite in perfection.

HOLY TRINITY: There are three Persons in God, equal, and of the same substance: the Father; the Son, begotten of the Father; the Holy Spirit, proceeding eternally from the Father and the Son. All three are eternal and infinitely perfect; all three are the same Lord and the same God.

CREATION AND THE FALL: God created the angels to be with Him forever; some of them fell from grace, were consigned to hell, and became devils. God created Adam and Eve, the first parents of the human race, and He placed them in Paradise, whence they were justly banished in consequence of Adam's sin. Because of the fall of Adam, all are born in the state of original sin and would be lost if God had not sent a Saviour.

JESUS CHRIST, REDEEMER: The Saviour is Jesus Christ, the Son of God—equal to the Father and Holy Spirit in all things—and perfect Man—with a human soul and body. The divine Person of Christ unites His divine and human natures.

Christ was conceived in the womb of the Virgin Mary by the power of the Holy Spirit, without any man for His father; Mary, His Mother, remained a pure virgin. During His life Christ founded the Catholic Church. He offered Himself as a sacrifice for the sins of the world by dying on the cross to gain mercy, grace and salvation for mankind.

After His death and burial Christ arose on the third day and manifested Himself to His disciples for forty days before ascending into heaven, where He continually intercedes for us.

Pope Gregory I, 590-604

He sent down the Holy Spirit upon His Apostles to guide them and their successors in truth.

THE CHURCH: Christ is the invisible head of the Catholic or Universal Church; the Holy Spirit is its guiding Spirit of Truth (Soul of the Church). Christ founded the Church on a rock of infallibility and invincibility. The Church has these marks: one, because its members profess one faith and one communion under one pastor (the pope), the successor of St. Peter, to whom Christ committed His whole flock; holy, because the Holy Spirit abides in the Church, which teaches holiness in doctrine and morals, has the supernatural means to holiness, and in every age produces living examples of holiness; catholic, because it has existed in all ages, has taught all nations the truth, and teaches the whole body of divine revelation; apostolic, because it derives its doctrines, mission and succession from the Apostles.

RULE OF FAITH: The Scriptures, Old and New Testaments, were deposited by the Apostles with the Church, which is their guardian and protector, and the interpreter and judge of all controversies concerning them. The Scriptures and Tradition, as authentically interpreted and taught by the Church, comprise the proximate rule of faith.

SACRAMENTS: Christ instituted seven sacraments: Baptism, Confirmation, Holy Eucharist, Penance, Extreme Unction, Holy Orders, Matrimony.

MASS: Christ instituted the Sacrifice of His Body and Blood as a remembrance and unbloody renewal of His Passion and death, which is perpetuated in the Mass. Christ is immolated upon the altar at Mass, being Himself both priest and victim. Through the Mass, men participate in the sacrifice and merits of Christ, adore God, thank Him, make reparation for sin, and petition for blessings.

COMMUNION OF SAINTS: In the Church there is a communion of saints, i.e., a union of grace and good works, embracing the faithful on earth (Church Militant), in purgatory (Church Suffering) and in heaven (Church Triumphant). Members of the Church Militant are in communication with each other through prayer and good works. They communicate with the Church Suffering by prayer for the souls in purgatory. The faithful on earth communicate with the blessed in heaven by imitating them, by honoring them by prayer, and by seeking their intercession with God. The blessed in heaven communicate with the Church Militant and the Church Suffering by praying for the souls on earth and in purgatory. Souls in purgatory, probably, communicate with the Church Militant by intercession for the faithful on earth.

NECESSITY OF GRACE: Without divine grace man cannot make even one step toward heaven; all merits result solely from cooperation with the grace of God. Christ died for all men. God is not the author of sin. His grace or His knowledge does not take away the free will of man. Prayer and Good Works are necessary for salvation.

DEATH, JUDGMENT, HEAVEN, HELL: Christ will judge all men in a particular manner at the time of death; according to their spiritual condition, they will be consigned to heaven, purgatory or hell. At the end of the world, the dead, good and bad, shall rise from their graves to be judged

Pope Leo III, 795-816

in a general judgment, according to their works: the good shall go to heaven, body and soul, to be happy for all eternity; the wicked shall be condemned, body and soul, to the everlasting torments of hell.

SUMMARY OF CATHOLIC MORALITY [2]

The basic moral obligations of Catholics are contained in the Ten Commandments of God and the six Precepts of the Church.

COMMANDMENTS OF GOD

The Ten Commandments are the Decalogue given by God to Moses on Mt. Sinai (Exodus 20: 1-17). They bind the conscience of all mankind, since they make known explicitly the moral obligations arising from man's nature and his relation to God. Their observance enables man to attain to everlasting salvation.

1. I AM THE LORD THY GOD; THOU SHALT NOT HAVE STRANGE GODS BEFORE ME.

Commands us to give to God alone the supreme worship that is due Him by the virtues of faith, hope, charity, and religion: by faith— by embracing all truths which God has revealed and proposed for belief through the Scriptures, Tradition and the infallible teaching of the Catholic Church; by hope—the expectation of grace and salvation through the merits of Christ, in fulfillment of God's promises, and in accordance with His goodness, power and mercy; by charity —loving God above all because He is infinitely perfect, and all men as oneself, for God's sake; by religion—through interior sentiments and ex-

2. From *The Catholic Almanac,* pp. 235-36. Copyright © 1963 by St. Anthony's Guild. Reprinted by permission of Doubleday and Company, Inc.

ternal expressions of adoration, thanksgiving, penance and petition.

(The veneration given to saints, respect for their relics, and the use of statues, etc., in religious worship are not in violation of this commandment, since all of these practices and things are related in various ways to divine worship.)

Forbids: idolatry, false religion, superstition, fortune-telling, witchcraft, observations of omens, the use of charms, spells, dreams and astrology; apostasy, heresy, indifferentism, participation in non-Catholic worship; presumption and despair; hatred of God and neighbor, envy, sloth and scandal; sacrilege; irreverence toward the saints and their relics, and toward representations of God and the saints which are useful in fostering religious devotion.

2. THOU SHALT NOT TAKE THE NAME OF THE LORD THY GOD IN VAIN.

Commands reverence in speech toward God, the saints and holy things; truthfulness in taking oaths, and fidelity in fulfilling oaths and vows.

Forbids the irreverent use of God's name, cursing, blasphemy, perjury, and failure to fulfill vows.

3. REMEMBER THOU KEEP HOLY THE LORD'S DAY.

Commands the worship of God in a special manner on Sunday, by assistance at the Holy Sacrifice of the Mass.

Forbids unnecessary servile work on Sunday.

(The first precept of the Church, below, extends these obligations to holy days of obligation.)

4. HONOR THY FATHER AND THY MOTHER.

Commands: children, to respect and love their parents, to obey them in all that is not sinful, to help them when they are in need; all persons, to respect and obey lawful superiors, and to discharge the duties of citizenship; parents, to provide for the spiritual and physical welfare of their children; superiors, according to their varying degrees of responsibility, to care for those entrusted to them.

Forbids disrespect, unkindness, and disobedience to parents and lawful superiors; neglect by superiors of their responsibility for the care of those in their charge.

5. THOU SHALT NOT KILL.

Commands all persons to take proper care of their spiritual and physical welfare and that of their neighbor.

Forbids murder and suicide, mutilation of self and others, fighting, anger, hatred, revenge, gluttony, drunkenness and bad example.

6. THOU SHALT NOT COMMIT ADULTERY.

Commands purity and modesty in behavior.

Forbids all impurity and immodesty in words, looks and actions, whether alone or with others.

7. THOU SHALT NOT STEAL.

Commands respect for the belongings and property of others, fulfillment of business agreements, payment of just debts, restitution for theft and damage of the goods of others.

Forbids stealing, cheating, unjust keeping of what belongs to others, unjust damage to the property of others, and the accepting of bribes by public officials.

8. THOU SHALT NOT BEAR FALSE WITNESS AGAINST THY NEIGHBOR.

Commands that the truth be spoken in all

St. Peter's Basilica in the Vatican City at Rome

things, but especially in what concerns the good name of others; that secrets be kept when sealed by promise, when one's office requires it or when the good of another demands it; that restitution be made, when possible, for the damage done to the good name of another.

Forbids lies, rash judgment, detraction, calumny, and the telling of secrets one is bound to keep.

9. THOU SHALT NOT COVET THY NEIGHBOR'S WIFE.
Commands purity in thought and desire.
Forbids all thoughts and desires contrary to purity.

10. THOU SHALT NOT COVET THY NEIGHBOR'S GOODS.
Forbids envy at the success of others and all desire to take or keep unjustly what belongs to others.

PRECEPTS OF THE CHURCH

The Church, a perfect society equipped by God with all the authority and means necessary to provide for the spiritual welfare of its members, has the power to make laws. The Precepts of the Church oblige Catholics to:

1. Assist at Mass on Sundays and holy days of obligation. (Also, to desist from unnecessary servile work on these days.)
2. Fast and abstain on the days appointed.
3. Confess their sins at least once a year.
4. Receive Holy Communion during the Easter time.
5. Contribute to the support of the Church.
6. Observe the laws of the Church concerning marriage.

4
Roman Catholicism

A PERSON'S CONVERSION IS often preceded by inner conflict, introspection, fear of death, renunciation of sin, and the keen desire to be united with God. The crisis, which may be spiritual, moral, or physical, urges the convert to change himself for God. Humility is paramount to conversion.

The theology of conversion involves grace, a supernatural gift of God. Grace makes the recipient a "child" of God and enables him to participate in God's divine nature. Man freely cooperates in this process; Grace is *given* but is ineffectual unless it is *accepted*.

Conversion is the active acceptance of God's supernatural gift[1] and requires the surrender of one's pride. In other words, conversion requires the use of human reason and will power in cooperation with divine grace.

The effects of conversion are both psychological and theological. Psychologically, the convert reorients his life and all its values toward conscious intellectual growth, changes his way of life, and experiences peace of soul through certainty of belief.

The spiritual effects of conversion include the presence of God and the incorporation of the individual into the Mystical Body of Christ, that is, the Church.

1. *Peace of Soul* (Garden City, N.Y.: Image Books Division of Doubleday and Co., 1954), pp. 236-37.

In the early days of the Church, the term *conversion* meant a moral change in favor of God and the true religion. In the Middle Ages, it often meant the renunciation of the world to enter the religious state, the return of a sinner, heretic, or schismatic to a moral life within the Catholic Church, or the turning of an infidel to Catholicism. Conversion always meant more than a change of Church membership. It represented a change of heart, acceptance of Church doctrines, and submission to Church laws.[2]

The Roman Catholic system of conversion is based on natural law and Church law. The natural law challenges every person to seek the true religion, embrace it, and live according to its principles and precepts. Catholic dogma asserts that a person can attain knowledge of God through reason. Although faith is a gift of God, it is a supernatural act of the intellect and will. It is not a blind act but one of understanding, influenced by the will.

The Church appeals to the nonbeliever as the guardian and teacher of revealed truth. The Church claims to bear the "credentials" of the one true religion, which are called the "marks of credibility." They are Unity, Sanctity, Catholicity, and Apostolicity.

The Church recognizes three steps of conversion; they are considered supernatural acts. First, the prospective convert is stimulated by a variety of motives (such as dissatisfaction with his present condition, or intellectual curiosity) and influenced by external grace to investigate the credentials of the Church. The next step is "the good will to believe." The final step is the Act of Faith: "I believe what the Church teaches because God has revealed it."

2. *The Catholic Encyclopedia Dictionary* (New York: The Gilman Society, 1910), p. 254.

After the three steps of conversion are completed, the sacrament of baptism is administered. The convert is thereby formally received into the Church.

The Church teaches that, since salvation depends on conversion, no power can interfere with the prerogative of the Church to accept all who wish to enter. But the Church has the power to stipulate conditions for acceptance. To convert, a person must have knowledge of the Catholic religion, make a profession of Catholic faith, and resolve to live in accordance with the teachings and precepts of that faith. Heretics (baptized Christians who reject Church dogma) must be reconciled to the Church. Protestants fall into the category of "heretics" only in an informal sense. To meet the conditions of reconciliation, a heretic must make an abjuration of heresy or a profession of faith. He must receive conditional baptism if there is doubt about the validity of the Protestant baptism. He must go to confession and receive conditional absolution.

The Roman Catholic Church does not reject every kind of non-Catholic baptism. Each case is examined and judged on its own merits. Generally, the Church recognizes the validity of baptism administered by the Eastern Orthodox Church and the Old Catholics, but it finds baptism administered by the majority of the Protestant denominations to be unacceptable.

In many parts of the world, a prospective convert who, in the opinion of the Church, was validly baptized in another religion is merely required to fulfill the steps required by the Church that were not included or properly fulfilled as part of the original baptism. The only requirements for the validly baptized non-Catholic are an abjuration of heresy or a profession of faith, and absolution from censures (spiritual punishment for wrongdoing).

Because it is difficult to determine the circumstances attending the original baptism, such as the intention of the administrator and the mode of administration, the usual procedure in the United States is to baptize all converts, either conditionally or absolutely. The procedure for conditional baptism calls for an abjuration of errors or a profession of faith, conditional baptism, and sacramental confession followed by absolution. The formula recited by the officiating priest for a conditional baptism is: "If thou art not yet baptized, then I baptize thee in the name . . ."

When baptism is conferred absolutely, the convert need not make an abjuration of errors or profession of faith. He is also excused from the confession of sins and the need for absolution.

The Roman Catholic Church offers many opportunities for religious instruction, which are one of the conditions for admission into the Church. Making instruction available to applicants is a sacred duty of clergymen.

The Catholic Church will not admit a convert unless it feels certain that "he sees clearly it is credible." The instructions a prospective convert receives are intended to give him this clear insight on his own intellectual and social level. The instructions are not limited to the cerebral sphere. The Catholic-to-be is also encouraged to practice the exercises of Christian perfection.

The needs of the individual determine the amount of time devoted to instructions as well as the level of teaching. Religious training should include going to Mass and becoming familiar with the inside of the church.

Many Catholic groups have made the dissemination of Catholic information to non-Catholics their

The Sistine Chapel in the Vatican is the place of the con-clave during the election of a Pope

sacred vocation. The Paulist Fathers, who are among the most active Catholic missionaries, maintain information centers in many large American cities. The Paulists offer a course of studies leading to conversion. They also publish a variety of pamphlets on conversion to Catholicism.

The Knights of Columbus is a large and effective Catholic laymen's group engaged in proselytizing. Clubs are active throughout the United States, in Puerto Rico, the Philippine Islands, Canada, and Mexico. The Knights of Columbus aim to soothe points of controversy and to make Catholicism an integral part of American life.

Anyone interested in learning about the Catholic faith will find Catholic information centers conveniently located in most of the major cities. In addition to providing information and offering correspondence courses, some centers have classroom instruction.

Many clergymen believe that Catholic information centers are powerful instruments in conveying the message of Catholicism to the American public and bringing countless non-Catholics into the Church.

The abundance of instructional material for the prospective convert makes his chief problem one of discriminate selection. The great variety of guides, handbooks, and catechisms provides a wealth of information designed to make the neophyte feel at home in the Catholic religion with minimum effort and maximum speed.

The *Handbook for Converts*,[3] published in Cork, Ireland, is "designed as an aid for both convert and priest during the course of instruction." The prospective convert is reassured that his decision to investigate the

3. Rev. A. Bullen, *Handbook for Converts* (Cork, Ireland: The Mercier Press, Ltd., 1961).

teachings of the Catholic Church does not commit him to any course of action.

He is encouraged to ask questions and even express his dissatisfaction with unacceptable evidence advanced in support of doctrines and practices. He is urged to supplement his interest in study with prayer for divine help.

Attitudes Towards Mixed Marriage

Planning to marry a Catholic motivates many non-Catholics to look into Catholicism. If the non-Catholic ultimately decides against conversion, he enters into a "mixed marriage."[4] The Church has voluminous literature on mixed marriage. Mixed marriages are strongly discouraged, but the Church is flexible on this point.

At the time of publication of this book, marriage between a Catholic and non-Catholic is forbidden unless a dispensation has been granted. However, the matter of mixed marriage has been under study by canonists and theologians since it was brought up during the Ecumenical Council Vatican II, and it is possible that modifications might be made in Roman Catholic Church regulations for mixed marriages. A person contemplating a mixed marriage that involves a member of the Roman Catholic Church should consult a representative of the Church for information on current regulations.

At present, the following conditions prevail. If there is any danger to the faith of the Catholic partner or the children of such a marriage, mixed marriage is forbidden by canon law.[5] In certain cases, the Church

4. By a "mixed marriage" is meant a marriage in which the non-Catholic partner does not convert to Catholicism.

5. Canon 1060: "The Church most solemnly and everywhere forbids marriage between a Catholic and a person enrolled in a heretical or schismatic sect. If there is danger of perversion for the Catholic party and the offspring, such a marriage is forbidden also by divine law."

grants conditional dispensations. Approval of the Church, however, can never accompany the dispensation. A mixed marriage is never sanctified with a Nuptial Mass and blessing. The *banns*, that is, the announcement of an intended marriage in a parish church, are not published.

A mixed marriage that involves a baptized non-Catholic is called "mixed religion" and is unlawful but not invalid. Marriage to an unbaptized non-Catholic is both unlawful and invalid.[6] This condition is called "disparity of worship."

Conditions of dispensation for a mixed marriage are: grave cause, a written promise from the non-Catholic partner not to interfere with the religion of the Catholic, along with the promise of both parties to have all their children baptized and educated as Catholics, and moral certainty that the promises will be fulfilled. In addition, the Catholic party must assume the task of trying, prudently, to convert the non-Catholic partner.

A Catholic entering into a mixed marriage without dispensations, while not subject to excommunication, is *ipso facto* excluded from receiving the sacraments. A Catholic who, in addition, contracts a marriage before a non-Catholic clergyman or with implicit or explicit agreement to raise the children as non-Catholics incurs excommunication *ipso facto*. The Church's rules on mixed marriages are due to her concern that the Catholic may endanger his faith and that of his children. Moreover, the Church has found through experience that mixed marriages are often the cause of marital strife.

Reverend D. F. Miller, C.S.S.R., in a pamphlet en-

6. Cannon 1070: Marriage between a Catholic and a person who was not baptized is "null and void."

titled *Can Mixed Marriages Be Happy?*,[7] points to the notion current among Catholics that mixed marriages can be happy, an attitude uncovered by a recent poll. The Church differs on this count. First, there is the prohibition in Canon Law (1060 and 1070). A good Catholic will submit to the laws of the Church or ask for a dispensation. Second, a true Catholic will sacrifice the mundane and sensual pleasures he sees in a mixed marriage for the true happiness which is only in Heaven. He will also consider the dangers to home and children inherent in a marriage with a non-Catholic mate. Third, happiness in this world requires complete union of husband and wife, which can never be attained in a mixed marriage because the partners, coming from different religions, cannot be united in soul, a union indispensable to a true marriage.

Reverend Miller feels that a good Catholic will draw the following conclusions:

1. In view of the fact that mixed marriage is forbidden, that it poses a danger to the soul of the Catholic and the children, and that complete union is impossible in a mixed marriage, a Catholic should marry only a fellow Catholic.

2. If the Catholic keeps company with a non-Catholic, the latter should be informed at an early date that if he wishes to pursue the courtship he must resolve to learn the Catholic faith and be prepared to convert to it.

3. If a mixed marriage is unavoidable, the Catholic party must be prepared not to complain when suffering comes his way. He must be willing to sacrifice, but not to compromise, for the sake of his faith. He must elect to live the life of a "heroic Catholic."

7. *Can Mixed Marriages Be Happy?* (Liguori, Mo.: Liguorian Pamphlets, 1957).

Reverend John A. O'Brien,[8] Catholic authority on conversion, explains why the Church is opposed to mixed marriage. First, the Church is solicitous for the happiness of both partners, a state which experience shows is difficult to achieve when both partners are not of the same faith. Second, the Church wishes to preserve the Catholic partner from cooling to the Catholic Church, a situation which usually comes about with mixed marriage. Finally, the Church is concerned with the Catholic training and education of the children, which cannot be guaranteed in a mixed marriage.

The reader is assured that the Church's concern for her communicants is not motivated by a feeling of its own weakness. Rather, it is influenced by the knowledge that the home environment and, in some cases, inadequate religious training are difficult for the Catholic to withstand. The Church is fully aware of the influence of parental example and home environment on children.

The Catholic Church is not out to ensnare non-Catholics. It is not interested in using mixed marriage as an instrument to acquire new members. Converts must embrace Catholicism freely; they must have thorough instruction and inner conviction. Conversion must come from within as an act of the intellect and the will.

Pope Pius XI condemned mixed marriage because it lacks "that close union of spirit" that must mark Christian wedlock and because it is a danger to the religious upbringing of the children. The Roman Catholic Church's attitude toward mixed marriage is summed up in a *Handbook for Converts*.[9]

8. *Marriage: Catholic or Mixed* (Huntington, Ind.: Our Sunday Visitor Press, undated).
9. *Op. cit.*, p. 84.

. . . The Church, anxious over the "here and now" of her sons and daughters, discourages marriages between Catholics and members of other religions.

While it is not impossible for a good Catholic to be united in soul in a limited way with a non-Catholic, this union is much more slender than the great bond of a common Faith which unites two Catholics. A mixed marriage, therefore, is less likely to be a nice and happy marriage. It is for this reason, and because of the danger to the Faith of the Catholic partner and offspring, that the Church requires some serious reason before she will allow one of her children to marry a non-Catholic.

Yet, despite her opposition, the Church will permit the marriage of a Catholic to a non-Catholic under certain circumstances. When she realizes that the ideal is not possible, that the welfare of her children is at stake, she will grant a dispensation. Dispensations are usually granted in the cases of a Catholic living in a non-Catholic area where the circle of possible suitors is limited to non-Catholics, an older person whose chances of marriage to a Catholic are slim and diminishing with time, and when the non-Catholic shows an immediate and sincere interest in the Catholic religion.[10]

In their pamphlet called *Six Premarital Instructions for Catholics and Non-Catholics*,[11] Fathers Leslie Rumble and Charles Mortimer Carty enumerate the promises required of a couple about to contract a mixed marriage. They include a guarantee of full freedom for

10. *Can Mixed Marriages Be Happy?*, *op. cit.*
11. *Six Pre-Marital Instructions for Catholics and Non-Catholics* (St. Paul, Minn.: Radio Replies Press, undated).

the Catholic party to practice the Catholic religion, prayer and good example by the Catholic partner to lead the non-Catholic to the true faith, and the understanding that all children born to them will be brought up as Catholics. The pamphlet also presents instructions [12] on Catholicism to be given in cases of mixed marriage *before* any promises are made.

Individual bishops of the various dioceses have the power to determine the conditions for a mixed marriage. The amount of instruction to be given the non-Catholic partner and the use of the church building for the marriage rite vary from one diocese to another. Everywhere, however, the following agreement is required:

> I, the undersigned, not a member of the Catholic Church, wishing to contract marriage with ...., a member of the Catholic Church, propose to do so with the understanding that the marriage tie is indissoluble except by death, and promise on my word of honor that .... shall enjoy free exercise of religion according to his/her belief, and that all children of either sex born of this marriage shall be baptized and educated exclusively in the faith and according to the teachings of the Roman Catholic Church; and furthermore, that no other marriage ceremony than that before the Catholic priest shall take place.[13]

12. These instructions are grouped under the chapter titles:
    1. "The True Church"
    2. "The Commandments of the Church"
    3. "The Holy Eucharist"
    4. "Why Catholics Attend Mass"
    5. "The Sacraments and Penance"
    6. "The Sacrament of Matrimony"

13. *Yes . . . I Condemned the Catholic Church* ("Knights of Columbus Series," No. 15 [St. Louis, Mo., 1949]), p. 30.

It is important to note that Catholics may be joined in marriage exclusively by a Roman Catholic priest, not by a clergyman of another faith or a justice of the peace.

Another booklet on mixed marriage[14] summarizes the highlights of the "promises" as follows:

1. Indissolubility of the marriage bond, and complete adherence to the rules of the Church
2. Baptism, instruction, education and training of children according to the rules, regulations, disciplines and teachings of the Church
3. Freedom for the Catholic partner and children to practice the Catholic religion, and burial for them in a Catholic cemetery.

After the agreement and promises are expedited satisfactorily under circumstances legitimate in the eyes of the Church, a dispensation is granted.

The concern of the Church does not end with the marriage ceremony. This is clearly spelled out in *A Program for Catholics in a Mixed Marriage.*[15] It presents a

> . . . definite program of principles, actions and habits to preserve themselves and their families from the very tragedies they have been warned against by the experience and the authority of the Church.

The fourfold program in a mixed marriage requires the Catholic partner to take precautions for:

1. The preservation of his faith

14. Richard Ginder, *A Mixed Marriage* (New York: Catholic Information Society, undated).

15. D. F. Miller, C.S.S.R., *A Program for Catholics in a Mixed Marriage* (Liguori, Mo.: Liguorian Pamphlets, 1960).

2. Fidelity to the Catholic principles of morality
3. The Catholic upbringing of the children
4. The right attitude toward his partner.

To counteract the erosion of Catholic faith that often occurs in the case of mixed marriage, the author prescribes a specific program for the Catholic partner. He is urged to subscribe to a program of:

1. Deeper reading and intensification of faith
2. Confession for regular guidance and devotion
3. Tenacious adherence to habits of prayer and reception of Holy Communion
4. Loyalty to Catholic morals regarding birth prevention, abortion, sterilization, etc.
5. Recognition of dangers to children stemming from example and counteracting them with intensive home training and Catholic school education
6. Sharing the Catholic religion with the non-Catholic by means of fearless patience and understanding, prayer, good example, and even silence and suffering when necessary. The Catholic must strive to obtain a clear and increasing knowledge of the foundations of his faith. He should supplement this program with an invitation to his non-Catholic mate to join him at Catholic services, lectures, and other functions, with the hope that these experiences will ultimately bring him into the Church.

Many Protestants, however, believe that sweeping reforms in the Catholic law are needed as a prerequisite for a rapprochement between the Catholic Church and Protestantism. Many Protestants feel that the Catholic Church should not threaten those about to enter a mixed marriage with sanctions, that the validity of mixed marriage should be recognized and the various religions should cooperate to stabilize the marriage, and that the Catholic Church should not claim exclusive priorities. Protestants believe that one Church should not force a member of another Church to abide by her laws, that both partners should be permitted to continue as members of their own Churches, and that the religious affiliation of the children should be left to the consciences of the parents and the children.[16]

Within the Catholic Church itself a new attitude on mixed marriage may crystallize in the future. A writer in an influential national Catholic weekly recently called for more kindliness in mixed marriages in terms of:

1. Revised promises (perhaps a witnessed verbal agreement to replace the written one which must be signed)
2. Some announcement of the banns
3. A liturgical ceremony (designed to emphasize the sacramental character of marriage which current practice tends to dismiss in the case of a mixed marriage).[17]

Can this be understood as indicative of a new mood which may revolutionize the entire position on mixed marriage held by the Catholic Church? Only time will tell.

THE RECEPTION OF CONVERTS

A Catholic Dictionary[18] presents the following

16. Erwin Wilkens, "Reform of the Roman Catholic Law of Mixed Marriage," *Ecumenical Review World Council of Churches,* XIV (1962), p. 103.

17. Joe Breig, editorial in *Ave Maria,* July 21, 1962, p. 19.

18. *A Catholic Dictionary* (3rd ed.; New York: Macmillan Co., 1961), p. 122.

Form of reconciliation of heretics (i. e., Protestants and schismatics readmitted into the Church) used in Great Britain:

> *Veni Creator Spiritus* is said or sung, followed by a prayer; the convert then kneels with his right hand on the gospels and reads his profession of faith (the Creed of Pope Pius IV) and abjuration of heresy; the Psalm *Misere* is then said and a prayer for absolution: here follow the Baptism or conditional Baptism if either be necessary, and the Priest pronounces release from excommunication and imposes a small penance; unless the convert has been baptized absolutely, Confirmation and sacramental absolution then follow; *Te Deum* and a prayer are said or sung, and the convert is dismissed with a blessing and exhortation.

The *Handbook for Converts*[19] gives the following account of the reception of a convert:

> Although it is simple and short, you will undoubtedly find the ceremony of your reception into the Church very moving. It will not be trying, for apart from two witnesses, it is quite likely that there will be no one but you and the priest in the church at the time.
>
> If you don't know two Catholics (of the same sex as yourself) who will be able and glad to stand as witnesses, the priest will find them for you.
>
> You will all go to the Communion rails and kneel down. The priest will say alternately with you this hymn to the Holy Ghost:

Come, Holy Ghost, Creator, come
From Thy bright heavenly throne

19. *Op. cit.,* pp. 113-16.

Come take possession of our souls
And make them all Thine own.

Thou who art called the Paraclete
Best gift of God above
The living Spring, the living Fire,
Sweet unction and true Love.

Thou who art sevenfold in Thy grace,
Finger of God's right hand,
His promise, teaching little ones,
To speak and understand.

O guide our minds with Thy blest light
With love our heart inflame
And with Thy strength which ne'er decays
Confirm our mortal frame.

Far from us drive our fiendish foe
True peace unto us bring
And through all perils lead us safe
Beneath Thy sacred wing.

Through Thee may we the Father know
Through Thee th' eternal Son
And Thee the Spirit of them both,
Thrice-blessed Three in One.

All glory while the ages run
Be to the Father, and the Son
Who rose from death, the same to Thee,
O Holy Ghost, eternally. Amen.

Send forth Thy Spirit, and they shall be
created.
And Thou shalt renew the face of the earth.

Let us pray
O God, who hast taught the hearts of the faithful

by the light of the Holy Spirit, grant that by the light of the same Spirit we may be always wise and ever rejoice in His consolation. Through Christ Our Lord, Amen.

With your hand on the Missal, you will then make this profession of Faith. [Convert makes profession of Faith. See Appendix A.] Next, the priest will say a psalm asking for God's mercy.

Out of the depths I have cried to Thee, O Lord:
> Lord, hear my voice.
> Let Thine ears be attentive to the voice of my supplication.

If Thou, O Lord, wilt mark iniquities:
> Lord, who shall endure it?

For with Thee there is merciful forgiveness:
> And by reason of Thy law I have waited for Thee, O Lord.

My soul hath relied on His word: My soul hath hoped in the Lord.

> From the morning watch even until night, let Israel hope in the Lord.
> Because with the Lord there is mercy: and with Him plentiful redemption.
> AND He shall redeem Israel from all his iniquities.
> Glory be to the Father and to the Son and to the Holy Ghost.
> As it was in the beginning, is now, and ever shall be, world without end. Amen.

Then follows the Baptism. If you have definitely not been previously baptised, the priest will administer Baptism with the full ceremonies. If, however, it is only possible, but not certain that you have previously been baptised, he will perform the very brief ceremony of conditional baptism.

Pope Nicholas I, 858-67

You will then return to the Communion rails where the priest will absolve you from possible excommunication:

"By the authority of the Apostolic See committed to me for this purpose, I absolve thee from the bonds of excommunication which (perhaps) thou hast incurred, and restore thee to the Holy Sacraments of the Church, to the communion and fellowship of the faithful. In the name of the Father, and of the Son, and of the Holy Ghost. Amen."

This is followed by the *Te Deum,* a prayer of thanksgiving for the gift of faith you have received.

After this ceremony you make your first Confession.

A slightly different ceremony is described in *A Catechism for Inquirers:* [20]

1. The "Profession of Faith," which is read by the convert to a priest, usually in the church. The priest sits vested in surplice and violet stole, and a book of the gospels is conveniently placed so that the convert may touch it with his hand. After the Profession has been read, the priest reads a psalm, some prayers, and a form of Absolution.
2. Then follows immediately Conditional Baptism, and
3. Confession by the convert and Conditional Absolution.

Profession of Faith

Regulations for the use of this short form are as follows: (1) The shorter form, recommended by the Catho-

20. Rev. Joseph I. Mallon, C.S.P., *A Catechism for Inquirers* (Revised ed.; New York: Paulist Press, 1960), pp. 92-3.

lic bishops of the United States of America, is to be used only for those who have not reached the age of puberty and for those who are uneducated. All those who find the longer form beyond their religious education can be considered as uneducated persons. (2) But for better educated Catholics the longer form must be used. (Decree of the Supreme Sacred Congregations of the Holy Office, N. 211/54, July, 1956.)

> Then while the convert is still kneeling, the priest sitting say the *De Profundis* or the *Miserere*.
> Lord, have mercy.
> Christ, have mercy.
> Lord, have mercy. Our Father (silently).
> and lead us not into temptation.
> But deliver us from evil.
> Grant salvation to Your servant(s).
>
> For his (her, their) hope, O my God, is in You.
> O Lord, hear my prayer.
> And let my cry come to You.
> The Lord be with you.
> And with your spirit.
>
> ### Let Us Pray
>
> O God, whose property is always to have mercy to spare, receive our petition, that this Your servant (these Your servants), who is (are) bound by the sentence of ex-communication, may mercifully be absolved by the compassion of Your goodness. Through Christ our Lord. Amen.

The priest then sits down and gives the following absolution:

By the Apostolic authority, which I exercise here, I absolve you from the bonds of excommunication which (perhaps) you have incurred; and I restore you to the Holy Sacraments of the Church, to the communion and unity of the faithful, in the Name of the Father, and of the Son, and of the Holy Ghost. Amen.

Conversion Procedure

How does a person go about converting to the Roman Catholic religion? The following answer is the usual procedure.

The average Catholic-to-be becomes somewhat doubtful about his own religion or curious about Catholicism. He may begin reading on his own. Eventually he enrolls in a course of instruction in the teachings of the Catholic Church. He enrolls either at the parish church nearest his home (privately or in a group), or at one of the many Catholic information centers.[21] Instructions vary in length depending on the individual's ability to learn, the depth of his previous education, the amount of time he can spend studying, etc. Usually, a parish priest uses a catechism as his textbook. A catechism is usually composed of separate sections on dogma, morals, and the sacraments. The material is presented in question-and-answer format.

21. One of the Paulist Information Centers, operated by the Paulist Fathers, is located at 2 Columbus Avenue, New York, New York.

St. Patrick's Information Center is located at 31 E. 50th St., New York, New York.

The Religious Information Bureau of the Knights of Columbus —4422 Lindell Boulevard, St. Louis 8, Missouri—offers a free correspondence course.

Pope Adrian IV, 1154-59

After completing his instructions, the prospective convert is ready to decide whether or not he accepts the teachings of the Church. If he does, he presents himself to the priest in church to make his profession of Faith. The ceremony (described on page 97) is usually private.

The parish priest takes a personal interest in his prospective converts. When a non-Catholic tells a priest of his interest in Catholicism, the priest tries to ascertain his present knowledge of Catholicism and the sincerity of his determination to live as a Catholic. In most cases, this results in a series of instructions, either private or in a class, or both, on Catholic teachings.

Usually, during these instructions, a personal relationship is established between the priest and the person involved, which enables the priest to know the sincerity of the person's convictions and to offer him the necessary personal guidance. Priests generally look for a deep desire to discover and abide by the will of God.

A director of St. Patrick's Information Center in New York City summarizes:

> . . . There is, for me, a great temptation to oversimplify . . . and to repeat the answer of Peter the Apostle on Pentecost when his audience asked what they must do. He told them to repent of their sins and to be baptized. This, of course, required faith in Jesus. Our conclusion, then, would be faith in Jesus and all He taught, and baptism.
>
> With this oversimplified answer, you will find that the Catholic Church's laws agree. One law states that Baptism makes a person a member of the Church . . .

As for the requirements for conversion, he wrote:

> An adult should be well instructed in what

he believes, as well as convinced of it; there should be knowledge plus conviction. For this purpose, the usual procedure is a course of instruction. During the weeks of instruction, the person is encouraged to develop habits of prayer and to become familiar with the worship of the Church, the Mass. At the close of this period, the person is interviewed, to make sure that he knows enough, to make sure that he believes all the doctrine, and to make sure he is properly motivated . . .

Bethlehem

Documents

A Profession of Faith (short form)

I, ... touching with my hand God's Holy Gospels, enlightened by divine grace, profess the faith, which the Catholic, Apostolic, Roman Church teaches. I believe that Church to be the one true Church, which Jesus Christ founded on earth: to which I submit with all my heart.

I believe in God, the Father Almighty, Creator of heaven and earth; and in Jesus Christ, His only Son, Our Lord; who was conceived by the Holy Ghost, born of the Virgin Mary, suffered under Pontius Pilate, was crucified, died, and was buried. He descended into Hell; the third day He arose again from the dead; He ascended into Heaven, sitteth at the right hand of God, the Father Almighty; from thence He shall come to judge the living and the dead. I believe in the Holy Ghost, the Holy Catholic Church, the communion of saints, the forgiveness of sins, the resurrection of the body, and life everlasting. Amen.

I believe that seven sacraments were instituted by Jesus Christ for the salvation of mankind: namely, Baptism, Confirmation, Holy Eucharist, Penance, Extreme Unction, Holy Orders and Matrimony.

I believe that the Pope, the Bishop of Rome, is the Vicar of Jesus Christ on earth, that he is the supreme visible head of the whole Church, and that he teaches infallibly what we must believe and do to be saved.

I also believe everything which the Holy, Catholic, Apostolic and Roman Church defines and declares we must believe. I adhere to her with all my heart, and I reject every error and schism which she condemns.

So help me God and these holy Gospels which I touch with my hand.

Profession of Faith (Long Form)

I ....

.... years of age, born outside the Catholic Church, have held and believed errors contrary to her teaching. Now enlightened by divine grace, I kneel before you, Reverend Father ....

.... having before my eyes and touching with my hands the Holy Gospels; and with a firm faith I believe and profess each and all the articles that are contained in The Apostles' Creed, that is, I believe in God, the Father Almighty, Creator of Heaven and Earth; and in Jesus Christ, His Only Son, Our Lord, who was conceived by the Holy Ghost, born of the Virgin Mary, suffered under Pontius Pilate, was crucified, died and was buried; He descended into Hell, the third day He rose again from the dead; He ascended into Heaven and sitteth at the right hand of God, the Father Almighty; from thence he will come to judge the living and the dead. I believe in the Holy Ghost; the Holy Catholic Church; the communion of saints; the forgiveness of sins; the resurrection of the body, and life everlasting. Amen.

I admit and embrace most firmly the apostolic and ecclesiastical traditions and all the other constitutions and prescriptions of the Church.

I admit the Sacred Scriptures according to the sense which has been held and which is still held by Holy Mother Church, whose duty it is to judge the true sense and interpretation of the

Pope Boniface VIII, 1294-1303, painting by Giotto

Pope Innocent XI, 1676-89

Sacred Scriptures; and I shall never accept or interpret them except according to the unanimous consent of the Fathers.

I profess that the Sacraments of the New Law are, truly and precisely seven in number, instituted for the salvation of mankind, though all are not necessary for each individual: Baptism, Confirmation, Holy Eucharist, Penance, Extreme Unction, Holy Orders and Matrimony. I profess that all confer grace and that of these Baptism, Confirmation and Holy Orders cannot be repeated without sacrilege.

I also accept and admit the ritual of the Catholic Church in the solemn administration of all the above mentioned Sacraments.

I accept and hold, in each and every part, all that has been defined and declared by the Sacred Council of Trent concerning Original Sin and Justification. I profess that in the Mass is offered to God a true, real and propitiatory sacrifice for the living and the dead; that in the Holy Sacrament of the Eucharist is really, truly and substantially the Body and Blood together with the soul and Divinity of Our Lord Jesus Christ, and that there takes place what the Church calls transubstantiation, that is the change of all the substance of bread into the Body and of all substance of wine into the Blood. I confess also that in receiving under either of these species one receives Jesus Christ, whole and entire.

I firmly hold that Purgatory exists and that the souls detained there can be helped by the prayers of the faithful. Likewise I hold that the saints who reign with Jesus Christ should be venerated and invoked, that they offer prayers to God for us and that their relics are to be venerated.

I profess firmly that the images of Jesus

Christ and of the Mother of God, ever Virgin, as well as of all the saints should be given due honor and veneration. I also affirm that Jesus Christ left to the Church the faculty to grant Indulgences and that their use is most salutary to the Christian people. I recognize the Holy Roman, Catholic and Apostolic Church as the mother and teacher of all the Churches and I promise and swear true obedience to the Roman Pontiff, successor of St. Peter, Prince of the Apostles, and Vicar of Jesus Christ.

Besides I accept, without hesitation, and profess all that has been handed down, defined and declared by the Sacred Canons and by the general Councils, especially by the Sacred Council of Trent and by the Vatican General Council, and in a special manner concerning the primacy and infallibility ·of the Roman Pontiff. At the same time I condemn and reprove all that the Church has condemned and reproved. This same Catholic Faith, outside of which nobody can be saved, which I now freely profess and to which I truly adhere, the same I promise and swear to maintain and profess, with the help of God, entire, inviolate and with firm constancy until the last breath of life; and I shall strive, as far as possible, that this same faith shall be held, taught and publicly professed by all who depend on me and by those of which I shall have charge.

So help me God and these Holy Gospels.

Eastern Orthodox Church

Mount Sinai, commonly accepted as the mountain where
Moses received the Ten Commandments, is the site of the
Greek Orthodox Monastery of St. Catherine

Introduction—Eastern Orthodox Church

FOR AN INTRODUCTION TO the Eastern Orthodox Church the author decided to go to an official source and therefore presents the following excerpt from the *Year Book* and Church Directory of the Russian Orthodox Greek Catholic Church of America. [1]

The Orthodox Church is the unity of faith and love (St. Ignatius of Antioch) of all Churches which have preserved Orthodoxy, i.e., the Tradition of Faith, Order, Worship and Piety, as confessed from the beginning "everywhere, always and by all." And, although historically she was for a long time confined to the Eastern part of Christendom after the separation of the Christian West from her, the Orthodox Church rejects the idea that hers is a "partial" or "oriental" expression of the Christian faith. On the contrary, she confesses her faith to be full, catholic, and universal. She sees herself as the One, Holy, Catholic and Apostolic Church.

1. Reprinted with permission from the Introduction by the Very Reverend Alexander Schmemann, Dean of St. Vladimir's Orthodox Theological Seminary, to the *Year Book* and Church Directory of the Russian Orthodox Greek Catholic Church of America (New York, 1963), pp. 7-11.

115

The Tradition of Faith stems from Divine Revelation as recorded in Holy Scriptures and understood and interpreted by the Church in the continuity of her teaching ministry: by her Councils, Fathers, Teachers, Saints, by her worship and by the whole of her Divinely inspired life. Of especial normative character are the dogmatical and canonical decisions of the Seven Ecumenical and Ten local Councils, the writings of the Holy Fathers, the testimony of the liturgical and iconographic tradition and the universal consensus of doctrine and practice.

The Tradition of Order is based on the unbroken continuity of the Ministry and above all on the Apostolic succession of Bishops who are, in each Church, the guardians of the catholic fullness of faith and the Divinely appointed bearers of the Church's priestly, pastoral and teaching power and authority. Their unity expresses the unity of the Church; their agreement is the voice of the Holy Spirit. They govern the Church, and in this they are helped by the priests and deacons. They are also helped by the whole body of the Church, for, according to Orthodox teaching, all the faithful are entrusted with responsibility for the purity of faith. Church order is preserved in the Holy Canons, which constitute an integral part of Tradition.

The Tradition of Worship includes the seven Sacraments: Baptism, Chrismation, Eucharist, Holy Orders, Matrimony, Unction and Penance; the order of the daily, weekly and yearly cycles of prayers; the Fasts and Feasts; the commemoration and veneration of the Mother of God, the Saints and the Angels; the veneration of Holy Icons; the prayers for the departed members of Christ's Body; the sanctification—through rites of blessing and intercession—of all human life as life in Christ.

The Tradition of Piety is expressed primarily in the lives, achievements, and teachings of the saints, who bear witness to the presence and action of the Holy Spirit in the Church and are, therefore, our guides and helpers on the way to the Kingdom of God.

All those—individuals, groups or churches—who reject the whole or any part of this Tradition, who deform it or deviate from it, are, according to the teachings of the Orthodox Church, alien to Orthodoxy and cannot be admitted to the Sacraments, for these are the signs and the fulfillment of the Church as unity of faith and love.

The following Orthodox Churches exist at present: the four ancient Patriarchates of Constantinople, Antioch, Alexandria, and Jerusalem; the national Churches of Russia, Greece, Serbia, Georgia, Bulgaria, Rumania, Poland, Czechoslovakia, Albania, and the churches of Cyprus and Sinai. Each of these is autocephalous, i.e., independent in its Hierarchical and administrative structure and united to other churches by the identity of tradition and communion in sacraments. The Ecumenical Patriarch of Constantinople is recognized as the first bishop among equals and has the primacy of honor. Each autocephalous church, in turn, has its Primate who assures its unity with all other churches.

At the end of the eighteenth century, the Orthodox faith was brought to Alaska, then a Russian territory, by a group of Russian monks from Valamo. They converted the Aleuts, and in 1848 the first bishopric was established in Sitka. From Alaska it spread along the Pacific Coast and then moved to the East, encountering a wave of Orthodox immigration that began in the second part of the nineteenth century. Prior to

**Monastery of Gregorious, Mount Athos, Greece, founded
in the 13th century**

World War I, all Orthodox parishes, regardless of their national origin, were under the canonical jurisdiction of the Russian Church, forming a Diocese with the Bishop, who, since 1906, resided in New York. After the war, virtually every ethnic group formed its own Diocese with direct dependence on its national mother-Church in the Old World. The years 1920–39 were the peak of this acute "nationalisation" of Orthodoxy in America. There existed, in the U.S.A. and Canada, more than ten Orthodox jurisdictions which, although in communion with one another, maintained very loose contacts among themselves. After World War II the need for cooperation, the challenge of a new generation— American born and American educated—and many other factors raised the inescapable question of greater unity. . . . After several unsuccessful attempts, a first concrete step was taken with the establishment of The Standing Conference of Orthodox Bishops in America.

5

Eastern Orthodox Church

THE EASTERN ORTHODOX CHURCH claims to be the "ancient Church of the World," the very Mother and source of Christianity. For ten centuries, it was the one Church of the Holy Apostles, of the Holy Fathers, and of the martyrs of old. It maintains that Western Christianity, though derived from the East, split away from its source and is now divided into a multiplicity of sects known as Roman Catholicism, Protestantism, Greek Catholicism, etc. The original, ancient Church of the East, known as the Eastern Orthodox Church, remains ever the same, immutable and Orthodox.

Orthodox clergymen state that a precise definition of the Eastern Orthodox Church is difficult, if not impossible. This is the closest they can come to a definitive description of their Church: The Church is "the Mystical Body of Christ" with Jesus as her Head, Source, and Essence. The Eastern Orthodox Church exists both on earth and in heaven. On earth are her members in the flesh; and in paradise are her members who have departed to be with their Savior. Yet, all are one in Him.

The Eastern Orthodox Church is described as a living body composed of vibrant parts whose Head and Lord is the founder of the faith. For this reason, Orthodoxy is violently opposed to any attempt by a mortal to assume the title "Head of the Church." The Church will never desert her immortal Lord for a mortal one on earth. Exponents of Catholicism have seen fit to find fault with this Orthodox doctrine, calling the Church "headless," and arguing that every visible body must have a visible head. Orthodox spokesmen call this a childish sophism that is undeserving of rebuttal. To them a Church with a "visible head" is a Church with an "absolute monarch."

The Eastern Orthodox Church, however, does have a hierarchy. It is governed by an Ecumenical Council, with the Patriarch of Constantinople (Istanbul) first in rank among the Orthodox patriarchs. Although he has the right to act as President of the entire Church, he does not enjoy the position of "head of the Church." No member of the Church may assume the title of "infallible teacher of the Church" because, in conformity with the teachings of Christian Scripture, only the Holy Spirit can be called an infallible teacher and guide of the Church; the Holy Spirit alone "shall lead us into all truth."

Orthodox leaders are emphatic in their position that the Eastern Orthodox Church is not a political organization. It has never possessed temporal power, nor has it ever coveted the scepter of Caesar.

Since the Church is visible, it must utilize visible means of imparting her invisible graces, called "Sacraments." The greatest of these sacramental means are the seven mysteries ordained by Jesus and His apostles. They are:

1. Baptism
2. Myrrh or Chrism (Confirmation)
3. Eucharist
4. Penitence

5. Priesthood or Holy Orders
6. Marriage
7. Prayer Oil or Holy Unction.

Official definitions of the Orthodox Church identify it with original Christianity:

> The Orthodox Church began with Christ and His Apostles at the very beginning of the Christian Era. There was no time in this Era when the Orthodox Church did not exist, and there has been no interruption of the life of the Orthodox Church up to today. Throughout the centuries the same teachings, the same principles, the same Head have remained. In its monuments is recorded the original and first birthday celebrated by the Apostles themselves. The Orthodox Church did not originate with Chrysostom, or Basil the Great, or Gregory the Theologian, or any such personality of the Church, but with Christ Himself and His Apostles. It is in fact an Apostolic Church, and its age is the same as that of Christianity itself.
>
> The word "orthodox" is derived from two Greek words: "orthos," right or true, and "doxa," opinion. It means "sound in opinion or doctrine, especially in religious doctrines; hence, specifically, holding the Christian faith as formulated in the great church creeds and confessions." The Orthodox Church bears the full meaning of the connotations of the "One, Holy, Catholic and Apostolic Church." It is not only "One," not only "Holy," or "Catholic," or "Apostolic;" it is all of them, that is: it is "Orthodox." "Orthodox," again, does not mean conservative, nor its antonym, radical . . . The term "orthodox" was used in olden times to define the faith of the Church against the heresies which arose for awhile denying mainly the truth of the Holy Trinity,

which the "heterodox" holds, and thus the term "Orthodox" became the chief title of the Church. Specifically, the Church is "ONE," for Christ is One, its Founder and Head, who preserves it and keeps it united. The Church is "Holy" because it is the sacred Institution for the sanctification of its faithful by the Holy Spirit. It is also "Catholic," a word which derives from the Greek "Kath-olou," which is a historical expression implying not only that its truth is unique everywhere and always, but also that it teaches the absolute Kath-olou Truth, and it is the only efficient one which unites the universe of man "so there shall be one flock, one Shepherd" (John 10: 16). Finally, the Church is "Apostolic" because its teaching and its active mission have been handed down by the Apostles in a continuous and unique succession to the leaders and members of the Church.[1]

The power and prestige of Eastern Orthodoxy has not been felt in America because Eastern Orthodox communicants form a relatively small minority of Christians in the United States. The nine autonomous ethnic churches comprising the Eastern Orthodox Church of America—the Greek, Russian, Albanian, Bulgarian, Carpatho-Russian, Rumanian, Serbian, Syrian, and Ukranian Churches—are self-governing institutions founded over half a century ago.

Although individual worshippers might think in terms of membership in the ethnic church, each of which is a self-governing institution, Eastern Orthodoxy is recognized as the mother-Church to which the smaller bodies look as an all-embracing institution with national differences erased by religious similarities. With the Americanization of the immigrants who brought

1. Rev. George Mastrantonis, *What Is The Eastern Orthodox Church?* (St. Louis, Mo.: Ologos, 1956), pp. 7-8.

this branch of Christianity to these shores and the increasing use of the English language for worship by their American-born children, an ecumenical spirit has been gaining momentum for the consolidation of the constituent bodies into a united Orthodox Church of America. The Church is a participating member of the world ecumenical movement involving most of the Protestant denominations and is one of the Confessional Bodies in the World Council of Churches.

Eastern Orthodoxy is not known for an aggressive missionary program. At the same time, however, Orthodoxy extends a hand of welcome to all who wish to join the Church. One Orthodox missionary group, which goes by the name of *Ologos* (Orthodox Lore of the Gospel of Our Savior), of St. Louis, Missouri, is listed as "a non-profit missionary team which publishes and distributes leaflets, pamphlets and booklets on the Eastern Orthodox Faith."

Conversion Procedure

Conversion in the churches comprising the mosaic of Eastern Orthodoxy adheres to the following pattern:

A person expresses his interest in joining the Church. His sincerity established by a priest, with the approval of a bishop, he is invited to undergo an undefined period of catechetical instruction with a local priest. The candidate, now called a *catechumen,* determines the length of time needed for the preliminary studies by the pace of his progress. He is required to acquaint himself with his new religion by reading the literature assigned to him by his instructor.

Following this period of instruction, the catechumen is required to accept the obligations of membership in the Orthodox Church. Now he is prepared to receive baptism, chrismation (confirmation) and the Holy

Eucharist, the three sacraments associated with admission into the Orthodox Church; he then signs an official document of conversion. The bestowal of these sacraments includes the avowal and recitation of the Nicene Creed, the symbol of faith for Orthodoxy that includes the acceptance of the divinity of Jesus, the Trinity, life eternal, baptism for the remission of sins, and chrismation as a spiritual "circumcision," etc.[2] With the fulfillment of these requirements and procedures, the catechumen becomes a full member of the Orthodox Church.

In the case of Christians baptized in the name of the Holy Trinity coming from a Protestant church and who are able to produce proof of baptism, acceptance

2. THE NICENE CREED

I believe in one God, the Father Almighty, Maker of Heaven and earth, and of all things visible and invisible.

And in one Lord Jesus Christ, the only-begotten Son of God, begotten of His Father before all worlds, Light of Light, Very God of Very God, Begotten, not made, being of one substance with the Father, by Whom all things were made.

Who for us men, and for our salvation, came down from Heaven; and was incarnate by the Holy Ghost of the Virgin Mary, and was made man.

And was crucified also for us under Pontius Pilate; He suffered and was buried.

And the third day He rose again according to the Scriptures.

And ascended into Heaven, and sitteth on the right hand of the Father.

And He shall come again with glory to judge both the quick and the dead; Whose kingdom shall have no end.

And I believe in the Holy Ghost, the Lord the Giver of Life, Who proceedeth from the Father[*]; Who with the Father and the Son together is worshipped and glorified; Who spake by the Prophets.

I believe in one Holy, Catholic and Apostolic Church.

I acknowledge one Baptism for the remission of sins.

I look for the resurrection of the dead.

And the life of the world to come. Amen.

[*] Point of difference with Roman Catholicism which holds that the Holy Ghost proceeds from the Father and the Son.

is through the sacrament of chrismation alone. Because the Orthodox Church recognizes the validity of the Catholic sacraments of Baptism and Confirmation, converts from Roman Catholicism are also excused from the sacrament of Chrismation and are admitted through the sacraments of penance and Holy Communion. The Orthodox Church differs from other Christian denominations in requiring the sacrament of Confirmation to follow immediately that of Baptism, even in the case of infants.

Converts must be accompanied by two sponsors of either sex who are members of the Church. Under certain conditions a single sponsor of the same sex as the convert is acceptable.

In the ordinary performance of the sacrament of baptism the priest blesses the water according to the prescribed ritual and then immerses the candidate in the font three times—in the name of the Father, and of the Son, and of the Holy Spirit. The Church recognizes, however, that there are certain instances when trine immersion is not possible and, consequently, provides for exceptions to this rule. "Baptism of the bed-ridden" by sprinkling water may be administered to the sick. In cases of extreme emergency, when water is not available and there is no time for a priest to be called or the service to be read, "aerobaptism," performed by any Orthodox Christian, is valid.

The baptismal formula is: "The Servant of God (name)is baptized in the name of the Father (first immersion, and of the Son (second immersion) and of the Holy Spirit (third immersion). Amen."

No baptism can be considered valid unless the name of the Trinity is invoked.

When this sacrament has not been performed in the name of the Holy Trinity or when the celebrant is not an Orthodox Christian then it must be repeated. However, the Church using leniency or "Economia" recognizes as valid the baptism performed by other Christian denominations if it is performed with water and in the name of the Holy Trinity. To such Christians coming into the Orthodox fold the Church administers only the Sacrament of Chrismation, or as it is known in the Western Churches, the Sacrament of Confirmation.[3]

The Bishop of Meloa, Mgr. Emilianos, representative of the Ecumenical Patriarchate to the World Council of Churches,[4] discusses conversion:

If the person to be converted belongs to a non-Christian religion, his initiation and baptism must precede the confirmation of his conversion to Orthodoxy. These are the two fundamental requirements.

Converts belonging to other Christian persuasions and turning to the Orthodox faith are obliged to sign an official document of acceptance of the Orthodox creed which is followed by a ritual ceremony called confirmation—"chrisma."

On principle, each person applying for membership to the Orthodox Church is classified at the beginning as "catechumen," otherwise "proselyte." The period of catechism may be shortened or prolonged according to one's own personal assimilation into the new faith. During this stage, the criteria of the Orthodox Church as to whether the proselyte merits the confirmation of his conversion, are based on the sincerity of his oral confession and his religious manifestations and spirituality towards the new faith . . .

The chief aim of our Church is not to proselytize

---

3. Bishop of Nazianzos Ezekiel, *The Sacrament of Holy Baptism* (New York: The Greek Archdiocese Publication Dept. undated).
4. 17 Route de Malagnou, Geneva.

people in order to increase the number of its believers but to make them consistent with the commandment of our Lord.

Arthur Dore, director of the Office of Information of the Greek Orthodox Archdiocese of North and South America,[5] states:

> The procedure in brief for conversion to the Greek Orthodox Church is as follows. The prospective convert first discusses his intentions with an Orthodox Priest and obtains instructions from him. The Priest decides whether or not to proceed with the conversion, which must also have the approval of the Bishop. Baptism, sponsored by a Godparent who is a member in good standing of the Greek Orthodox faith, is a requirement; but the Orthodox Church accepts as valid a Baptism previously performed in a Christian Church in the name of the Holy Trinity. Confirmation, Chrismation and Holy Communion are performed at the baptismal ceremony.
>
> Greek Orthodoxy welcomes converts, but does not solicit them. It is the policy of the Church not to proselytize among other Christian faiths. Mixed marriages are allowed but not encouraged. In such marriages, the non-Orthodox spouse must give assurances to the priest that the children will be brought up in the Greek Orthodox faith, before the marriage is performed in an Orthodox Church.

Ernest A. Villas, director of the Department of Laity of the Greek Orthodox Archdiocese of North and South America adds:

> Conversion to Greek Orthodoxy must be initiated by the prospective candidate seeking admission to membership in the Church. The Greek

5. 10 East 79th St., New York, N. Y. 10021

Orthodox Church has taken an adamant position against any and all forms of proselytizing, which is unfortunately practiced by some denominations under the guise of missionary activity. Orthodoxy welcomes any and all persons to its fold, regardless of race. This welcome is extended, however, only after the person indicating such interest has been found to be sincere in his desire for further steps into full communion.

The candidate would first undergo a period of catechetical instruction by the particular priest in his area. He would be given materials to read.

Following this instructional period, the length of which is largely determined by the pace of the candidate, and after acceptance by the candidate of the obligations of membership in the Orthodox Church, he is then prepared to receive the sacraments which will consummate his membership. These sacraments are Baptism, Chrismation and the Holy Eucharist. (Readings on these sacraments and familiarity with their significance would, of course, have been an important part of the instructional period.)

Following the bestowal of these sacraments, which includes avowal and recitation of the Nicene Creed, the applicant would be joyously accepted into full membership as one of the faithful, a true member of the "One, Holy, Catholic and Apostolic Church."

Historically speaking, and by no means do I pose as a source of historical data, we find that conversion to Orthodoxy was largely effected by the Orthodox laity whose examples of Christian piety were the Church's greatest attraction for new members. The equality of action between clergy and laity, the lack of discrimination against other peoples and minorities, and partici-

pation in the life of the civil community won for
the Orthodox the admiration and respect of
those about them. Eventually, conversion came
about as a natural process. In Africa this is
apparent today where the Greek community in
all large metropolitan areas is widely accepted
and respected. In short, it is a case of the people
bringing their Church with them, not the Church
imposing its emissaries upon any given nation or
country.

This does not mean to imply that Orthodoxy is bereft of missionaries or missionary activity. Quite the contrary. Entire nations were
converted to Orthodoxy by missionaries who not
only devoted their lives to such activity, but
even incurred martyrdom in the process. Two of
Orthodoxy's greatest missionaries, Cyril and
Methodius, to whom history credits the conversion of the Slavs to Christianity, were sent upon
their mission in the true sense of mission as interpreted by the Orthodox Church. That is, with
the consent of the peoples involved. Cyril and
Methodius were official representatives of both
the Byzantine Church and State to the Slavs at
the invitation of the Slavs. It is this principle
of mutual consent that underlies the spirit of
Orthodox mission.

George J. Bacoulos, director of the Department
of Inter-Church Relations [6] describes conversion requirements and procedures:

Briefly, the minimum requirements for a person
to become an Orthodox Christian, and coming
from another Christian denomination, would be
to receive the Sacrament of Chrismation or Con-

6. Inter-Church Building, 475 Riverside Drive, New York,
N. Y. 10027

firmation. This, of course, would be preceded by
a period of instruction which would vary in
length according to the ability and background
of the candidate. However, conversion into
Orthodoxy to one not of a Christian denomination would entail, in most instances, a more
thorough and specialized course of instruction,
followed by the Sacrament of Baptism and that
of Chrismation.

As an example of the opinion of local priests, the
men who are actively engaged in the ministry, the Very
Reverend Neophytos Spyros, pastor of the Annuncia-
tion Greek Orthodox Church in Elkins Park, Pennsylvania, who holds the office of Evangelismos of the Greek
Orthodox Community of Philadelphia, explains:

> I would like to inform you that the Orthodox
> Church in general is against proselytizing people
> from other Christian denominations.
>   As for conversion from other religions we
> follow first a period of instructions and a test;
> and second, we baptize and confirm the person
> into the Orthodox Church according to the rites
> of our holy church.

The Very Reverend Alexander J. Fedoronko, pastor
of Saint Michael's Orthodox Catholic Church in Philadelphia explains:

> Every candidate must undergo a period of in-
> struction in the basic principles, doctrines, his-
> tory, liturgies, etc. of the faith. Even if the
> candidate expresses a conviction in the tenets of
> the faith, he should be required to take these
> instructions so that the instructor (priest) can
> determine whether or not the candidate is defi-
> nitely convinced.

The actual office of conversion depends upon the candidate's former belief. If he is a convert from Judaism, Mohammedanism, or another non-Christian faith, or has had no religious background, he is accepted through the Sacraments of Holy Baptism and Holy Chrismation (Confirmation). Non-Trinitarian Christians, such as the Unitarians and some of the Mormon groups, are received through the same procedure.

Those who were baptized in another Christian denomination, providing they were baptized in the Name of the Holy Trinity, are, after showing proof of baptism, accepted through the Sacrament of Holy Chrismation. Duly baptized and confirmed members of the Roman Catholic Church are accepted through the Sacraments of Holy Penance (Confession) and Holy Communion, inasmuch as the Orthodox Church recognizes the validity of the Sacraments of Baptism and Confirmation as performed in the Roman Catholic Church. All converts, regardless of the office used for conversion, are required to receive the Sacraments of Penance and Communion almost immediately after conversion.

Each convert must have at least one sponsor, although the general custom is to have two, and these must be of the Orthodox faith. Where only one sponsor is used, he or she must be of the same sex as the convert.

All the above refers to the conversion of adults. At the conversion of infants or small children (up to the age of seven) the same procedures are used, with the exception of the initial instruction period and the Sacrament of Penance. Children of this age are accepted upon the expression of faith made by their sponsors and upon the expressed desire of their parents.

The essence of conversion is summed up by Father Gregory Adakr of the Cathedral of Our Savior in New York:

> Briefly . . . one might say that any "convert" to Orthodoxy would be faced with acceptance of those teachings which are contained within the Nicene Creed (Symbol of Faith): e.g., Divinity of Christ, Trinity, Resurrection, Life Eternal, Baptism for remission of sins, Chrismation as a spiritual "circumcision," etc.
>
> (As to the "history of conversions," one need only be reminded that all Christians come from "converted ancestry"; a handful of men, only, were followers of Christ. These men, as apostles and disciples, brought the "Gospel" and "Baptism" to the hearts of all mankind. Hence, the "history of conversions" is a history of Christianity.)

In the Orthodox churches the sacrament of baptism is as a rule administered to infants. It is a rare exception when adults present themselves to be baptized—all the more so as the Orthodox churches have only a very limited organized mission in non-Christian areas. The Office of Holy Baptism is based, however, on adult baptism and is in actual fact addressed to adults. This is shown quite clearly in the baptismal rite which implies that an infant to be baptized is not treated in any other way than an adult. The same liturgy is applied in both cases and this is clearly illustrated by the fact—as we have seen above—that baptism is immediately followed by confirmation.

Looking at the Orthodox liturgies we first find prayers which are related to child-birth and delivery and which are not part of the liturgy proper. They are offered at different stages and must be considered separately. There are first the "prayers on the first day after a woman hath given birth to a child." Then follow the prayers "at the naming of a child when he receiveth his name, on the eighth day after his birth." This time the child is brought to the church by the midwife. The priest makes the sign of the cross upon the forehead, lips and breast of the child and says a prayer of intercession. Later, there are the prayers "for a woman on the fortieth day after child-birth." This time, the mother brings the child to the church in order that he be "churched," i.e. introduced into the Church. The priest offers again a prayer of intercession and, if the child has already been baptized, performs the "churching": he carries the child to the doors of the sanctuary, saying, 'The Servant of God is churched . . ."

The Office of Holy Baptism begins with the *reception of the candidate as a catechumen.* The priest removes the person's clothes except for one garment. He places him with his face towards the east, breathes three times in his face, makes the sign of the cross upon him three times, lays his hand upon his head and prays for him. He says the three exorcisms, ordering the Devil to leave this person: "The Lord layeth thee under ban, O Devil: He who came into the world and made his abode among men . . . Begone, and depart from this creature, with all thy powers and thy angels." After further prayers for delivery from evil the priest breathes upon his mouth, his brow and his breast, saying, "Expel from him every evil and impure spirit, which hideth and maketh its lair in his heart. The spirit of error, the spirit of guile, the spirit of idolatry and of every concupiscence; the spirit of deceit and of every uncleanliness . . . And make him a reason-endowed sheep in the holy flock of thy Christ . . ."

Then follows the renunciation of the Devil —for our aspect of the subject this is one of the most important parts in the liturgy. The priest turns the person to the west and asks three times, "Dost thou renounce Satan, and all his Angels, and all his works, and all his service, and all his pride?" And each time the catechumen answers, "I do." If the person to be baptized comes from a different tradition, or is an infant, his godparent ("sponsor") answers in his place. The priest questions him three times, "Hast thou renounced Satan?" And the catechumen, or his sponsor, responds each time, "I have." He is then requested to spit upon Satan, and the priest turns him again to the east, asking him three times, "Dost thou unite thyself unto Christ?", and then, also three times, "Hast thou united thyself unto Christ?" When the catechumen has answered these questions, he says the Holy Symbol of the Faith, the Nicene Creed. This is also said three times, whereupon the question, "Hast thou united thyself unto Christ?" is repeated three times again. When the catechumen has affirmed, for the third time, "I have," the priest orders him, "Bow down also before Him!", and he answers, "I bow down before the Father, and the Son and the Holy Spirit, the Trinity, one in Essence and undivided." A short prayer of intercession concludes this part of the liturgy.

The *Office of Holy Baptism* proper begins with the priest entering the sanctuary, putting on white vestments and lighting all the tapers. He censes the font and then prays to God in a long prayer of petition. He then sanctifies the water, praying, "O King who lovest mankind, come thou now and sanctify this water, by the indwelling of thy Holy Spirit. And grant unto it the grace of redemption, the blessing of Jordan. Make it the fountain of incorruption, the remission of sins, the remedy of infirmities, the final destruction of demons . . ." Three times he makes over the water the sign of the cross, and, breathing upon it, says, "Let all adverse powers be crushed beneath the sign of the image of thy cross." A similar act is performed with specially prepared oil. The priest pours some of the oil into a vessel. He dips two fingers into the oil, makes the sign of the cross upon the catechumen's brow and breast and between his shoulders, saying, "The Servant of God is anointed with the oil of gladness; in the name of the Father, and of the Son, and of the Holy Spirit." As he anoints the breast and shoulders he adds, "Unto the healing of soul and body"; anointing the ears, "Unto the hearing of faith"; and the hands, "Thy hands have made me and fashioned me." Lastly, he anoints the feet, saying, "That he may walk in the way of thy commandments."

When the whole body is anointed, baptism is administered. The priest holds the candidate upright, looking towards the east, and immerses him three times, saying, "The servant of God is baptized, in the name of the Father, and of the Son, and of the Holy Spirit, Amen." After the third immersion, priest and congregation sing the 32nd Psalm: "Blessed is he whose unrighteousness is forgiven and whose sin is covered." Then the priest puts the garments upon the baptized, saying, "The servant of God is clothed with the robe of righteousness; in the name of the Father, and of the Son, and of the Holy Spirit."

A prayer of thanksgiving and praise leads to the *Office of Holy Chrismation*. The priest anoints with the holy Chrism the person who has been baptized, making the sign of the cross on the brow, on the eyes, the nostrils, the lips, the ears, the breast, and on the hands and feet, saying each time, "The seal of the gift of the

Holy Spirit. Amen." Then the priest, accompanied by the sponsors and the baptized, makes the circuit of the font three times, and all sing, "As many as have been baptized into Christ have put on Christ. Alleluia." Two lessons from Holy Scripture are then read; first, Romans 6:3-11, and then, Matthew 28:16-20. Read at this point of the service, both lessons have their specific significance. The passage from the Epistle to the Romans points to the life in the power of the Holy Spirit to which the newly baptized has been called. The lesson from Matthew recalls Christ's commandment to teach and baptize all nations. Both texts confirm the commitment of the newly baptized. The service ends with a prayer of intercession.

The office of baptism is still not yet complete. On the eighth day after baptism the person is brought again to the church for *Ablution*. The priest prays for him, asking God to "maintain the shield of his faith unassailed by the enemy." He sprinkles him with water and says, "Thou art justified. Thou art illumined. Thou art sanctified. Thou art washed: In the name of our Lord Jesus Christ, and by the Spirit of our God." With a sponge, the priest washes the face and head of the person, and his breast, and the rest, saying, "Thou art baptized. Thou art illumined. Thou hast received anointment with the holy Chrism. Thou art sanctified. Thou art washed: in the name of the Father, and of the Son, and of the Holy Spirit." This act symbolizes the lasting effect of baptism, even when all outward signs disappear.

Ablution is followed immediately by the ceremony of the *cutting of the hair*. After several prayers, the priest cuts the hair in the form of a cross, saying, "The servant of God is shorn: in the name of the Father, and of the Son, and of the Holy Spirit." This act shows once more that the baptized person is henceforth dedicated to the service of God. This service also ends with an intercession.[7]

We find that conversion requirements, practices, and procedures according to the rite of the Eastern Orthodox Church and all its ethnic subdivisions are very similar to those of most Christian churches. They begin with a period of instruction and culminate in the administration of the sacraments, which in the Eastern Orthodox Church are baptism, chrismation, penance, and Communion for non-Christians admitted into the Church.

Eastern Orthodoxy is opposed to an aggressive evangelistic program, but admits all sincere applicants who are prepared to follow the prescribed steps to conversion. Father Christopher Condeleon, pastor of St. Demetrios Church in Newark, New Jersey, acknowledged that it is not common for candidates for conversion to come off the streets. He only knows of candidates who come in a mixed-marriage situation.

On the subject of mixed marriage the Orthodox Church maintains the usual attitude—*a priori* opposition with provisions in the event that such a marriage cannot be prevented. In the case of mixed marriage, the non-Catholic partner must sign an agreement to raise the children in the Orthodox religion.

7. Lucas Vischer, *Ye Are Baptised,* World Council of Churches, Geneva, July, 1961, pp. 15-18. Reprinted with permission.

Protestantism

The door of the castle church, Wittenberg, Germany, where Martin Luther posted his 95 theses against the sale of absolutions by the Church

Introduction—Protestantism

B EFORE TREATING THE SUBJECT of Protestant conversion, we must answer the question: "What is Protestantism?" Religous sociologists have been unable to create a universally acceptable definition of Protestantism. Several particulars, however, are affirmed by all Protestants.

Henry D. Van Dusen, president of the faculty of Union Theological Seminary in New York City lists the following points of agreement among Protestants in *A Guide to the Religions of America*:

Faith in Jesus Christ as Lord and Savior;

The Bible as the primary source of what is true and right;

The loving concern of God for every human being;

Direct and constant fellowship between God and every believer;

God's forgiveness in response to each person's penitence and faith;

The Church as the community of followers of Christ;

The responsibility of every Christian for his faith and life (the "priesthood of all believers");

The duty to discover and do God's will in

his daily work (the divine significance of every "calling");

The obligation to seek to advance the Kingdom of God in the world;

Eternal life with God in the "Communion of saints." [1]

Included in this section on Protestant Christianity are only those communions which subscribe to these standards of belief. This choice, despite its obvious shortcomings, is necessary as a working hypothesis. It seems as practical as any current definition of Protestantism. A representative group of those religious entities which are on the periphery of Protestant Christianity will be studied later.

The world has hundreds of Protestant denominations. Only the World Confessional Bodies, several major denominations, and a number of smaller groups will be discussed. The World Confessional Bodies, which are associations of churches holding common hisorical traditions and doctrinal standards, include the Lutheran World Federation, the Lambeth Conference (of Anglicans), the Presbyterian World Alliance, the Baptist World Alliance, and the Congregationalists, Disciples, and Friends Conferences.

The four main types of Protestantism to be discussed are

1. Lutheran
2. Presbyterian (Calvinist or "Reformed")
3. Anglican or Episcopalian
4. "Independent," "radical," or "free Church."

The fourth group, including the Disciples of Christ, Evangelicals, Baptists, Congregationalists, Methodists,

1. "What Is A Protestant?," *A Guide to the Religions of America,* ed. *Leo Rosten* (New York: Simon and Shuster, 1955), p. 112.

and Friends, is the predominant type of Protestantism in the United States.

Essentially, every Protestant denomination expects a convert to accept its practices and values. These vary widely. Some faiths consider Sunday the day for religious observance; others, Saturday. Some denominations look upon the Bible as the history of God's revelations to man leading him to a higher spiritual life; whereas some consider the Bible a completed revelation, others consider it a step in a continuing chain.

There are denominations whose members recount the place of conversion and the moment when they were converted—to the year, day, hour, and even minute. Others look upon conversion as a gradual process—the result of family influence, church training, and other factors. The first type of conversion may be an electrifying, traumatic, emotional experience; the latter type, though equally important, may be a continued dedication to, rather than a change in, a mode of life.

Some denominations believe that the world must come to an end because of its wickedness and that God will take the saved into Heaven with Him. Some denominations associate the conversion experience with "the gift of tongues."

It is only natural that a religious mosaic like Protestantism should be characterized by a multiplicity of customs and practices. Yet, in regard to conversion, there appears to be a basic spirit of unanimity.

Milton Cox Sealey, Pastor of Erieside Church on the Boulevard, an independent undenominational church in Willowick, Ohio, summarizes the Protestant approach to conversion:

As to our procedure, it is simple. We teach and preach the Word of God, the old and new covenants, emphasizing basically repentance for sin, and faith in the Lord Jesus Christ. Each of us needs to see that God has provided a sacrifice in Himself, as in Genesis 22:8—"My son, God will provide himself a lamb for a burnt offering" —as in Isaiah 53, and as in Psalms 22 and 69. Under such whole Bible emphasis, we see, first, our utter need of God's salvation, second, His perfect substitutionary offering, Hebrews 10:10, 12, 14—a "once for all" sacrifice, and thirdly, we come to a personal decision of accepting God's free gift of redemption, as in Romans 6:23— "the gift of God is eternal life . . ." and Romans 10:9, 10—"if thou shalt confess with thy mouth the Lord Jesus, and shalt believe in thine heart that God hath raised Him from the dead, thou shalt be saved. For with the heart man believeth unto righteousness; and with the mouth confession is made unto salvation."

The procedure summarized would be: 1. The individual confesses himself to be a guilty lost sinner before God, without hope or merit of any kind; 2. he sees in God's eternal Son, the Lord Jesus Christ as the Lamb of God, for his cleansing and redemption; 3. he believes (accepts) God's way of salvation (Acts 4:12; John 3:16, 18, 36; John 5:24, John 8:24) and enters the family of God (the line of faithful Abraham, Galatians 3:13-16, 29).

Dan M. Potter, executive director of the Protestant Council of the City of New York, describes the Protestant requirements for conversion:

. . . The various denominations related to the Protestant Council have different requirements for religious conversion. The basic element in most of them is belief that Jesus Christ is Messiah, Son of God and Savior of Mankind from sins. There are varying elements in expression of this basic belief, and therefore some denominations require at least six weeks of instruction and the passing of various examinations before membership is permitted.

The use of the term *conversion* presents a special problem. In the case of those churches that are committed to the ecumenical movement, the word "transfer" would be more appropriate in describing the change of membership from one denomination to another. The assumption is that the faith is the same although the forms in which it may be expressed may vary.

Some denominations, however, believe that every true Christian must have a "conversion experience." In this case the use of the term *conversion* would be appropriate. Its use would also be legitimate for one who comes over from one of the "Catholic" churches. In such a case, it is, of course, a matter of changing from one view of Christianity to a widely diverging view. The Reverend William A. Norgren, director of the National Council of the Churches of Christ in the U.S.A., explains:

> Even here, however, there is in no sense a denial of the reality of the baptism of the person "converted" or of his religious experience. There will be only the feeling that this experience has been incomplete and/or partially in error.

The use of the term *conversion* here will thus be confined to cases of new members acquired by Protestant churches from the ranks of the unchurched or non-Protestant persuasions. *Transfer* will designate a change of membership from one denomination to another within the ecumenical family.

To present the conversion practices of every Protestant church would be a Gargantuan task of meaningless repetition. For this reason, only major bodies will be discussed fully, with a passing reference to some representative smaller denominations.

Attitudes Towards Mixed Marriage

Protestants generally oppose mixed marriages. This is to be expected from any religious group that is concerned with survival, and this is certainly the case with the various bodies comprising Protestant Christianity. Nevertheless, one encounters a more lenient attitude among most Protestant circles than among Roman Catholics.

Indeed, one of the major objections to mixed marriage from the Protestant camp is that the Catholic Church requires "promises"—the Catholic education of all children issuing from a mixed marriage and the obligation of the Catholic mate never to cease in his efforts to bring about the conversion of his non-Catholic partner.

The opposition of Protestantism to this kind of marital arrangement is summarized in a pamphlet, *If I Marry a Catholic,* published by the National Council of Churches.[2] It is agreed that mixed marriages in general should be avoided because more than twice as many mixed marriages end in divorce or separation than do marriages in which both parties come from the same religious background. Generally, one of the basic ingredients of a happy marriage is similarity in background, a most important element of which is a common religious heritage.

2. Dr. L. Foster Wood, *If I Marry a Catholic* (New York: National Council of Churches of Christ in the U.S.A., 1945).

Compounding the existing problems are the questions of contraception, therapeutic abortion, getting along with in-laws, rites of burial, and other issues on which Protestants and Catholics do not see eye to eye.

Although Protestantism is emphatically opposed to mixed marriage on principle, it is willing to join other churches in a spirit of mutual respect and good will to help make mixed marriages happy and successful ones. However, Protestantism cannot abdicate its position, which calls for complete religious equality in a mixed marriage. This includes equal instruction of the children in both religions until such time as they are old enough to make a choice between the two.

Within Protestantism there is a multiplicity of denominations, but a virtual unanimity of attitude, prerequisites, practices, and procedures related to conversion. Even the word *conversion* does not seem to please most Protestant clergymen, who prefer to call the conversion procedure *admission into the church,* or membership.

Generally, there is a spirit of agreement in all quarters that conversion must be preceded by the recognition of sin, of the hopelessness of man, and of his need

The Reformation Monument in Geneva, Switzerland, contains statues of four of the Reformation leaders: (left to right) Guillaume Farel, John Calvin, Theodore deBeze, and John Knox

for a savior and for redemption. This is followed by belief in and acceptance of Jesus as the Messiah, Son of God, and Savior of Mankind. The convert then enters into the community of the faithful.

All groups require the applicant to devote a period of time to study, under capable instructors, followed by examinations. Various professions of faith based on common theological principles must be declared by him before his formal admission into the church.

Baptism is required by all who come from the army of the unchurched and from non-Christian religions. Most Protestant churches accept baptism administered by the Catholic Church as valid. A communicant in good standing in one denomination who wishes transfer to another church is generally admitted "by letter." The word *transfer* in this instance is more accurate than *conversion.*

Methods of baptism employed by the various denominations include infant baptism, adult baptism, adult rebaptism, sprinkling with water, total immersion, and trine immersion. Baptism with flowers, as practiced by the Unitarians, is not accepted as valid.

Protestant churches characteristically prefer the simpler and less formal approach to conversion. After the basic requirements just listed, most of them would rather stay away from dogmatic, formalized rules and procedures.

Protestantism, like other religious persuasions, is opposed to mixed marriages on practical as well as religious grounds. Yet, when faced with the inevitability of such a union, it is willing to work with other churches for a joint attempt to make the marriage secure and give it a maximum chance to succeed. However, Protestantism insists that this be done by the participating churches in a spirit of cooperation and mutual respect.

6
Lutheranism

Martin Luther ushered in the Protestant Reformation on October 31, 1517, when he officially protested against the Catholic use of indulgences. Today, the millions of Protestants all over the world who follow his teachings are known as Lutherans. Almost the entire population of Denmark, Norway, Sweden, Finland, and Iceland, two thirds of all Germans, most Estonians and Latvians, and millions in other parts of the world are Lutherans.

Lutheranism emphasizes the importance of salvation by faith, a doctrine essential to the theology of its founder. Lutheranism retains many of the Catholic forms of worship, in simplified form, and also observes the festivals and seasons of the Church year. The traditional worship services, including the use of vestments and altars, survive in the Lutheran Church, not because they are sacramentally indispensable, but because they add beauty and traditional sentimental value dating back to antiquity. The services are conducted in the vernacular.

Conversion Procedure

Peter L. Kjeseth, a member of the Department of

Theology of the Lutheran World Federation[1] discusses the question of conversion to the various Protestant groups:

> . . . The requirements for conversion from any non-Christian religion would be the same, that is, instruction which leads to both baptism and confirmation. In the case of Roman Catholicism or Protestant groups, most generally the process would be instruction leading to confirmation, since our church recognizes the validity of Roman Catholic and of most Protestant baptism . . .

A Lutheran minister outlines the conversion procedure he follows in his particular church:

1. It is required that a course of Christian doctrine be attended, which is given in the form of ten lectures of 1½ hours each. The six chief parts considered and presented at these lectures are:
   a. The Ten Commandments
   b. The Apostles' Creed
   c. The Lord's Prayer
   d. The Sacrament of Holy Baptism
   e. The Office of the Keys and Confession
   f. The Sacrament of the Altar (Holy Communion)
2. The candidate for membership must embrace these doctrines and accept and confess his allegiance to the Lord, Jesus Christ as his personal Savior.
3. It is required that the verbal inspiration of the Bible be accepted, as the source and norm of all teaching.

Further details are presented in the folder, *How to Join the Lutheran Church*.[2]

1. Route de Malagnou 17, Geneva, Switzerland.
2. *How to Join the Lutheran Church* (New York: American Lutheran Publicity Bureau, undated.)

Martin Luther, German leader of the Protestant
Reformation

The Lutheran Church expects its members to accept in all simplicity God's statements in the Bible. God says:

> All of us are sinful and, so long as we do not believe in Jesus Christ, the wrath of God rests upon us. We are helpless to save ourselves and need a Savior. Jesus Christ, the Son of God, came into the world and in our place did all that was necessary for salvation. All that Christ did for us is offered freely in the Gospel; when we believe the Gospel, God's forgiveness becomes our own by faith in Jesus Christ. Faith in Jesus Christ is the work of God's Holy Spirit operating on our hearts through God's word.

You will find that it is not hard, nor will it take a long time to learn these basic truths of Christianity.

Any Lutheran pastor will always be glad and willing to explain the doctrines of the Bible and point out the true and only way to heaven. Give him an opportunity.

Most Lutheran pastors arrange lecture courses at regular intervals on the fundamentals of Christianity, and on the position and practice of the Lutheran Church. By attending these lectures, which are more in the nature of heart-to-heart talks, no one is placed under any obligation to join the Church. If after having heard these talks any person finds himself not ready to join the Lutheran Church, he will not be made to feel uncomfortable or embarrassed simply because he has the courage of his convictions and states the reasons why he cannot join. But almost invariably the experience has been that these talks made a deep impresion on the hearts of those attending. The talks are given in such a way that no one need feel ill at ease, no matter what his intellectual and spiritual background happens to be.

The pastor's one aim is to make clear the way of salvation. In presenting the Bible teachings he will not rely on human reasoning and tricks of oratory to convince you of their truth. He knows that "no man can say that Jesus is the Lord, but by the Holy Ghost," and that the power of the Spirit alone can work faith. As soon as he is satisfied that you understand and believe what has been presented to you from the Bible, you are ready to join the Lutheran Church, if you so desire, and you may be received into membership formally, either in public service or privately before witnesses.

Do you see any difficulties there? It is a simple matter to join the Lutheran Church.

Do you wish to join the Lutheran Church? Then give your name and address to one of the members, who will notify the pastor. Or come and meet the pastor at one of the services. Or tell him of your desire by mail. He will take care of everything else that might be necessary. If it is impossible for you to meet with others to hear the pastor's talks, arrangements can be made for private meetings. However, the great majority of those who wish to become acquainted with the truths of the Bible prefer to meet with the regular discussion groups organized by the pastor. Once the time is set for the talks, you need only listen to God's Word, with an open mind and a receptive heart. Yes, it is a simple matter to join the Lutheran Church. We extend a hearty invitation to you!

Reprinted below is the Lutheran service for the reception of new members:

Will the congregation please arise?

Beloved in the Lord:

You have applied for membership in this First Lutheran Church. You have met and counseled with the pastor. Evidence of your sincerity of purpose has been conveyed to the Church Council.

I now ask you before God and this Christian fellowship, will you in accordance with the requirements of the constitution of this congregation, by the help of God, strive to lead a consistently Christian life, strive to promote the unity and welfare of this congregation, diligently and prayerfully study God's Word, keep the Lord's Day holy, regularly attend the worship services, faithfully and reverently partake of the Lord's Supper (as parents see to it that your children are diligently nurtured in the Christian faith), and in recognition of God's mercies to us and in accordance with the degree in which the Lord has blessed you, exercise Christian stewardship of your talents and means to the end that God's Kingdom at home and its benevolent enterprises throughout the world may be furthered?

Recognizing also the dire need of witnessing unto the world of the power of Christ's resurrection unto newness of life, will you cherish and proclaim by word and life our most holy Christian faith?

If so, answer, "I will."

To the congregation—

You have now heard the sincere statement of purpose and desire by these fellow Christians (whose application for membership in this congregation has been heartily approved by your Church Council according to our constitution). I now ask you, do you wish me as your pastor on your behalf to welcome these Christians into our congregational fellowship and will you promise

before God to help make them feel at home
among us as we share the full meaning of membership in Christ's redemptive fellowship ad-
monishing, consoling, encouraging and edifying
one another in our holy faith.

If so, the congregation will answer, "Yes."

Gladly I now declare you members of this
First Lutheran Church and welcome you most
heartily to our fellowship to share with us the
joys, the blessings and the responsibilities of
God's Kingdom here.

Let us pray:
O Lord God, who dwellest on high yet de-
lightest to have Thy habitation in the hearts of
men; Who has built Thy Church as a city upon
a hill, and laid the foundations of it upon the
Apostles and Prophets, Jesus Christ Himself
being the Chief Corner-Stone: Make us to be a
spiritual building fit for the indwelling of Thy
Holy Spirit, grounding us in faith, building us
up in hope, and perfecting us in love, that we,
joined in the union of the Church Militant on
earth, may enter in Thy Church Triumphant in
heaven; through Jesus Christ, our Lord. Amen.
Our heavenly Father—we give Thee hearty
thanks that Thou dost continually preserve and
increase Thy Holy Christian Church. Grant unto
these who now stand before Thine altar the ful-
ness of Thy Divine Grace and Power. Grant unto
their lives the benediction of Thy presence and
Thy peace. Fill all our hearts with an undying
love of Thee and a mutual love of one another.
And send, O Lord, Thy rich blessing to this
church through the godly profession of these
Thy servants made before Thee this day. This
we pray in the name of Jesus Christ, our crucified and risen Lord. Amen.

John Calvin, French Protestant theologian of the Reformation

7
Presbyterian Church or
Reformed Churches

THE PRESBYTERIAN CHURCH STEMS from the Calvinist Reformation. Churches that descended from Calvin are generally called "the Reformed Churches." This type of Protestantism is found in England, Scotland, Switzerland, France, Hungary, Germany, the Netherlands, and the United States.

Presbyterianism has a representative form of Church government, consisting of a series of ascending judicatories with the congregation as the basic source of power. Congregational power is vested primarily with duly elected members of the session, or "court," which sends representatives to the presbytery and the synod. The presbytery then elects from its official membership commissioners to the general assembly, the highest authority in the denomination.

Although the Reformed Churches still subscribe to the Calvinist doctrine of predestination, liberals within the churches are veering away from the strict orthodoxy of Calvinism. This spirit of theological liberalism is evident within most contemporary Protestant denominations.

Conversion Procedure

The World Alliance of Reformed Churches—World Presbyterian Alliance,[1] one of the prominent World Confessional Bodies, is a communion of eighty-nine member Churches, each of which enjoys autonomy in forming its own rules. Nevertheless, most, if not all, of them adhere to a basic position on conversion. This spirit of unanimity is not confined to those churches bound together in a particular World Confessional Body. The Reformed Churches are not notably different from other Christian bodies in their policy on the theory and practice of conversion.

This fact is illustrated in a statement by Rev. Lewis S. Mudge, secretary of the Department of Theology of the World Alliance of Reformed Churches—World Presbyterian Alliance:

> A convert to a Presbyterian Church from outside the Christian faith is required, a. to profess his faith in Jesus Christ as Lord and Savior, b. to undergo a course of instruction in the Christian faith or otherwise to satisfy the Church concerning his knowledge, c. to be baptized in the name of the Trinity, and d. to be received into membership of some particular congregation. The instruction given will normally be based on both the Old and the New Testaments, and the convert will be expected to know at least the Ten Commandments, the Lord's Prayer and the Apostles' Creed. You will note, however, that his actual profession of faith is a simple one that he believes in Jesus Christ. It would not be normal to ask specific adherence to any

1. Route de Malagnou 17, Geneva, Switzerland.

longer confession of faith. The latter is usually expected of ministers, but not members. The difference lies in the degree of theological sophistication required, of course, rather than in the substance of the faith expected. Converts from Roman Catholicism would not be baptized a second time, as we regard the Roman Communion as part of the Christian Church. Persons coming to a Reformed or Presbyterian Church from another Protestant body are permitted to do so by "transfer of letter." This means that one congregation recommends the individual in question to another, so that the last of the four steps mentioned above will apply. . . . Certainly the formal requirements I have mentioned are the chief ones in missionary territories, just as they are in the West, but the particular conditions of missionary experience have imposed many special difficulties: in particular that of the convert's relation to the religio-cultural milieu from which he has come.

Rev. Donald W. Hoffman of Marble Collegiate Church in New York, New York which is affiliated with the Reformed Communion, states:

. . . Joining our Church is done through an act of confession of faith. This is true both for a child who has been brought up within the church by believing parents, as well as for persons who are brought up with no faith or in another faith (by another faith I mean a non-Christian faith). We accept transfer of membership from other Christian denominations. . . . .

The Waldensian Church, a 100,000-member group of evangelical Christians in Italy, whose history dates

Landmarks in Geneva, Switzerland, associated with John Calvin's life are (left) the site of Calvin's home and (right) the Cathedral of St. Pierre, where Calvin did much of his preaching

from the twelfth century (making it a pre-Reformation Protestant church), is affiliated with the World Alliance of Reformed Churches. Its leader in Italy, Dr. Ermanno Rostan, confirms the general attitude of his church and most other Protestant groups:

> Regarding the conversion from Protestantism to the Waldensian Church, we do not ask any special requirements apart from that of being a communicant member of the Church. The Waldensian Church also is a Protestant Church; therefore in this case we do not speak of conversion but rather of a change from one Church to another. The member of a Protestant Church (Reformed, Methodist, Lutheran, Congregational and so on) who wants to join the Waldensian Church needs to have a certificate from his own Church showing that he is a regular communicant member. In case he is not yet a member (young man) he will follow a course of religious instruction like any other boy or girl. I am speaking, of course, about Churches living in an ecumenical atmosphere, not about sectarian groups.

Non-Protestants who wish to enter the Waldensian Church, however, must take a course of religious instruction.

The various avenues by which an applicant may be admitted into the United Presbyterian Church are described in the booklet, *So You Are Going to Be a Presbyterian*:

> There are three methods by which individuals join the United Presbyterian Church, namely, profession of faith, reaffirmation of faith, and transfer of letter. In the first procedure, a person who has not been baptized may appear before

the session (not the congregation) and make known his intent to unite with the local church. The session shall then proceed to examine such a person with respect to his faith in Christ, his desire to lead a Christian life, his promise to support the Church and subject himself to its authority in the Lord. If this examination is sustained as being satisfactory, the session shall receive the individual, pending baptism. The sacrament shall subsequently be administered during public worship of the congregation.

The second method of joining the United Presbyterian Church is generally described as "reaffirmation of faith." Anyone who belongs to a Christian church which does not make a practice of transferring letters or anyone having allowed his former church affiliation to lapse may make known to the session his wish to unite with the local church. Thereupon, this individual is examined concerning vital matters of faith and life. Once the examination has been sustained as satisfactory, the person may be received by a majority vote of the session. Previous baptism in any Christian denomination, including the Roman Catholic, is accepted as adequate and effective.

Finally, a person may unite with a local United Presbyterian Church by transferring a letter of church membership from another local congregation of a Christian denomination. The person is received on the basis of the letter in hand by a majority vote of the session. Such people usually are asked to come before the session and they may or may not be examined by the elders. Letters are received from any evangelical church and are granted to the same.

After a number of people have been received by the session, they are customarily welcomed into the fellowship of the church at a congregational service; however, their membership is effective as of the day they are received by the session. Many churches now ask all members to attend classes or read appropriate literature dealing with church membership.[2]

Documents

Having become a member of the Presbyterian Church, the convert signs the following certificate of membership, which is filled out by his Pastor:

This is to Certify that

....

was received ....

....

....into full membership in the

.... Church

of ....

on the.....................day of...............................19..............

....
Pastor

....
Clerk

(*This is not to be used as a letter of transfer or dismissal*)

2. Carl G. Howie, *So You Are Going to Be a Presbyterian* (Philadelphia: Dept. of Chaplains and Service Personnel of the United Presbyterian Church in the U.S.A., 1959), p. 14.

John Calvin depicted conferring with the Geneva City Council

My Covenant with God and the Church

I. In uniting with this Church, I subscribe to the following declarations:

   1. Believing Jesus Christ to be the Son of God, I accept Him as my Savior and acknowledge Him as my Lord. (*Luke 12:8*)
   2. Trusting in the Holy Spirit for guidance and grace, I shall seek to lead a consistent Christian life, honoring Christ in all my relationships. (*John 15:14*)

II. As a member of this Church, I accept the following responsibilities:

   1. I shall strive to be faithful in attending its services.
   2. I shall endeavor to render some form of Christian service.
   3. I shall give regularly to the support of the Church.
   4. I shall pray regularly for myself, for others, and for my Church.

Signed ....

Date ....

8
Anglican or Episcopalian Church

T HE PROTESTANT EPISCOPAL CHURCH is a branch of the Anglican Communion, a worldwide body of churches, with a membership of over forty million, that are in communion with the Church of England. The word *episcopal* comes from the Greek *episkopos*, meaning "bishop." In the Episcopal Church, the bishop symbolizes the unity of the Church and serves as the chief pastor of the flock.

The Episcopalian or Anglican Church is sometimes called "the bridge church" because of its position between Protestantism and Roman Catholicism. As are other Protestant groups, Episcopalianism is independent of Rome. On the other hand, it retains the ancient sacraments and creeds of the Roman Catholic Church.

Episcopalianism is Protestant in doctrine and Catholic in liturgy. Three trends are discernible within the Church—High, Low, and Broad. The High Church is Catholic with no papal affiliation; the Low Church is Protestant; the Broad Church is liberal, sometimes almost in a Unitarian sense.

However, all Episcopalians, and all Anglicans, are bound together by their membership in the parish under the care of the same minister and by their use of the Book of Common Prayer.

Parishes receive suggestions on policy from the

Trinity Church, New York City, founded by Royal Charter in 1697, is known as the parent Episcopal Church in the United States

Lambeth Conference, the national church body, or the diocesan office. However, unless a local rector, a clergyman in charge of a parish, teaches doctrines that are contrary to the faith, little can be done to shape local religious programs.

Conversion Procedure

The Lambeth Conference is the World Confessional Body of Anglicans-Episcopalians, which comprises the eighteen churches (one of which is American, the Protestant Episcopal Church) included in the Anglican Communion. Although minor differences in procedures and requirements for conversion may exist because of the autonomy enjoyed by the rectors, those generally accepted in the Anglican Communion, as outlined by an executive officer of the Advisory Council on Missionary Strategy of the Consultative Body of the Lambeth Conference,[1] are:

> First, the basic requirement for "conversion" would be a willingness to make (or renew) the promises which are required of those being baptized. I append the questions which are asked of an adult coming to Baptism, as they are contained in the Prayer Book of the Protestant Episcopal Church in the United States. The promises in most other Anglican bodies would be of this same general character:
>
> "Well-Beloved, you have come hither desiring to receive holy Baptism. We have prayed that our Lord Jesus Christ would vouchsafe to receive you, to release you from sin, to sanctify you with the Holy Ghost, to give you the kingdom of heaven, and everlasting life.
>
> "Dost thou renounce the devil and all his

1. Chester Street, London S.W. 1, England.

works, the vain pomp and glory of the world, with all covetous desires of the same, and the sinful desires of the flesh, so that thou wilt not follow, nor be led by them?

Answer. I renounce them all; and, by God's help, will endeavour not to follow, nor be led by them.

Minister. Dost thou believe in Jesus the Christ, the Son of the Living God?

Answer. I do.

Minister. Dost thou accept him, and desire to follow him as thy Saviour and Lord?

Answer. I do.

Minister. Dost thou believe all the Articles of the Christian Faith, as contained in the Apostles' Creed?

Answer. I do.

Minister. Wilt thou be baptized in this Faith?

Answer. That is my desire.

Minister. Wilt thou then obediently keep God's holy will and commandments, and walk in the same all the days of thy life?

Answer. I will, by God's help."

Second, the formal steps required for conversion would be Baptism (if not already baptized) and Confirmation, which is the completion of Baptism. But Confirmation, if it had already been administered by a bishop in historic Catholic succession, would not be repeated. Nor would Baptism, of course. Baptism would presuppose a willingness to accept the Apostles' Creed, as a minimum statement of Christian faith, and also active participation in the life and worship of the Church.

Third, Anglican churches do not have any particular denominational or confessional position. They regard themselves simply as parts of the Catholic Church, and requirements for conversion or admission into an Anglican church would not be different from those we would regard as qualifying one to call himself a "Christian." With almost no exception, Anglican churches have not been interested in proselytizing. That is to say, no Anglican church would adopt as a matter of policy a mission for the conversion of other Christians. Although there are a good many Christians of other traditions who become Anglicans, they do so on their own volition, and in almost every case because their former allegiance is no longer acceptable to them.

With respect to non-Christian faiths, conversion to Christianity would be regarded as the normal object of missionary endeavour. Most Anglican thought on this question would not, I think, presuppose that a convert's former religious faith was valueless or wrong. Rather, Anglican thought would tend to look on becoming a Christian as a completion or fulfillment of what the one God had begun in the former allegiance. This would be particularly true with respect to members of the Jewish religion.

As a whole, Anglican churches are strongly influenced by the principle of the national church, as exemplified in the Church of England. Thus in any "Christian" land, there would be little interest in the conversion of other Christians; and in countries where the church of the majority is not Anglican, the chances are that converts from the majority church would be received only after fairly careful exploration, to be sure that their conversion was not in any sense the result of proselytizing activity.

Anglican churches do not regard themselves as "denominational" in the general sense of the word, and concentrate their missionary efforts in "non-Christian" cultures, as a general rule. Where there are exceptions to this, as in Latin America, it is generally a recognition of the purely nominal character of the supposed Christian affiliation of this country.

A member of the New York Protestant Episcopal City Mission Society[2] summarizes the steps involved in entering the Episcopalian Church:

It is general procedure if someone wishes to join our Church he inquires about it and we inform him that he must first go through a period of instruction before he is baptized. Then, after baptism, comes another period of instruction after which he is confirmed by a bishop, and this completes his membership in the Church.

2. 38 Bleecker Street, New York, N. Y. 10012.

9
Baptist Church

B ECAUSE OF THE MULTIPLICITY of Baptist groups, a
definition of the Baptist Church is almost as
difficult to formulate as a definition of Protestantism itself. There are the Northern and Southern
Baptists, white and Negro Baptists, rural and metropolitan Baptists, not to mention the official listing of
twenty-eight Baptist bodies. Baptists trace their origins
back to the Anabaptist movement of about 1515. They,
like their precursors, believe that Christians should be
rebaptized in adult life—at an age when they are able
to appreciate the experience of saving grace.

The Baptist Church in America is proud of its
tradition of religious tolerance, which dates back to
1630 when Roger Williams, a Baptist, established the
first modern government founded on the principle of
religious toleration in what became known as Rhode
Island.

Organizationally, the Baptists, Congregationalists,
and Methodists are similar in that their basic unit is the
congregation, and in each church all the congregations
are bound together in an "association" of congregations
rather than in a hierarchy. The "congregational" type
of organization is the third form of church government. The other two, mentioned earlier, are the Episcopalian form, which is a hierarchy led by the bishops,

and the Presbyterian system which, described in the simplest terms, invests the highest authority in councils of elders who represent the local churches.

The Baptists, Methodists, and Congregationalists are gradually shifting away from their distinctive informal manner of worship toward a more formal and liturgical one.

Conversion Procedure

A popular pamphlet, *Why I am a Baptist*,[1] distributed by the Baptist Church, presents a list of eleven reasons for joining the church. This list can also serve as a brief description of the Baptist faith for those who contemplate membership in this branch of Protestant Christianity.

Why I Am A Baptist:
1. Because I am a Christian.
2. Because I want to promote the interests of the kingdom of God in the most effective way.
3. Because I believe the New Testament, rightly interpreted, is the only sufficient guide of faith and practice for the Church.
4. Because I believe in religious liberty.
5. Because I believe in democracy in the Church.
6. Because I believe the Church should be composed only of those who believe in

1. J. Sherman Wallace, *Why I Am A Baptist* (Philadelphia: The American Baptist Publishing Society, 1957). This should not be regarded as an official statement. Actually, the Baptists do not issue official documents of this type, for there is no fixed or formally approved statement of Baptist doctrine which would be binding on all our members. There are many who would agree with all that Dr. Wallace has written, and many who would disagree with him on at least some of his points.

Jesus Christ as Savior and Lord; who give evidence of a transformation of life through the influence of the Holy Spirit.

7. Because I believe the ordinances of the Church are material symbols of spiritual realities and have value only as symbols.

8. Because I believe that Christian baptism is the immersion in water of a Christian believer, and that nothing else is baptism.

9. Because I believe that the Lord's Supper is for those who are believers in Christ and who have acknowledged Him in baptism.

10. Because I believe in a spiritual Church.

11. Because I believe in a missionary Church.

The Director of the Baptist Educational Center in New York[2] summarizes the Baptist requirements for conversion:

I wish to advise that persons are accepted in the Baptist denomination on the basis of their Christian faith. After acceptance of the Christian faith, Baptism by immersion follows.

2. 453-455 West 143 Street, New York, N.Y. 10031, Dr. Horatio S. Hill, Director.

John Wesley, English evangelical preacher and founder of Methodism

10
Methodist Church

METHODISM BEGAN WITH JOHN WESLEY (1703–1791), a minister in the Church of England who was reared in the High Church, the group within the Anglican Church that emphasizes authority. Wesley was dismayed by the apathy within the Established Church. Consequently, he devoted his scholarship, administrative ability, and energy to the development of a "popular" Christianity—one with a more powerful appeal to the people. He sought to revitalize the people's enthusiasm for their religion.

His movement caught on despite the opposition of the established clergy, who took exception to his flaming evangelism and, especially, to his denunciation of the emasculated spirit of the Established Church. He completely rejected the Calvinist doctrine of predestination; he preached that all men could be saved.

Methodism is distinguished by its emphasis on (1) "Sanctification," also called "Christian Perfection" or "Perfect Love," shown through grace, and the flowering of the spirit, which are the outward marks of one who is saved; (2) "Universal Atonement," or salvation for all men; (3) "Salvation by Faith" (man's faith in God and God's goodness); (4) "The Witness of the Spirit" (When a man is saved he may know it because God's Spirit will reveal it to him).

Although John Wesley never intended to create a new church, the seeds he sowed have brought forth one of the largest and most influential Protestant denominations in the world. It met with its greatest success in the United States. Early Methodism, with its circuit riders, hymn singing, and religious warmth, won the hearts of the countless men and women of the rapidly expanding American frontier and rural areas, who were hungry for a dynamic, personal religion.

The best definition of a Methodist is still that given by John Wesley himself:

> A Methodist is one who has the love of God shed abroad in his heart by the Holy Ghost given unto him, one who loves the Lord his God with all his heart, with all his soul, with all his mind, and with all his strength.

The General Rules of Methodism[1] are: (1) Do no harm; (2) Do all the good you can; (3) Observe the ordinances of God. The General Rules, drawn up by John Wesley and his brother Charles and adopted without alteration by the first Methodist Societies in America, are part of the Discipline of the Methodist Church. The rules also state that

> one condition required of those who desire admission into these societies—"a desire to flee from the wrath to come, and to be saved from their sins." But wherever this is really fixed in the soul it will be shown by its fruits. It is therefore expected of all who continue therein that they shall continue to evidence their desire of salvation. . . .

1. *The General Rules of Methodism* (Nashville, Tenn.: Methodist Evangelistic Materials, undated).

Members of the Holy Club, led by John and Charles Wesley while students in Oxford University, were called Methodists for their methodical devotion to study and religious duties

Conversion Procedure

Leroy H. Walker, in charge of Membership Care and Attendance, General Board of Evangelism of the Methodist Church,[2] sums up the Methodist position on conversion:

> . . . In general The Methodist Church does not demand a rigid adherence to any particular theological formula, viewpoint, or procedure. It is our belief that conversion is performed by God. We try to lead an individual to an acceptance of Jesus Christ as Lord and a commitment to follow Jesus in all of their living, and to leave to God the kind of an experience He wants them to have.
>
> It might be helpful to you to know that we sometimes feel that there are about five steps to a true Christian experience, or to full conversion. They are as follows: *First,* a desire to know God and to be right with Him; *Second,* there must be confession of sin and repentance. Following this, *Third,* there must be faith that God through Jesus Christ does forgive the sin confessed for which we have repented. Then the next step is *Fourth,* peace, or we might say that having accepted God's forgiveness and pledging one's allegiance to Jesus Christ, to follow Him in all things, one has a sense of peace, joy, happiness, and deep satisfaction.
> *Fifth,* we also assume that when one is converted he will want to commit his life and heart to Jesus Christ, recognize Him as Lord, and follow Him in all aspects of life. We believe that this would involve being baptized and received into membership into the Church.

2. 1908 Grand Avenue, Nashville 5, Tennessee.

II
United Church of Christ

IN RECENT YEARS, THE Protestant churches have shown an increasingly strong desire for amalgamation. Nowhere has this desire been carried out with more force and practical application than in the recently established United Church of Christ. This religious body was formed on June 25, 1957, by the union of the Evangelical and Reformed Church and the General Council of the Congregational Christian Churches of the United States. This union was effected to dramatize the unity of the Christian churches, to make their common witness in its founder more effective, and to serve his kingdom in the world more powerfully.

Both of the uniting fellowships were the results of former unions. The Evangelical and Reformed Church was formed in 1934 by the union of the Evangelical Synod of North America and the Reformed Church in the United States. The roots of both are deep in the history of this country and in the Reformation movement of continental Europe.

The Evangelical Synod was founded in Missouri in 1840, and the Reformed Church in the United States was begun in Pennsylvania in 1725. These groups traced their lineage to Calvin, Luther, Melanchthon, and Zwingli. Their Protestant heritage was expressed in their use of the Heidelberg Catechism, Luther's Catechism, and the Augsberg Confession as their creeds.

The Congregational and Christian Churches united to form the General Council of Congregational and Christian Churches in 1931. Both of these groups had been enriched through several previous unions. Congregationalism in America stems from the founding in the 1620's of Plymouth Colony by the Pilgrims and of Massachusetts Bay Colony by the Puritans. The Congregationalists were joined by the Congregational Methodists in 1892, by Evangelical Protestants in 1923, and by German Congregationalists in 1925. The Christian Church, in 1820, united Methodists from North Carolina, Baptists from Vermont, and Presbyterians from Kentucky. The Congregational Christian Churches, for the most part, trace their ancestry to Reformation movements in England.

The United Church of Christ, formed without breaking the historic continuities of the two uniting groups, aims to fulfill those characteristics most highly prized in both the Evangelical and Reformed Church and in the Congregational Christian Churches.

The union of these religious bodies may serve as the pattern for future mergers leading towards an amalgamation of the greater part of Protestantism into one united Church. It is noteworthy that these two combining churches, which had diverse forms of church government and different historical backgrounds, placed Christian unity above denominational differences.

Congregationalism was founded in the controversial days of the early seventeenth century as one of several groups within the Church of England. The early exponents of this movement sought greater autonomy for the local congregation and less for the bishops. They flourished in the free atmosphere of Colonial America, retaining ties with the Church of England until King Charles II demanded strict conformity to the Book of Common Prayer, at which time they became independent in theory as well as in practice.

Congregationalism emphasizes the preeminence of the congregation; the congregation has supreme authority. In the congregation the sacraments are celebrated, the Word is preached, the will of God is revealed to the worshipper, and the brotherhood of Christians is established. The Church is governed by the people who constitute the congregation.

Congregationalist churches are united in a fellowship or association on the county, state, and national levels. However, the final authority rests with the congregation. The power of the association is limited to counseling and brotherly persuasion.

Some historians maintain that the liberal, democratic institution of Congregationalism has had a profound and lasting influence on American democracy.

Conversion Procedure

Typical of the liberal Congregationalist attitudes is its position on conversion. Ralph G. Calder of the International Congregational Council,[1] one of the Confessional Bodies connected with the World Council of Churches, states:

> . . . We as Congregationalists have no formal procedures, this lack being in many respects characteristic of our Churchmanship.
>
> I would not think that we differ from other Christians as to the way in which we would seek

1. 110, Memorial Hall, Farrington Street, London, E. C. 4, England.

to be assured that a conversion was genuine, though we would not require subscription to any detailed confession of faith. Our Congregational Churches are not "Confessional" in the sense that our members or even our ministers are not committed to a precise and particular formulation of Christian belief.

It would, however, be sufficient for us that such a convert conveyed an impression of complete sincerity as to his new Christian convictions of faith. With us confession of faith has always been allied to Church Membership. We would therefore require that such a person also become a member of a local Congregational Church. Here again no precise and generally accepted formula is laid down for such membership. Most Churches ask simply for a general confession of Christian Faith, and a covenanted loyalty to the local Church. It would, however, in addition, be normal for us, though not necessarily imperative, that an unbaptized person should receive Christian baptism.

Sheldon E. Mackey, the executive secretary of the Stewardship Council of the United Church of Christ,[2] also discusses the Church's position on conversion:

. . . both the Evangelical and Reformed Church and the Congregational Christian Churches have for many years followed a procedure of confirmation instruction designed both for children and adults. After a period of instruction using such materials as "My Confirmation," children or adults were confirmed and became, through this process, communicant members of the Church. This period of instruction has varied

2. 1505 Race Street, Philadelphia 2, Pennsylvania.

anywhere from three months to two years depending upon practice in a local church . . .

The United Church of Christ would receive persons from other denominations by letter of transfer (if the member from the other denomination were in good standing in his or her local church) or by renewal of Profession of Faith (if the person in question had not maintained himself in good and regular standing in the Church from which he was coming). Persons who might apply for membership from the Roman Catholic Church (or other non-Protestant persuasion) would receive instruction, and after such instruction, would be received through the process of Confirmation or Profession of Faith . . .

The usual liberal Protestant attitude also emerges in a statement by Dr. Willis E. Elliott, in charge of the Department of Literature of the United Church Board for Homeland Ministries: [3]

. . . As for the requirements for conversion in the United Church of Christ, we do not have a dogmatic approach either theologically or psychologically: there is a very wide difference among us, though we are somewhat on the left of the American Protestant theological spectrum. . . . Requirements for conversion (in terms of) requirements for Church membership . . . also would vary over a wide range in our denomination . . .

Several spokesmen of the United Church recommend that prospective converts read *My Confirmation: A Guide for Confirmation Instruction.*[4]

A practicing minister in the United Church of

3. 2969 W. 25 Street, Cleveland 13, Ohio.
4. *My Confirmation: A Guide for Confirmation Instruction* (Philadelphia: Christian Education Press, undated).

Christ serving the Broadway Congregational Church in New York City epitomizes the matter thus:

> The Congregational Church as a denomination has no specific program on the matter of conversion, save the general program of evangelism. It is our way to treat every case as an individual problem.

That the United Church of Christ gladly welcomes converts is evident in their highly developed program of evangelism and the extensive literature used in its advancement. Literature includes the pamphlets, *Evangelism in the Local Church,* and *A Parish Program of Evangelism, The Need for Evangelism, A Strategy of Evangelism, Visitation Evangelism,*[5] *How To Make an Evangelistic Call.*[6] Church members are urged to share their faith with others.

Documents

Once a prospective convert has decided to become a member of the United Church of Christ, he will generally be given an application for membership similar to the following sample.

Application for Membership

in the

UNITED CHURCH of CHRIST

---

5. *Evangelism in the Local Church; A Parish Program of Evangelism; The Need for Evangelism; A Strategy of Evangelism; Visitation Evangelism* (Cleveland, Ohio: Commission on Evangelism, undated).

6. *How to Make an Evangelistic Call* (Nashville, Tenn.: Tidings, undated).

"The Christian Church is the only organization in the world where one of the conditions for membership is the admission that you are not perfect. If you will confess that you have come short of God's perfect will, that you need His forgiveness and grace to live the Christian life and that, accepting the Lordship of Christ over your life, you purpose to join hands with other Christians, to accomplish God's will on earth, the Church opens her doors to you."

I hereby make application for membership in the United Church of Christ

Name ....
       (Last)   (First)   (Middle)

Residence...

City...

Phone...

Business Address.................................... Phone...........

I believe Christ to be the Son of God, and the Savior of the world. I promise to follow Him as my Lord and Master. I am resolved, with God's help, to serve Him, to keep His commandments, to become a maturing, useful member of His Church, to attend its services, to be faithful in my attendance upon the Lord's Supper; to give generously of my material possessions for the furthering of its program at home and abroad, to take, as far as is possible, an active part in its work, and unselfishly to seek to make His will effective in my community and in the world.

Date........................   Signature..

Have you been baptized? (yes or no) ....

Are you uniting: (a) On confession of faith?...........

(b) By reaffirmation of

faith? ....

(c) By letter of transfer?.............

Appropriate literature on membership in the United Church is available on request. Titles include: *Why Join the Church* (Congregationalist); *Christian Teachings,* subtitled "A Manual for Those Preparing for Church Membership"; *Christian Faith and Purpose,* subtitled "A Catechism," and *The Manual for Church Members.*[7]

7. *Why Join the Church?; Christian Teachings; Christian Faith and Purpose; The Manual for Church Members* (Philadelphia: United Church Office, undated).

12
Religious Society of Friends,
or "Quakers"

THE RELIGIOUS SOCIETY OF FRIENDS, or Quakers, have spoken out on vital matters such as peace and the freedom of speech, assembly, worship, and conscience. The Quakers were among the first to raise their voices against slavery. They also gained a reputation as pacifists, refusing to participate in war except in the capacity of relief and reconstruction workers—ambulance drivers, hospital workers, etc.

All worship and business is conducted in a series of four "meetings": the preparative or congregational meeting and monthly, quarterly, and yearly meetings.

Contrary to popular belief, Quakers do have church officers. Men and women recognized for their spirituality are chosen by acclamation to act as elders and ministers.

Quaker worship—prayer, testimony, scripture reading, preaching, and singing—is characterized by spontaneity. The most striking feature, however, is the use of silence as an element in worship and the practice of "inquiring into the condition," permitting the "still small voice" within each worshipper to speak. Prayer in fellowship is the most important part of a

Quaker religious service. Quaker worship is non-liturgical; it has no established order of service, sacraments, ritual or rites, choirs, altars, organs, pulpits, or collections. Quakers are generally averse to gambling (including betting, raffles, lotteries, and the stock market), attending movies to excess, engaging in controversy, selling liquor, or taking oaths.

The distinctive essence of Quaker belief is the concept of the "Inner Light," a divine spark that resides in all men and helps them to resist evil. Quakers believe that God is always close. From this flows their optimistic belief in the perfectibility of man. Man's goal is perfection rather than sacramental holiness.

The "Peculiar People," as the Quakers were often called because of their insistence on being themselves, evolved out of the revolutionary activities of George Fox (1624–1691), an English "seeker" after spiritual truth and peace. The early history of the Society was marked by heroism and martyrdom at the hands of the members of the established religion in England. Since those dark days, the Quakers have earned universal respect for their good works.

Conversion Procedure

Blanche W. Shaffer, general secretary of the Friends World Committee for Consultation,[1] explains the European Quaker method of admitting new members:

> The Quaker groups on the continent have generally followed the practice of having "the candidate for membership" be visited by two members who try to find out how long this person has been in touch with Friends, and why

1. Woodbrooke, Selly Oak, Birmingham 29, England.

he or she would like to become a Quaker. The requirements for membership vary, and there are no strict rules.

The following is a statement on membership in "Church Government," the third part of *Christian Discipline in the Religious Society of Friends in Great Britain* (the Official Manual for British Quakers):

COUNSEL (pp. 13-16)

(It is recommended that the whole of this paragraph should be carefully studied by those appointed to visit applicants for membership before carrying out this duty.)

The Meaning of Membership. Membership in the Christian Church is a high privilege which entails a corresponding responsibility. Ideally, it is the outward sign of an inner union with Christ the living head and with the other members of a living body. This true and inner union cannot be infallibly discerned by men, and outward membership can never perfectly mark it; there are doubtless real members of the invisible Church who do not belong to any recognized Christian body. The Society of Friends may be compared to a family of which the young children are as much members as their parents and in which all, down to the youngest, can and may bear their rightful share in the family life and interests. We may readily grant that an ideal Christian Society cannot be secured on the basis of Birthright Membership, but neither can it be ensured by the imposition of outward tests of creed or practice nor even by the profession of conversion. Yet, there are certain broad principles of belief and conduct that afford a basis for an association in and through which living membership can find expression. In the case of our own Society unity is essential upon the spiritual and practical nature of Christianity—the deep and penetrating reality of worship and the claim of Christ to rule our whole life, both inward and outward.

There are, no doubt, some to whom membership in a Christian Society appears so lofty an attainment that they doubt whether they can with sincerity profess it and whether their lives would justify such profession. It is, however, certain that we were not intended to be isolated units, and an essential condition of the full flowering of our best life is close association and cooperation with others. Hence those who appear suitable for membership in the Society of Friends but who hesitate to make formal application for it may need encouragement both for their own good and that of the Society.

Advice to Visitors. To enable the Monthly Meeting to come to a right judgment as to the suitability of an applicant for membership the chief conditions to be looked for are that he is a humble learner in the school of Christ, that his face is set towards the light and that he is able to find spiritual help and teaching in our Meetings for Worship notwithstanding the absence of outward form. If it seems clear that an experience of the reality and power of God is being manifested in him he should be warmly welcomed into association with us. We believe that habitual dependence on the unseen Guide and Teacher, aided by the help the Church can give, will lead him forward on the path of spiritual and practical Christianity.

We are convinced that our distinguishing testimonies arise directly out of the central experience of Friends, but complete agreement with us, whether of formal belief or practice,

George Fox, English religious leader and founder of the
Society of Friends

need not be asked for. Care should nevertheless be taken to ascertain how far the applicant unites with the views and practices of Friends not only from an intellectual standpoint but in the realization that these are based on a sincere and living faith in God as manifested in the life of Jesus Christ and as he is ever manifested as a light in the hearts of men. Therefore besides enquiring into the attitude of the applicant to our distinguishing testimonies, visitors should inform themselves of the applicant's own views on Christian discipleship and their necessary expression in conduct.

Stress should be laid on the importance of regular attendance at our Meetings for Worship, not only as a joy and privilege to the individual and as a means of growth in grace, but for the sake of the congregation. Each true worshipper in the silent waiting upon God will help his fellow man even if not called to the ministry of the spoken word.

Visitors should endeavour to ascertain whether our method of worship has been helpful to the applicant in his spiritual life and if the Society of Friends is likely to be the body best fitted to meet his real needs. Though the applicant may be well informed in theory, he may have very slight knowledge of Quakerism in practice. Possibly he may be drawn to the Society through appreciation of the ministry and associations in the particular meeting he has been attending, or through one special tenet on which he places emphasis, without realizing that these are embodiments of a deeper underlying experience, which Friends have proved to be true. Should the teaching and practice of another religious body appear to meet his spiritual needs, it is unlikely that his right place is among us.

The method of holding our Meetings for Church Affairs under a sense of Divine guidance should be carefully explained to the applicant, together with our concern that Friends should work with one another in a humble and loving spirit, each giving to others credit for purity of motive, notwithstanding differences of opinion, and being ready to accept the decision of the Meeting even when it may not accord with his own judgment. The mutual forbearance and understanding which are produced by a constant dwelling under the power and control of Christ do much to prevent jealousies, misunderstandings or any breach of love.

The applicant should be informed of the responsibilities involved in membership and of the work of the Society, and it should be made clear to him that he can neither give nor receive all that true membership offers unless he is a regular attender of our Meetings for Church Affairs and takes his proper share in, and responsibility for, the Society's activities. It should be pointed out that there is ample scope for every gift, exercised in harmony with our loyalty to Christ and a desire to do his work in whatever way he may direct.

It is important that a new member should, after admission, receive kind and sympathetic help from the members of the Meeting which he has joined. Though it is primarily the work of the Overseers to exercise continuous Christian care over all the members of our Society, it is very desirable that those who visited the new member on his application would continue their interest and sympathy after he has been received.

Paul Myers, chairman of the Committee of Overseers of the New York Preparative Meeting states:

> We do not, in Quakerism, practice conversion
> (as such) and the procedures for admitting new
> members vary from Meeting to Meeting.
>
> However, the generally accepted approach
> to this matter is outlined in a folder under the
> title, *How to Become a Member of the Religious
> Society of Friends:* [2]

How to Become a Member
of the
Religious Society of Friends

Many people today are becoming interested
in Quakerism as a religion of sincerity, truth,
and freedom, which expresses itself in worship
without ritual and in practical Christian living.
Often they do not realize how simple is the
procedure of becoming members of the Society
of Friends.

You may have been attracted to Quakerism
by the relief work of the American Friends
Service Committee. Or perhaps you find yourself
in accord with the emphasis on those principles
of good will that tend to remove the cause of
war and of numerous social inequities. Some
people, motivated by a desire to see what a
Friends' Meeting is like, have wandered into one
on a Sunday morning. There they have found
perhaps a warm fellowship, and they have felt
the deep spiritual power of a devoted meeting
for worship at its best. You may be one of those
who are searching for something more vital and
more satisfying to your religious longing than
you have heretofore found. May we say that we

2. *How to Become a Member of the Religious Society of
Friends* (Philadelphia: The Representative Meeting, Philadelphia
Yearly Meeting of Friends, undated).

too are earnest seekers, striving to know ever more of God and to live more nearly as He would have us live?

If you too are a seeker, you may wish to investigate more fully the Quaker ideals and practices. You probably know already that among Friends there is no theological formula or creedal statement to which members must assent. Friends wish to respect the integrity of your personal beliefs and do not try to establish conformity to established dogmas. We regard freedom just as essential to the search for religious truth as it is in other fields in our scientific age.

You will find, however, a few principles that are generally accepted. George Fox, the founder of our religious society, believed that he "knew God experimentally," and later generations have felt that they too have had this close relationship to the Father. "The true light that lighteth every man" flooded into the world with the advent of Jesus, as it had been coming into the world in various degrees with holy men and women of many lands and in many ages. It shines today in the soul of man. God is transcendent, but more important to human beings, He is also an immanent Spirit, "in whom we live and move and are." Out of this belief grow principles and practices which are cherished characteristics of Friends. You will find them set forth in *Faith and Practice*.

To join the Religious Society of Friends there are four things to do:

FIRST—You should attend meeting for worship for a considerable period of time. This will help you to understand our Society, its ideals and way of worship and to know that it meets your needs. You should get acquainted with the people who compose it. You should occasionally attend some of the meetings for business, in order to learn of Friends' business principles and methods.

SECOND—While you are familiarizing yourself with Quakerism in action, you should learn to know the book entitled *Faith and Practice*. You should read Parts I and II thoroughly, and to some extent Part III also. You will find that Part III is an anthology, setting forth various expressions of belief of many Friends over the centuries. It is not a section to be read straight through, but should be considered thoughtfully in smaller portions over a period of time. Some parts of it may become the basis for deep and prayerful meditation. Let it sink in and become part of your religious background. Long before you have completed the reading of Part III, you may feel ready for the third step, which is the formal application for membership.

Some people are mystified when, after considerable attendance and study, no one asks them to join. There are several reasons for this, no one of which is indifference. Fundamentally we wish each person to be so desirous of joining that he will take the first step without waiting for a suggestion from us. Then too we do not want anyone to feel that he must become a member in order to continue his meeting attendance, but we hope that, when he is ready, he will speak. It may be that in some cases we are remiss, when we should give a word of encouragement.

THIRD—The third step is the application. *Faith and Practice,* provides as follows:

"An applicant for membership should address a letter to the Monthly Meeting of his choice, stating why he feels drawn into the fellowship of Friends, and indicating that he is in unity with its principles and testimonies. This letter, addressed to the Monthly Meeting, is to

A Quaker meeting

be sent to the Clerk of Overseers, who should acknowledge it promptly.

"The Overseers, or Friends appointed by them, will then instruct and guide the applicant as seems appropriate. They should inquire by personal visits, if possible, into his earnestness and conviction concerning Friends' principles, and should try to discover whether his life and conduct are consistent with his religious profession.

"If the Overseers find no obstruction to the acceptance of this application they now forward it to the Monthly Meeting which, after considering it, will postpone action until a subsequent meeting in order that Friends may become better acquainted with the prospective member. If, after such an interval, the application is approved, the Monthly Meeting records the acceptance into membership and appoints a committee of two or more Friends to welcome the new member promptly and warmly, inviting attendance at all our meetings. This committee also obtains the necessary statistical data for the meeting records."

Persons living at a distance from any meeting may have to be content with correspondence. Children under 12 years of age may be admitted with their parents. If only one parent is joining with the child, the written consent of the other parent is desired. Children over 12, if sufficiently matured intellectually, may apply on their own behalf like adults. The meeting will wish, however, to be assured of parental approval.

FOURTH—Meetings like to feel that they have extended full Christian courtesy to other religious organizations. Therefore, before accepting an applicant into the meetings, they expect him to clear past membership. You should, therefore, notify your former church of your desire to terminate your membership. Some churches will issue a church letter of transfer of membership to the Society of Friends. Such letters will be cordially received. If your former church is one that will not release its members, it will be sufficient for you to tell it of your intent.

We trust that, whether or not you join the Religious Society of Friends, you will ever know the fellowship of believers and feel the unfailing love of the Heavenly Father.

A fitting conclusion to this chapter is the statement on the religion of the Quakers contained in a folder entitled *Quaker Worship—An Invitation*:[3]

Friends meeting for worship is a united search for truth and understanding that helps us clarify our purposes and strengthen our resolve to live up to them.

The expression "that of God in every man" means, for Friends, not merely our individual spiritual potentialities, but the awareness that we are all part of something greater than ourselves. This Divine spirit within us, strengthened by common worship, makes the meeting for worship our deepest expression of group experience.

Because of this inner experience, worship after the manner of Friends is spontaneous and unplanned. Until we have gathered and settled into silence as a group, no one of us can foresee how this common experience may develop, since no one of us knows in advance what the needs or creative powers of the group may be. Each meeting for worship is a new adventure, and a planned program might stand in the way of

3. *Quaker Worship—An Invitation* (Philadelphia: Friends General Conference, undated).

some fresh insight which the group might achieve.

Since we believe there is "that of God in every man," we feel the group insight may be expressed by anyone sharing in the meeting. As we do not leave the arrangements for worship with a minister, we are charged with responsibility for participation, if the group is to function creatively.

We begin participation in meeting for worship as we still our body and direct our mind beyond the distractions of the immediate environment. Perhaps a phrase of poetry, a passage from the Bible, an arresting idea from our reading may serve to focus attention away from crowding, irrelevant thoughts. It is not easy for any of us, without practice, to clear our minds of outside concerns. Sometimes we can surmount the insistence of self by dwelling on the needs of others, or our sense of community with our fellow men, near and far. As we quiet our senses and "center down" each in his own way, we reach a deeper level within ourselves and approach the spiritual center of the meeting, and a sense of greater nearness to the divine source of all truth and reality.

On this deeper level of meditation, we may become aware of a clearer insight, a fresh understanding of, perhaps, some passage in the Bible and its spiritual application to us today. Or it may be some deep concern we want to share, or a recent experience giving a new meaning to life. If some urgency within us makes us feel that the idea belongs not only to us but to the group, then we must share it with the others. At times, when the meeting is most creative, messages by different speakers may follow each other symphonically, with variations on a theme,

The Friends Meeting House, Flushing, New York, built in 1694, is one of the oldest houses of worship in the United States

enriching and fulfilling each other until the end of the meeting.

Participation in meeting for worship means both disciplining oneself and attuning oneself to the group. Whether one is moved to speak or to keep silence, what matters, for the meeting, is that he be sensitive to the inner prompting that should be his guide.

We feel that in the practice of the Friends' manner of worship we have found a method which is free and vital. Wherever our search for truth and spiritual growth may lead us, we feel it is high adventure, and we invite you to share it with us.

13

The Christian Church

(Disciples of Christ)

THE DISCIPLES OF CHRIST originated as a movement back to "Pristine Christianity" and away from sectarianism. The Disciples claim the Bible as their only written creed. Their form of Church organization is Congregational.

Conversion Procedure

Rev. Leon A. Smith, minister at the Tioga Heights Christian Church in Philadelphia, Pennsylvania, states:

> The procedure followed by a large majority of our Churches for membership is belief that Jesus Christ is the Son of God, and the acceptance of him as personal Savior. This is followed by baptism through immersion. We consider Christianity to be primarily a way of living and we expect those who are received into membership in our Church to accept Jesus' way of living and to follow his teachings and example, as fully as possible in their daily lives.

Rev. Hampton Adams, minister of the Park Avenue Christian Church in New York City enlarges on the requirements and procedures of conversion, from the standpoint of the liberal wing of the Disciples of Christ:

> Our Church does not have a carefully defined doctrine of conversion. There is a fundamentalistic segment of our denomination of which this could not be said; but I speak for the more liberal and larger portion of our denomination. We counsel with persons who manifest an interest in becoming Christians, disciples of Christ, as we sometimes refer to the matter. We have courses of instruction for children in preparation for church membership. With the adults we insist that there is room within the church for persons of different points of view and different levels of spiritual maturity.
>
> When a person comes before the church to be received into membership for the first time, we put a question to him in the form of the confession that Matthew records Peter as making in the sixteenth chapter of the first Gospel. Putting his confession into a question, we say to the person, "Do you believe that Jesus is Christ, the Son of the living God?" Then we ask further, "Do you accept him as your personal Savior?"
>
> We receive members from all denominations simply upon a statement that they consider themselves to be Christians and that they desire membership with our Congregation.

Jesse M. Bader, general secretary of the World Convention of Churches of Christ (Disciples) adds:

> . . . for those coming from another faith than the Christian Faith, requirements for conversion and membership in one of our congregations would be to attend a study class, at which time he or she would be taught some of the history of the Christian Church (Disciples of Christ); the

requirements for Church membership, and the meaning of Church membership. Also, there would be teaching of the present life and work of this communion at home and overseas.

With reference to those coming from another Christian group, such as Protestant, Orthodox, and Roman Catholic, these would be requested to attend a study class where doctrines, polity, and witness of the communion would be considered. Those who had not been baptized by immersion would be required to be immersed, in most of the congregations. Some congregations among us practice "open membership," which means the acceptance of the unimmersed into full membership in the congregation. . . . the formal steps required for conversion are *hearing, faith, repentance,* confession of Jesus Christ as Lord and Savior, and Baptism.[1]

1. Requests for literature on the subject of membership and Church history may be addressed to The United Christian Missionary Society, 222 S. Downey Avenue, Indianapolis, Indiana.

14
Mennonite Church

THE MENNONITE CHURCH IS an evangelical denomination that subscribes to the fundamental doctrines of Christianity. It was begun in Europe in 1525 during the Protestant Reformation. The name "Mennonite" came from Menno Simons, an early Dutch leader. One of the Church's guiding principles is that one's beliefs and the life he leads are inseparable. Mennonites do not practice infant baptism, but rather "Follower's" or "Believer's" Baptism. The Mennonites are unconditionally opposed to war, and subscribe to a policy of nonresistance.

Conversion Procedure

The details of conversion to the Mennonite Church are contained in *The Minister's Manual for the Mennonite Church:*[1]

When any person, by the grace of God, has come to a saving knowledge of the truth, and desires to enter into a covenant with God to be baptized and received into church membership, he should make known his desire to the bishop or minister, or to any member of the Church,

1. F. J. Funk, *The Minister's Manual for the Mennonite Church* (Scottdale, Pa.: Mennonite Publishing House, 1890).

who may inform the minister. The bishop or minister then inquires of the applicant whether he believes that his desire to live a better life is a call from God to the saving of his soul; whether he realizes that he himself is not able to do any part of the saving work, and that it is impossible for him of his own will to continue faithful in the good work begun in his heart; whether he believes that God, of His own grace and power, will, upon true repentance, forgive him his sins, give him a new heart, adopt him into the family of God, and receive him into the fellowship of saints. Also whether he is willing to submit himself to the Gospel of Jesus Christ, and His nonresistant doctrine, in all things to be advised and instructed by the Word of God; whether he is at peace with his neighbor and fellow men generally, so far as is possible, and whether he is connected with any secret society, or is in any other way living contrary to the teachings of the Gospel as we interpret it, and if so, whether he is willing unconditionally to withdraw from any such secret organization, and in every respect to renounce all the errors of his former life. If the applicant gives satisfactory evidence that he is prompted by the Spirit of God, and is willing to conform to the requirements of the Gospel, the bishop or minister publishes the request before the congregation, and admonishes the members to observe the walk and conduct of the applicant, to show him a good example in a pious spiritual life, and to pray for him.

The subject or subjects (if more than one) for baptism should then be well instructed in the doctrines of repentance, forgiveness of sins, regeneration, the life of God in the soul, the ordinances to be observed, the restrictions which the Gospel places upon the Christian, and the

Menno Simons, Dutch religious reformer, organized and led a division of Anabaptists

rules of church government. The meetings for this purpose may be held at the meetinghouse or at some other convenient place, on the afternoon of each meeting day, or any other appropriate time and place may be selected. The minister should give such instructions on the above-mentioned subjects and others, as he may consider suitable and necessary. The converts should be instructed to read and study carefully the eighteen articles of our Confession of Faith, and the minister should make it his duty to see that they understand them. They should also be made acquainted with the rules and requirements of the Church, as well as the duties which church membership imposes upon them, and the privileges it bestows.

The object of these instructions is to edify and confirm the subjects for baptism in their faith, and encourage them to persevere in the right way. All applicants for baptism and admission into the Church should be able to give satisfactory evidence that they have truly repented of their sins, and have found peace in their souls through faith in Jesus Christ, and that they have passed from death into life.

At least three or four of these meetings should be held before baptism. In some places they are held much oftener. These should be opened and closed with prayer, and if practicable, with the singing of a hymn. In many places the instruction meetings are held publicly, the members and the congregation in general being present, which is appropriate and profitable for both the members and the unconverted.

In some localities before baptism is administered a counsel of the Church is held for the purpose of ascertaining whether there is any Scriptural reason to prevent the admission of any of the applicants into the Church. If no cause is found, they are requested to meet again on the day preceding baptism, upon which occasion the eighteen articles of the Confession are read to them and explained, and they are asked whether they believe in and fully agree with these doctrines. If they answer in the affirmative, they are exhorted to stand firmly, and be faithful in the commandments of God, and to continue in good works unto the end.

In other places the names of the applicants are simply published in the meeting, and if no objection is presented, and the candidates have been sufficiently instructed, either publicly or privately, the time for baptism is appointed, and the exercises are proceeded with as follows:

After singing a hymn the minister or deacon may appropriately read John 1:1-36. After the usual opening services and prayer the bishop or another minister takes an appropriate text and preaches a discourse from it (observing not to preach too long). . . .

Addressing the applicants, the minister says: "And now, if it is still your desire to be baptized and received into church fellowship, you will arise."

He then addresses to the applicants the following questions:

1. "Do you believe in one true, eternal, and almighty God, who is the Creator and Preserver of all visible and invisible things?"

Answer: "I do."

2. "Do you believe in Jesus Christ, as the only begotten Son of God, that He is the only Saviour of mankind, that He died upon the cross, and gave Himself a ransom for our sins, that through Him we might have eternal life?"

Answer: "I do."

3. "Do you believe in the Holy Ghost which proceedeth from the Father and the Son; that

He is an abiding Comforter, sanctifies the hearts
of men, and guides them into all truth?"

Answer: "I do."

(Note—The foregoing questions are, by
some, combined in one; but it is better to ask
them separately, in order that they may be
better understood.)

4. "Are you truly sorry for your past sins,
and are you willing to renounce Satan, the
world, and all works of darkness, and your own
carnal will and sinful desires?"

Answer: "I am."

5. "Do you promise by the grace of God,
and the aid of the Holy Spirit, to submit yourself to Christ and His Word, and faithfully to
abide in the same until death?"

Answer: "I do."

After these questions have been asked and
answered affirmatively the minister and the subjects for baptism kneel, while the congregation
stands, and the minister prays for God's blessing
upon them, that they may have grace to remain
steadfast and be faithful to the end in the
promises they have made.

After prayer the minister arises, while the
subjects for baptism remain kneeling. The deacon or some other brother now brings a vessel
with water, and the minister, laying his hands
upon the head of the subject for baptism, says,

"Upon the confession of thy faith, which
thou hast made before God and these witnesses
(he now with both hands takes a quantity of
water from the vessel and pours it upon the
head of the applicant), I baptize thee with
water, in the name of the Father, and of the
Son, and of the Holy Ghost."

(Some, instead of saying "Which thou hast
made before God and these witnesses," say, "Repentance and sorrow for thy sins," etc.)

After all the applicants are thus baptized, the minister returns to the one first baptized, and taking him by the hand says:

"In the name of Christ and His Church I give you my hand. Arise! And as Christ was raised up by the glory of the Father, even so thou also shalt walk in newness of life, and as long as thou art faithful and abidest in the doctrine of His Word, thou art his disciple indeed, and shalt be acknowledged as a member of the body of Christ, and a brother (or sister) in the Church." He then gives him the kiss of peace and says: "The Lord bless thee and keep thee. Amen."

In the same manner he also raises the female converts, and the wife of the minister or deacon, or any sister of the Church, gives them the kiss of peace, and thus receives them into the fellowship of the Church.

The minister now takes his place again at the desk, and gives such further instruction as he may deem necessary, after which the services are closed in the usual manner.

If any person who has been connected with another denomination, and having been baptized upon the confession of his faith (persons who were baptized in their infancy cannot be received into the Church without being rebaptized) wishes to unite with the Church, he is not rebaptized, unless he desires it, but is taught the doctrines of the Bible, and the rules of order as we believe and practice them. If he agrees with these, and the Church has no cause against him, the minister, in the presence of the whole congregation, asks him the following questions:

"Do you confess that you are of the same mind with us in the doctrines and rules of the Church; and do you promise to remain faithful and obedient in the same until death?" If he

Bethel Theological Seminary, Oak Brook, Illinois, serves
the Church of the Brethren. Details show etched glass
windows and a large wood carving

answers this affirmatively the minister takes him by the hand saying:

"Upon this confession which thou hast made before God and these witnesses, thou shalt be acknowledged as a brother (or sister) in the Church: and as long as thou art faithful and abidest in the doctrine of His word, thou art His disciple indeed." The kiss of peace is then given, and he says: "The Lord bless thee and keep thee. Amen."

Some prefer the following more complete form:

"Do you acknowledge and confess that you agree and are of one mind with us in the doctrines and faith of the Mennonite Church, and that you acknowledge and accept them as in accordance with the teachings of the Gospel; and do you promise by the grace of God and the aid of His Holy Spirit to submit yourself to them, and also to her rules of order and forms of worship, and to remain faithful and obedient in the same until death?"

Answer. "I do."

"Then in the name of Jesus Christ and His Church I give thee my hand, and welcome thee to the communion and fellowship of this Church and congregation and to the Church in general, and as long as thou art faithful and abidest in the doctrine of His Word, thou art His disciple indeed, and shalt be acknowledged as a member of the body of Christ and a brother (or sister) in the Church."

The minister then gives the usual salutation and says:

"The Lord bless thee and keep thee. Amen."

Frequently applicants prefer to be baptized in the water. In this case the questions are sometimes asked, and the prayer offered in the house. The services here may be closed by the singing of a hymn before proceeding to the water. Here the minister, standing with the converts near the water, surrounded by the congregation, reads Acts 8:35-39, or some other short and appropriate Scripture. He may also add, as circumstances may suggest, a few words of comment, or admonition, or the congregation may sing a hymn. The minister then leads the applicants, one or two at a time, into the water, where the applicants kneel and the minister takes up water with both hands, pours it on their heads, and proceeds further as described above.

The Statement of Christian Doctrine and Rules and Discipline of the Mennonite Church (Lancaster Conference) gives the following conditions for instruction and acceptance of new members:

Article III
The Church

1. The Church consists of penitent, believing, and obedient members.

The ministry responsible for the instruction of applicants should be diligent in giving thorough teaching on the way of salvation, help in living the Christian life, and preparation for Christian service. After a period of such instruction, applicants shall be examined to learn whether they are at peace, are penitent, believing, and willing to submit to the evangelical doctrine of nonconformity and nonresistance, and the discipline of the Church. Upon such evidence and with the counsel of the congregation they shall be received into the Church upon confession of faith and water baptism.

15
Church of the Brethren,
or "Dunkers"

THE CHURCH OF THE BRETHREN, also called "Dunkers," from the German word "to dip," referring to baptism, is comprised of several bodies descended from the German Pietist movement of the seventeenth and eighteenth centuries. Rebelling against the formalism and ritualism characteristic of the state church, they turned to the literal Word of the Bible as an exact and detailed guide to life. Their observances are distinguished by an *agape* or "love feast," foot washing, greeting with a "kiss of peace" anointing the sick with oil, and other practices. The Brethren oppose the taking of oaths, going to war, and participating in lawsuits.

The Brethren bodies are the Church of the Brethren, the Conservative Dunkers; the Brethren Church, Progressive Dunkers; the Old German Baptist Brethren, Old Order of Dunkers; the Church of God, New Dunkers; and the Seventh-Day Baptists, a German group. The name "Dunker" derives from their distinct observance of baptism in the form of trine immersion —one immersion each for the Father, the Son, and the Holy Ghost.

Conversion Procedure

A pamphlet, *What Does Church Membership Mean?* [1] gives the following questions (with comments), which are asked of a candidate before baptism:

> Church Membership Means a Faithful Endeavor to Keep Baptismal Vows.
> Before baptism we ask the following questions:
> 1. Do you believe that Jesus Christ is the Son of God and that he brought from heaven a saving Gospel? This question calls for faith in Jesus as the Son of God and in his saving Gospel.
> 2. Do you willingly renounce Satan, with all his pernicious ways, and all the sinful pleasures of this world? This requires a renunciation of the old life of sin and a commitment to a new life of righteousness.
> 3. Do you covenant with God in Christ Jesus to be faithful until death? The Christian covenants with God to be faithful in this new life until death.
>   Church membership is not just a turning from; it is a turning to. It is giving up the old life of sin, with full commitment to the new life of righteousness.

The meaning of church membership is summarized as follows:

> 1. Your church expects you to grow in Christlikeness.
> 2. Your church expects you to cultivate the

1. Rufus Bowman, *What Does Church Membership Mean?* (Elgin, Ill.: The Brethren Press, undated.), pp. 4-5.

spirit of unlimited forgiveness.

3. Your church expects you to keep your baptismal vows.

4. Your church expects you to be loyal to her ideals.

5. Your church expects you to be active in winning others for Christ.

6. Your church expects you to bring offerings regularly.

7. Your church expects you to attend services and participate joyfully in the sacraments.

8. Your church expects you to lead a life of prayer and devotion and to study the Word of God regularly.

9. Your church expects you to cooperate in the work of the local church, the district and the general brotherhood. This includes the support of Christian missions, Christian education, the ministry, Bethany Biblical Seminary, peace, temperance and other phases of spiritual uplift.

Church membership means all of this, and more.[2]

2. *Ibid.*, pp. 7-8.

16
Evangelical Congregational
Church

NEAR THE CLOSE OF the eighteenth century, a Lancaster County, Pennsylvania, farmer and tile maker, Jacob Albright, who had been a soldier in the Revolutionary War, was converted by earnest pietistic preachers. Following this religious experience, he began to preach as a circuit rider, and he organized groups for prayer and worship. Many supporters gathered about him, and out of this humble beginning emerged the organization of the Evangelical Association.

Late in the nineteenth century the denomination was reorganized under the name of the United Evangelical Church. A split among the leaders after World War I resulted in the creation of the Evangelical Congregational Church.

Followers of this denomination have been described as "Methodists in polity, Arminian in doctrine," with emphasis on the inspiration and integrity of the Bible and the "fellowship of all followers of Christ."

Conversion Procedure

Robert S. Wilson, editor of the Church Center

Press, Inc., publishing house of the church,[1] discusses the Evangelical Congregational attitude on conversion:

> When we think of conversion, we do not think of it as a change from one religion to another, but a change of life—from a life of sin to a life of holiness. This, we believe, can only come about through the convicting power of God, who causes us to realize that we have sinned against Him. We believe that the Christ, or Messiah is the One who can provide the satisfaction for sin. He died for us on the cross, and became the lamb of God, able to provide full atonement for sin. Through faith in what Jesus Christ has done for us, we find forgiveness as well as power to live for Him.
>
> This is the position of Christians down through the years. Although some have strayed from this truth, we believe this is the teaching on conversion, briefly stated, as found among the early followers of Jesus in the first century. Our church endeavors to get back to the truth as we find it in the first century.
>
> Our particular church grew up as a spiritual revival movement in the early 1800's. The origin was in eastern Pennsylvania, among the people who had migrated from Germany in the latter part of the previous century. Their spiritual leaders were not too helpful in some communities and there was a desire for something which would satisfy the souls of men. Conversion, in that pioneer environment, became somewhat of an emotional experience, where people would feel the conviction of sin to such an extent that they fell on their faces and wept tears of penitence, before God. The people were expected to pray until they found peace of heart. In sub-

1. Myerstown, Pennsylvania.

stance this is still found in present-day conversions, though our modern civilization does not encourage as great an emotional response as formerly. However, we emphasize that conversion must be more than a mental change of mind, but should involve the soul and the life of the individual.

17
Moravian Church

THE MORAVIAN CHURCH TRACES its beginnings to the pre-Reformation awakening under John Hus, who subsequently died a fiery death at the stake as a martyr. His followers were formally organized in 1457 under the name *Unitas Fratrum,* and the United States' largest Moravian group still bears that name. A second group is called the Unity of the Brethren.

The history of the Moravian Church is one of near extermination and then revival. Missionaries introduced the religion to America during the Colonial period through their missionary efforts among the Indians. Evangelical in character, the Moravian Church teaches salvation through faith in Jesus as a personal Savior. The church is the resulting fellowship of believers who share this experience of faith. The church also teaches faith in the Bible as the Word of God and belief in the divinity of Jesus. It requires infant baptism and confirmation of the baptismal vow in the rite of confirmation, which follows a period of religious instruction. Moravians have the unique practice of accepting new members from other denominations—a transfer—by "the Right Hand of Fellowship." [1]

1. Further information is available from the Headquarters of the Moravian Christian Church in America, 69 W. Church Street, Bethlehem, Pennsylvania.

18
The Salvation Army

THE SALVATION ARMY WAS founded in London, England, in 1865 by William Booth, a minister of the Methodist Church, who had severed his connection with the church in order to preach in the slums. First known as the East London Christian Mission, of which Booth was general superintendent, the organization grew more militant in character, and in 1878 its name was changed to the Salvation Army. William Booth was its first general.

In 1880, a small band of one male officer and seven women members was dispatched to the United States to start the movement in this country. Landing at Battery Park in New York City, they held their first open-air meeting and became the object of ridicule, abuse, and scorn. So enthusiastic was the small band, however, that its work quickly spread and the ranks of its converts grew. Eight years later, in 1888, the Salvation Army was active in thirty-two states and the District of Columbia. Soon, the organization had been extended to many other countries.

The first endeavors of the Salvation Army were the simple preaching of the Christian missionary movement, but, before long, social work activities were begun in many countries. Its philanthropic work consisted principally of maintaining soup kitchens or low-priced food depots, shelters for the homeless, and the working with "fallen women" and neglected children.

In 1890, the founder of the Salvation Army published a book called *In Darkest England and the Way Out*. In it, he outlined a forward-looking proposal for alleviating some of the social ills in the overcrowded areas of Europe and for improving the situation of farmers and other workers in overseas areas. Because of the group's activity in the international field, it has been granted status (consultive Class B) as a nongovernmental agency related to the Economic and Social Council of the United Nations.

The Salvation Army does not use the sacraments of baptism and Holy Communion.

> This conception, however, does not lead to any fundamental opposition to the sacraments in the Salvation Army. Although, in the light of this understanding, they consider that they can dispense with baptism and Holy Communion, this dispensation does not become a matter for dispute. No one is denied the use of the sacraments who feels compelled by his conscience to observe them and be thereby strengthened in his faith. Any Salvationist who feels a conviction that he ought to observe the sacraments is at liberty to do so. This attitude is characteristic. The Salvation Army is concerned with the strengthening of the spiritual life of its members, and any polemic would only draw the attention to outward things.
>
> However, the Salvation Army has certain ceremonies of its own, among them the Dedication of Children, Confirmation, and, above all, the Enrolment as a soldier of the Salvation Army. These ceremonies are strictly differentiated from the sacraments, but are considered helpful to the spiritual life.

If salvationists wish, they can dedicate their children to God's service in a simple ceremony in which:

> . . . the presiding officer takes the child into his arms and prays: "Loving Heavenly Father, take this child to be Thine own." The Orders and Regulations for the Salvation Army mention explicitly that under no circumstances shall water be used.

In some countries, there is a Salvation Army ceremony similar to *Confirmation*. Having received religious instruction, the child is given opportunity to express his desire to ratify of his own free will the promises made by his parents in the Dedication Service. The officer asks: "Will you be faithful to your Heavenly Father, to the Church of the Redeemed which He has founded on earth? . . . Will you strive to live according to the teaching you have received? . . . Will you persevere in the reading of the Word of God . . . and take part in meetings?" When the child has answered these questions, the officer receives him into "the community of those who love Jesus Christ and wish to serve Him." He is not yet a full member of the Salvation Army, but has now undertaken to live in the service of Christ.

The most important ceremony is no doubt the *Enrolment* as soldier, that is, the reception of those who desire to become full members of the Salvation Army. Before this they must read, accept, and sign the "Articles of War" which contain the Articles of Doctrine of the Salvation Army and a number of promises to be made. The postulant declares that he has received God's salvation; that he believes that God raised up the Army, that he is convinced of the truth of the Army's teaching; that he realizes the necessity of and has experienced repentance, faith,

William Booth, English religious leader, was the founder
and first general of the Salvation Army

and conversion; that he believes the Bible to be inspired; that he believes that it is the privilege of the believer to be wholly sanctified; that he believes in the immortality of the soul . . . He promises to renounce the world and to abstain from the use of intoxicating liquor; that he will take no part in anything that is low, profane, or unclean; that he will act honestly and straightforwardly towards all men; that he will support the "Salvation War" as far as is possible; that he will obey the lawful orders of his officers and that he will at all times live as a soldier of Christ and of the Salvation Army.

Those who promise to live in accordance with these articles are enrolled into the Army. The officer welcomes them under the Salvation Army Flag: "In the name of the General, I accept your declaration and greet you as soldiers of the Salvation Army and comrades serving under the flag of blood and fire . . ."

The practices of the Salvation Army are meaningful in more than one sense. They put special weight upon the importance of personal faith. They warn against all false expectation in a sacramental event. They make it clear that faith in Christ calls us to true service. The whole of Christian life is developed from the concept of the *militia Christi*. The question arises, however, whether dispensing with the sacraments is really what is meant in the New Testament. Is it in this sense that Christ's message puts the weight upon the "inwardness" of religious life? And may it not follow that, in the light of the strong emphasis on the *militia Christi*, other aspects of the biblical witness necessarily recede into the background? These are questions which will always play a major role in discussions with the Salvation Army.

Conversion Procedure

The Salvation Army considers itself:

. . . basically a religious organization, a movement in the Christian Church, to preach the Gospel of Jesus Christ. Its social work is its expression of the spirit of Christ, His love and concern for people and their problems.

To become a salvationist a person must:

1. Be fourteen years of age (Juniors 7 to 14 years).
2. Be converted after having repented of sin and by faith accepted Christ as his personal Saviour.
3. Know something of the Army's spirit and program through active interest and participation for a period of at least a month.
4. Read and sign voluntarily the "Articles of War for Soldiers" (see below).
5. Be approved by the local Census Board of the corps, comprised of the Commanding Officer and soldiers who carry specific responsibility. These are called local officers.
6. Be publicly enrolled as a soldier under the flag of the Army, after which he may wear uniform and participate fully in Army activities. He still works at his regular employment, lives in his own home, and carries responsibility for his family, while giving as much time and money as possible for the extension of the Kingdom of God through the Army.

ARTICLES OF WAR (summarized)

The person to be enrolled as a soldier of

the Salvation Army declares that:

1. He has received salvation.
2. He believes that God has raised up the Army.
3. He is convinced of the truth of the Army's teaching.
4. He realizes the necessity of and has experienced repentance, faith and conversion.
5. He believes the Bible to be inspired.
6. He believes that it is our privilege to be wholly sanctified.
7. He believes in the immortality of the soul.

He promises that:

1. He will abstain from the use of intoxicating liquor.
2. He will not take part in anything that is low, profane, or unclean.
3. He will act honestly and straightforwardly with all with whom he has dealings.
4. He will support the Salvation Army so far as is possible.
5. He will obey his officers.
6. He is determined to show himself at all times a true soldier of Jesus Christ and the Salvation Army.[1]

The stated purposes of the Salvation Army are the spiritual, moral, and physical reformation of all who need it; the reclamation of the vicious, criminal, dissolute, and degraded; visitation among the poor and lowly and sick; the preaching of the Gospel and the dissemination of Christian truth.

1. From a leaflet entitled *With Banners and Bonnets They Come*. Published by the Salvation Army, reprinted with permission.

19
Churches of the New Jerusalem

READERS OF *The New York Times* and other newspapers are probably familiar with announcements calling attention to the teachings of Emanuel Swedenborg (1688–1772) and offering free information on request.

The denomination could be listed, with fidelity to classification, together with the liberal churches. The Churches of the New Jerusalem—the General Convention and the General Church—originated in the theological teachings of Swedenborg, an eighteenth-century Swedish scientist, distinguished in the fields of anatomy, mathematics, and cosmology. He turned to theology after he experienced a series of dreams and visions revealing to him secrets of the spiritual world, especially matters pertaining to the Last Judgment. He taught the end of the first dispensation of the Christian Church and the beginning of a new dispensation which he called the "Descent of the Holy City," or "the New Jerusalem."

The doctrines of the General Convention are presented in the *Liturgy:*

1. That there is one God, in whom there is a Divine Trinity, and that He is the Lord Jesus Christ.

Emanuel Swedenborg, Swedish religious teacher and mystic

2. That a saving faith is to believe on Him.
3. That evils are to be shunned, because they are of the devil and from the devil.
4. That good actions are to be done because they are of God and from God.
5. That these are to be done by a man as from himself; but that it ought to be believed that they are done from the Lord with him and by him.

Conversion Procedure

Hugo L. Odhner, secretary of the General Church of the New Jerusalem, Bryn Athyn, Pennsylvania, discusses the position of his group on conversion:

Those who as adults acknowledge the doctrines contained in the Theological Writings of Emanuel Swedenborg as a new Divine revelation, are given New Church baptism and are then accepted as members of the Church. Obviously, they must first become acquainted with these doctrines by reading them to some extent. Our children are educated in the Old and New Testaments and in the doctrines of the New Church, and, when confirmed at the ages of 18–21, become members of the Church.

No emotional "crisis" or "altar-call" is likely, for conversion to us means the sincere and rational conviction of the truth of the doctrine, which in time will regenerate both the understanding and the will of the receiver.

Rev. Richard H. Tafel of the First New Jerusalem Society of Philadelphia adds the following information:

Conversion is not the spectacular thing with us that it is in some churches. It proceeds from a person's quiet determination to follow our Lord God and Savior in the good life which he teaches us in his Holy Bible. As you will see from the copy of our Adult Baptism and Confirmation of Faith, the emphasis is on *Life* in the *Light* of our fuller Christian teaching.

Perhaps because we sincerely believe that everyone who is making a conscientious effort to live up to the faith that he professes is "saved" (and we do not like to use this expression because it has been cheapened by many churches), we have historically placed the emphasis less on "conversion" to our particular church than on conversion to the true spiritual life. It is to the fostering and deepening of this life, in the light of our particular teachings, that we invite others to join with us in seeking.

A person joins our church by announcing his intention to the minister, preparing himself under him in a grasp of the church's teachings, and by the church Service of Confirmation (and Baptism, if he so wishes). We look at this as an apprenticeship in spiritual living, which is a lifetime endeavor.

20
Interdenominational

BECAUSE OF THE ECUMENICAL spirit, interdenominational churches are becoming increasingly popular. One such church is the well-known Riverside Church in New York City. Its huge assembly of
worshippers is drawn from every walk of life and
from many different religions. The Riverside Church
maintains historic ties with the American Baptist Convention and the United Church of Christ. It proclaims
itself "an international, interracial and interdenominational fellowship of Christians."

The fame of the church, with its lofty bell tower
and beautiful windows, brings countless visitors from
every part of the country. And the book rack of every
pew contains a packet of cards inviting the visitor to
full membership, affiliate membership, or non-resident
affiliate membership.

Conversion Procedure

Below is a facsimile of part of a card with details
on how to become a member of the Riverside Church:

> The Riverside Church exists in the metro-
> politan community to bear witness to the Gospel
> of Jesus Christ. In worship and service its mem-
> bers seek to build the vital Christian fellowship

which becomes the church when loyalty to Christ is central in the lives of His followers.

Membership in The Riverside Church is open to persons of all racial, national, cultural or denominational backgrounds who wish to participate with others in the worship of God and who desire to practice Christianity in their individual lives.

Prospective members are accepted into The Riverside Church by a vote of the congregation at one of its regular meetings. Preliminary steps include a conference with one of the ministers, attendance at group sessions with others who are joining and action by the Board of Deacons. New members are received at a Communion Service.

Persons who have never been members of a Christian church are received into membership upon *Confession of Faith*. Such persons for the first time declare their belief in Jesus Christ and their desire to follow and serve him with other Christians. Baptism is administered in either mode.

Membership by Letter is open to all those who come from Christian churches of any denomination.

Membership on Reaffirmation of Faith is open to anyone who has previously been a member of another church, but who for some reason is unable to secure a letter of transfer. The previous experience and commitment are accepted as the basis for entering into the new relationship in this church.

Members of out-of-town churches who are to be temporarily in the city, but who wish to retain their home church membership, may become *Affiliate members*. Such members may participate in all phases of the worship and work of the church, with the exception of voting at occasional church business meetings.

Non-resident Affiliate membership is open to members of other churches in communities at a distance from New York City who desire to establish this relationship with The Riverside Church and to contribute in a measure to its work. Those who are dismissed to other churches from The Riverside Church may also become non-resident affiliate members in order to continue in association with this church in its wider ministry.

Non-member Contributors are friends of the church who prefer for personal reasons, to keep their regular membership elsewhere but who wish to take part in this church and to contribute to its support because they believe in its work and enjoy its fellowship.

ABOUT JOINING
INVITATION TO MEMBERSHIP

The Riverside Church seeks to be a Christian Fellowship devoted to expressing the Gospel. All are invited to make this their church home.

☐ I am interested in joining this church.

....
Name

....
Street   Apt. No.

....
City   State

....
Tel. No.

Inquiries are welcome.

Appointments may be made by calling one of the ministers.

21
African Methodist Episcopal
Zion Church

MOST AMERICAN NEGROES ARE Baptists or Methodists, with a growing number joining the Roman Catholic Church and other, smaller churches. Many Negro churches came into being as a result of the social conditions of the times. The African Methodist Episcopal Zion Church, an independent body, came into being when the Negroes broke with the John Street Church, a Methodist church in New York City, as a reaction against racial prejudice. The A.M.E. was organized in 1796 and their first church built in 1800. The new group continued to maintain good relations with the parent Methodist Episcopal Church and drew up a formal agreement to be served by ministers of the latter group, a practice which continued for two decades.

Conversion Procedure

Rules of membership and reception of new members are the following: [1]

1. Reprinted with permission from *The Doctrines and Discipline of the African Methodist Episcopal Zion Church* (Charlotte, N.C.: A.M.E. Zion Publication House, 1948), pp. 39-44, 280-89.

RECEPTION OF MEMBERS

Form for Receiving Persons Into the
    Church on Probation.

*Those who are to be received into the Church
as Probationers shall be called forward by
name, and the Minister, addressing the Congregation, shall say:*

DEARLY BELOVED BRETHREN: That none may
be admitted hastily into the Church, it is our
custom to receive all persons seeking fellowship
with us on profession of faith, into a preparatory
membership on trial, during which time such
persons may have opportunity to become acquainted with the Rules and Doctrines of our
Church; and the Church may learn that sincerity
and depth of the motives which prompt them to
seek such fellowship.

The persons before you desire to be received
on Probation, and it is needful for me to remind
you that your lives should be holy examples to
them, that they may take no detriment from you,
but that through your help they may have reason to give thanks to God that they were led into
this fellowship.

*Then, addressing the Persons to be received on
Probation, the Minister shall say:*

DEARLY BELOVED: You have by the grace of
God made your decision to follow Christ and to
serve him, which decision we trust is not based
upon any worthiness in yourselves, but solely on
the merits of our Lord Jesus Christ, and on his
death and intercession for us.

That the Church may know your purpose,
you will answer the questions I am now to ask
you.

Have you an earnest desire to be saved from
your sins?

Ans. I have.

Will you guard yourself against all things

contrary to the teaching of God's word, and endeavor to lead a holy life, following the commandments of God?

Ans. I will endeavor so to do.

Are you purposed to give reverent attendance upon the appointed means of grace in the
ministry of the word, and in the private and
public worship of God?

Ans. I am so determined, with the help of
God.

*The Minister shall then announce that the Can-
didates are received on Probation, and shall
assign them to classes. He may then offer a
short extemporary Prayer.*

Form for Receiving Persons Into the
Church after Probation.

DEARLY BELOVED BRETHREN: The Scriptures
teach us that the Church is the household of
God, the body of which Christ is the head; and
that it is the design of the Gospel to bring together in one all who are in Christ. The fellowship of the Church is the communion that its
Members enjoy one with another. The ends of
this fellowship are the maintenance of sound
doctrine and of the ordinances of Christian worship, the exercise of that power of godly admonition and discipline which Christ has committed
to his Church for the promotion of holiness. It
is the duty of all men to unite in fellowship, for
it is only those that "be planted in the house of
the Lord that shall flourish in the courts of our
God." Its more particular duties are to promote
peace and unity, to bear one another's burdens,
to seek the intimacy of friendly society among
themselves, to continue steadfast in the faith and
worship of the Gospel, and to pray and sympa-
thize with each other. Among its privileges are

peculiar incitements to holiness from the hearing
of God's word and sharing in Christ's ordinances,
the being placed under the watchful care of
Pastors, and the enjoyment of the blessings
which are promised only to those who are of
the household of faith. Into this holy fellowship
the *persons* before you, who *have* already received the Sacrament of Baptism and *have* been
under the care of proper Leaders on Trial, *come*
seeking admission. We now propose in the fear
of God to question *them* as to *their* faith and
purpose, that you may know that *they* are
proper *persons* to be admitted into the Church.
Then, addressing the applicants for admission,
the Minister shall say:

DEARLY BELOVED: You are come hither seeking the great privilege of union with the Church
our Saviour has purchased with his own blood.
We rejoice in the grace of God vouchsafed unto
you, in that he has called you to be his followers,
and that thus far you have run well. You have
heard how blessed are the privileges and how
solemn are the duties of membership in Christ's
Church; and before you are fully admitted there-
to it is proper that you do here publicly renew
your vows, confess your faith, and declare your
purpose by answering the following questions:

Quest. Do you here, in the presence of God
and this Congregation, make the solemn promise
contained in the Baptismal Covenant, ratifying
and confirming the same, and acknowledging
yourselves bound faithfully to observe and keep
that Covenant?

Ans. I do.

Quest. Have you saving faith in the Lord
Jesus Christ?

Ans. I have.

Quest. Do you believe in the Doctrines of
the Holy Scriptures as set forth in the Articles

of Religion of the African Methodist Episcopal
Zion Church?

Ans. I do.

Quest. Will you cheerfully be governed by
the Rules of the African Methodist Episcopal
Zion Church, hold sacred the Ordinances of God,
and endeavor, as much as in you lies, to promote
the welfare of the Redeemer's kingdom?

Ans. I will.

Quest. Will you cherish friendly feelings toward all persons, as far as possible, especially toward the Members of the Church?

Ans. I will.

Quest. Will you contribute of your earthly
substance, according to your ability, to the support of the Gospel and the various benevolent
enterprises of the Church?

Ans. I will.

*Then the Minister, addressing the Church, shall
say:*

Brethren, you have heard the response given
to our inquiries. Have any of you reason to
allege why these persons should not be received
into Full Connection in the Church?

*No objections being alleged, the Minister shall
say to the Candidate:*

We welcome you to the communion of the
Church of God, and in testimony of our Christian
affection and the cordiality with which we receive you, I hereby extend to you the right hand
of fellowship; and may God grant that you may
be faithful and useful members of the Church
militant till you are called to the fellowship of
the Church triumphant, which is "without fault
before the throne of God."

Islam

The Koran is the revealed scripture of Islam

Introduction—Islam

MOHAMMEDANISM, WHICH THE RELIGION of Islam is often called in the Western world, is a misnomer. Muslims are quick to explain that Mohammed, though the greatest and "seal" of the prophets, was only a messenger who transmitted the religion of Islam from God to man.

The name *Islam* means submission and, in its fullest sense, means peace through submission to God. The word is associated with the submission of Abraham when he was prepared to sacrifice his son Isaac, an act which is called *Aslama* in the Koran. The Koran, the sacred book of Islam, is believed by Muslims to have been written by Mohammed, who transcribed revelations by God as they were told to him by the angel Gabriel. The Koran is the cornerstone of Islam; it is more important than the prophet himself.

Mohammed was born about 571 A.D. into the ruling tribe of the Saudi Arabian city of Mecca. He was well known for his virtuous life, and was unhappy with the immorality, feuds, and cynicism characteristic of his times. An ordinary caravan conductor until the age of about twenty-five, Mohammed entered the service of Khadija, a wealthy widow fifteen years his senior, who subsequently became his wife and inspiring companion. This step provided him with the

**Courtyard of the Haram, the Great Mosque in Mecca,
Saudi Arabia, encloses the Kaaba, Islam's most holy shrine**

economic freedom to devote his attention to spiritual matters.

Mohammed went to a cave outside the city of Mecca, where in 610 A.D. he received the call from Allah: "Recite thou in the name of the Lord who created." A new religion was born, the chief features of which were strict monotheism, emphasis on man's moral responsibility toward God, and judgment for all on the day of resurrection. It taught respect for order in nature, which led to the later blossoming of Muslim culture and science. Muslims must believe and fully understand the familiar cry of Islam, *"La ilaha illa Allah!"*—"There is no God but Allah!" The sentence is frequently translated, "There is no god but God!"

When Mohammed lived, countless *jinn* or "desert spirits" were worshipped by the Meccans. One of these spirits was Allah. Mohammed not only recognized his supremacy, but wiped his rivals from the face of the desert by making him the only God worthy of worship. Mohammed identified Allah with the God of ancient Israel and of Christianity.

Mohammed's initial preaching met with limited success; only a few hundred converts came under his banner in the course of a decade. The early abuse and ridicule by the Meccans eventually shifted to persecution. In 622 A.D. Mohammed was forced to flee for his life. Muslims regard this "flight" as the turning point of history and the beginning of the Muslim era.

Mohammed and his followers proceeded to the city of Yathrib, now Medina, Saudi Arabia, at the invitation of its citizens and took over the political administration of the city. Yathrib became known as Medinat en-Nabi, the City of the Prophet, or simply Medina.

In the years that followed, the prophet-turned-administrator devoted his enormous energy to the civil affairs of Medina and the consolidation of the feuding tribes into a harmonious confederation. He also proved himself an able military leader. He successfully defended himself against attacks from Mecca, whose inhabitants embraced the new religion *en masse* when the city fell to his military forces in 630.

Mohammed's career came to an abrupt end when, after a brief illness, he died on June 8, 632. But in his relatively brief span on earth, he managed to lay down a religious, moral, and socioeconomic code that became the foundation of a new civilization. Mohammed never claimed divine attributes, nor did he try to impress anyone as a miracle worker. His only claim was that he was selected by Allah to transmit a divine message.

Moslems at prayer

22
Islam

WHAT IS THE ESSENCE of the religion of Islam? Islam is based on the Word of God contained in the Koran and the *hadith,* or the sayings and traditions related to Mohammed and his followers. The Islamic articles of faith include belief in God, his angels, his divine books, his prophets, Mohammed as the last and greatest of the prophets (the first of whom was Adam), Judgment Day, and the predestination of good and evil. The only unpardonable sin is *shirk,* or "the worship of gods in addition to Allah."

The first of the famous Five Pillars of Islam is the profession of faith, called *shahadah.* It is expressed in the creed, "There is no God but Allah, and Mohammed is His prophet."

The second pillar, *salat,* or "ritual prayer," is offered five times daily in Arabic. The worshipper, who must be in a state of ritual purity, offers the *fatihah,* a prayer taken from the opening of the Koran, that is recited on almost every religious occasion:

> In the name of God, Lord of the worlds, the merciful, the compassionate, the ruler of the Judgment Day! Thee we serve and Thee we ask for aid. Guide us in the right path, the path of those to whom Thou art gracious; not of those

with whom Thou art wroth; nor of those who err.

The prayers are accompanied by genuflections and prostrations in the direction of Mecca.

In keeping with Islam's spirit of simplicity and informality, public worship is limited to the Friday noon service conducted by an *imam,* "religious leader," in a mosque. All adult males are obliged to attend. The noon service is accompanied with recitations from the Koran.

Zakat, or "the payment of an alms tax," is the third pillar. The practice of raising funds for the direct relief of human need originated as a voluntary contribution, evolved into a compulsory tax, and is once again a voluntary tax on income and holdings.

The fourth pillar, *ramadan,* is a month-long fast from dawn to dusk marking the month of God's commission of Mohammed as his prophet and the *hegira,* or flight of Mohammed from Mecca, ten years later.

The fifth pillar is known as *hajj* meaning "pilgrimage." A Moslem is required, if able, to visit Mecca at least once during his lifetime. Dressed in a simple white seamless ceremonial garment, he walks around the *kaaba* seven times and also visits other sacred shrines in Mecca. The chief advantage of the uniform garment is that it levels all social classes. Hajj also brings Muslims together from their far-flung homes to emphasize their unity and common heritage.

Islam's attitude against emphasizing racial differences has struck a responsive chord in the hearts of the new African nations. Some of Islam's economic views, especially its concept of sharing wealth, are also significant in an age when conflicting political ideologies are rooted in conflicting economic interpretations.

By a century after Mohammed's death, Islam had

spanned continents and had developed an admirable culture, literature, science, medicine, art, and architecture. Today, one in seven people in the world is a Muslim; some 300,000,000 people respond to the call of the *muezzin,* a Muslim crier who announces the hour of daily prayers from the mosque:

Allah is most great!
Allah is most great!
I testify that there is no God but Allah
I testify that Mohammed is the Prophet of Allah.
Arise and pray, arise and pray.
Allah is great;
There is no God but Allah!

On the subject of conversion we find a familiar paucity of subject matter—almost a vacuum—and an ambivalence of attitude.

On the one hand Mohammed's claim that he was the "seal of the Prophets," rendered all preceding prophecies, laws, and religions obsolete. Yet the Koran states: "Unto you your religion and unto me my religion."

The romantic figure of the brave Muslim warrior with scimitar in one hand and Koran in the other is equally anomalous in the light of the admonition in the Koran, "There is no compulsion in religion." Moreover, history records golden eras in the history of other religious groups living in tranquility under the shadow of the crescent.

Indeed, no recorded organized mission in Islam existed until recent times. Proselytizing activities were carried on informally by individual Muslims, such as merchants or travelers who came in contact with others. Today, Muslim missionaries are pressing an active and rewarding campaign for converts in the

Dome of the Rock, a Moslem Mosque built in the seventh
century, at the foot of Mount Moriah, Jerusalem

newly created states in Africa where the racial gospel of Islam has a ringing appeal.

The civil rights struggle in the United States has been accompanied by the growth of an islamic movement within the Negro community. This group, known as the Black Muslims, is not recognized by the World Muslim Congress. Led by Elijah Muhammad, the Black Muslims blend Islam with a racist policy advocating the separation of the races and Negro supremacy.

The missionary activities of the Muslim Brotherhood, U.S.A.[1] have attracted many members. The group publishes a tabloid called *Muhammad Speaks* and also publishes a mimeographed pamphlet on "The Fundamental Teaching of Islam," which adheres closely to the accepted pattern for presenting the doctrines of Islam.

Attempts have been made in various quarters to deny the Black Muslims the status of a religious body. The World Muslim Congress has denounced the sect.

The requirements for admission into the Black Muslim ranks are outlined by one of their leaders, Mustapha Hashim:

1. Technical steps such as affirmation, confirmation, baptism with water or flowers are not required, necessary or permitted as part of the procedure of conversion to Islam.
2. Ishmael, the first born son of the Patriarch Abraham (peace be upon them), and the

1. Offices at:
   5312 West Girard Avenue, Philadelphia 31, Pennsylvania.
   2618 East MacDougall Street, Detroit, Michigan.
   The School of Islamic and African Studies, 307 West 125 Street, New York, N. Y. 10027.
   Toduk West African Imports, Inc., 30 East 125 Street, New York 35, New York.

progenitor of the Arab people, was, according to the covenant between Abraham and Allah, circumcised when he was fourteen years of age and it was the custom of the Arab people before their acceptance of Islam to circumcise at this age.

3. Islamic custom requires circumcision to be performed at the age of seven days and the Arabs who have become Muslim follow this custom.

4. The Holy Prophet Muhammad (may peace and the blessings of God be upon him) has said, "Every child is born in a state of submission to the will of God, i.e., a Muslim, and it is his parents who make him a Jew, Magian or Fire-Worshipper." Therefore, the Muslim parent is concerned with preserving the state of spiritual purity in which his child is born, and technical steps for conversion are not necessary.

5. An adult or minor who has the permission of his parents or guardian may accept Islam by simply pronouncing the Declaration of Faith or "Kalimah" before two Muslim witnesses.

May Allah bless your efforts.

In recent years, sectarian Muslim groups such as the Ahmadiyya of India, which was founded by the energetic Mirza Ghulam Ahmad, have carried on extensive missionary work in various parts of the world. The group especially hopes to win the Western mind. Its primary aim, however, is sometimes said to be solely to spread knowledge of Islam, not necessarily to make converts.

Islam's missionary strength, in addition to its racial doctrine, lies in its simplicity. Directed to the average person, Islam's doctrines avoid ambiguous symbolism and excessive ritual. Islam has teachers and preachers, but no ceremonial priests. The emergent African peoples, long under foreign rule, find solace in Islam's message of kindliness, generosity, chivalry, and brotherhood. And conversion to Islam is a very simple procedure.

This explains in part the short supply of literature on the subject. One Muslim writer presents the entire procedure in two sentences:

> Upon conversion to Islam, the new believer is required to pronounce the formula once and hence becomes a member of the faith. There is no other ceremony involved.[2]

Muslims practice circumcision on all males at the age of one week, a rite derived from the biblical account of the circumcision of Ishmael. However, circumcision may be waived in the case of an adult convert.

Akil Serdaroglu of the Turkish Information Office in New York outlined the practical requirements for conversion as circumcision, five daily periods of prayer, the Ramadan Fast, giving alms, and repeating the necessary words before a Muslim religious leader.

The Koran states in several places that forcing nonbelievers to convert to Islam is to be shunned. "There is no compulsion in religion." Sura ii. 256. "And if thy Lord willed, all who are on earth would have believed together. Wouldst thou (Muhammad) compel men until they are believers?" Sura x. 100. "Lo! thou (O Muhammad) guidest not whom thou lovest,

2. Salina Biserlawy, article in *Living Schools of Religion*, ed. Vergilius Ferm (Paterson, N.J.: Littlefield, Adam and Co., 1961), p. 162.

but Allah guideth who He will. And he is best aware of those who walk aright." Sura xxviii. 56.

Dr. Mahmoud Hoballah, director of the Islamic Center in Washington, D.C., in the pamphlet entitled "Islam and Human Tenets," published by the Center, explains:

> From its very early revelation, the religion of Islam has made it explicitly clear to its adherents that the diversity of opinions, ideologies and creeds is natural to mankind. It is the result of their different methods of education, upbringing and of their reasoning power. The Muslims are thereby made to believe and act accordingly: do not let such a kind of natural diversity interfere in any way with the just dealing and kind treatment which man ought to give to his brothers in humanity. . . .
> These and similar Quranic instructions are not designed to illustrate natural phenomena, but to teach Muslims to look upon diversity of opinions as something natural and cannot be avoided. By the injunction of their religion, Muslims are, therefore, required to endeavor to cultivate within themselves an international character and attitude, with readiness to accept as a friend and good neighbor any and all human beings.[3]

As within Christianity, there are many sects within Islam. Islam, generally, is not a proselytizing religion. Some groups, however, such as the Ahmadiyah and the Pakistanis, have missionary activities. Information for those interested in conversion to Islam is available through information centers.

Mohammed Zarnegar of Arlington, Virginia, an

3. *Islam and Humane Tenets* (Washington, D. C.: Islamic Center, undated).

authority on Islam, discusses converting to Islam:

1. Concerning steps and procedures to become a Muslim:

The applicant goes to a "learned man," that is, the Muslim priest or pontiff, and in the presence of two witnesses, declares his intentions and professes the Faith as follows:

"There is no god but God (Allah); and Mohammed is the Apostle of God." Forthwith he is a Muslim. He may or may not select a Muslim name. If the convert is a man he must be circumcised (if not previously done). Thenceforth he has to perform all prayers and other duties prescribed for Muslims. In matters of marriage, he can marry a non-Muslim wife provided she is of the "People of the Book"—that is, Jewish or Christian and, to some authorities, Zoroastrian. But if a woman becomes a convert, she cannot marry anyone except a Muslim. Other points: If the convert is a woman married to a non-Muslim, either her husband has to become a Muslim or she must divorce him. And any children born in this marriage are considered, ipso facto, Muslims.

2. Concerning eligibility to embrace Islam:

Islam considers itself a universal religion, "the natural faith of all men," according to the Qoran and the "only faith acceptable to God." There is nothing to prevent a person from becoming a Muslim; no conditions are imposed, none is debarred. In fact, Muslims consider all children born all over the world as Muslims until they reach puberty. Then if the children are not born to Muslims, and if they do not become Muslims, they are considered non-Muslims. Should children of any faith or land die before puberty, they are considered to have been Muslims! Of

The Mecca Gate, Saudi Arabia, entrance to the holiest city of Islam

course, following conversion, they are duty bound (the adults) to perform duties imposed upon them by Islam or prescribed for Muslims. In the case of children, these become prescribed upon reaching puberty.

3. Concerning the attitude of Muslims to an active mission to the non-Muslim world:

It is generally believed among the learned Muslims that the age of proselytization is gone and Islam, being a fairly well-known faith, needs no active mission to court converts. Further, it is the duty of all Muslims to fully understand their faith and to be able to explain to others *when asked to do so by the others*. The latter clause is of prime importance for according to the Qoran, "There is no (and should not be any) compulsion in matters of faith." Thus few missions are sent abroad and if a center is at all established, its work should be to remove misunderstandings and false impressions and correct misinformation among others and produce harmony between Muslims and non-Muslims.

4. Concerning the "Muslim Brotherhood of the U.S.A." or the Black Muslims:

Muslims cannot recognize any group as Muslims that professes superiority of one race over another. The Nazi, the Fascist, this White or Black supremacy group, *et al.* cannot come under the fold of Islam because they refuse to accept one of the prime precepts of Islam and that is the equality of all mankind in the eyes of God. To Prophet Mohammed, the Koreish nobleman and the slave who became a convert occupy the same position of equality in the eyes of God. And the Qoran is specific and says: "The most respected before God is the most pious."

And since the Black Muslim movement

claims the superiority of one race over another, Muslims cannot recognize them as a sect of Islam. Further, Mr. Elijah claims to be a prophet and according to Islam, Mohammed is the Last Prophet. "After him there shall not be any prophet," is an article of faith and belief in the Muslim religion.

Returning to this question of racial supremacy, the very universality of Islam negates such claims and hence it is that Islam never identifies itself with one or more nations, not even with Arabs. Arabs only form a minority of Muslims. Thus it is against Islam for any race or nation to claim supremacy. The Qoran emphatically says: "All humanity one brotherhood is!"

An official of the Afghanistan mission to the United Nations provided the following summary of requirements for admission into the Muslim fold:

To become a Muslim one has to profess faith in "There is no God but one, and Mohammed is his prophet."

Although there is no ceremony required, in practice, this profession is made in the Mosque in the presence of two or more Muslims who choose a Muslim name for the person, and who explain to him the performance of his religious obligations. There are five principal obligations:

1. Profession of faith, as noted above.
2. Performance of prayers five times every day.
3. Fasting from dawn to dusk one month each year during the month of Ramadan.
4. Giving charity from one's income beyond his own and his family's necessities.
5. Pilgrimage to Mecca once in a lifetime if the person can afford it.

Conversion Procedure

To conclude, the following questions were submitted to the director of the main Islamic Center in Washington, D.C.:

1. What are the formal steps to conversion to the faith of Islam?
2. Is everyone accepted? Are there any restrictions or prerequisites?
3. What is the current attitude abroad in Islam toward an active missionary program designed to win the non-Muslim?
4. If an American should wish to embrace Islam, what would he have to do? Whom would he have to see? Where would he apply? Is there an office or institution which would take care of his request?
5. Is the "Muslim Brotherhood, U.S.A." recognized as a bona fide Muslim group?

The response:

1. There are no formal steps to conversion to Islam. The only prerequisites are the beliefs in the oneness of God, the prophecy of Muhammad and that Muhammad was the last Prophet, and belief in God's messengers including Abraham, Moses and Jesus.
2. Yes, everyone is accepted without restriction.
3. We don't know that there are any groups whose purpose is missionary work; however, every Muslim is enjoined to be a good example and to be ready to teach any non-Muslim who inquires about the religion. Islam believes that each individual must study and seek the truth to find which religion is God's. Then, he will be held respon-

Moslem Mosque at Nairobi, Kenya

sible for his decision before God on judgment
day.

4. An American who wishes to embrace Islam
must believe in the Books revealed to all
Prophets, the Angels and the day of judgment. He must pattern his life after the
Islamic code of laws and ethics and declare
openly that he is a Muslim.

5. The Islamic Center representing all Muslim
countries can not recognize the "Muslim
Brotherhood, U.S.A." as a bona fide Muslim
group because their beliefs and practices are
not compatible with those of real Islam. The
tenets of Islam are only humane and they
teach equality, brotherhood, justice, patience
and charity. On the contrary, the main teachings of Elijah Mohammed are as follows:

   a. Superiority of black men to white men.
   b. Elijah Mohammed is God's messenger
   (which contradicts Islam's teaching that
   the Prophet Muhammad, peace be upon
   him, was the last prophet, the seal of the
   prophets.)
   c. Deviation from essential Muslim obligations and commandments.

Dr. Mahmoud Youssef Shawarbi, director of The
Islamic Foundation of New York, has answered the
following questions:

Q: If a person should come with a request to
hear the "essentials of Islam," what would be
your response?

Dr. Shawarbi: We call the essentials of Islam
the "Five Pillars" or Principles. First is the declaration of the oneness of God—There is no God
but Allah, and that Mohammad is His Prophet.

Second, *Salat* or prayers, offered five times daily; beginning the day by communing with God, a break in the middle of the day at noon, another break later in the afternoon, a fourth period of prayer at sunset and a fifth before retiring for the night. The third Pillar is *Zakat* or charity, the Muslim "social security" and concern for the poor. The fourth Pillar is *Ramadan,* a month-long fast from dawn to sunset. The fifth Pillar is the Pilgrimage to Mecca once during one's lifetime. This is a great uniting force, bringing Muslims together from all parts of the world.

Q: How does one become a Muslim?

Dr. Shawarbi: It is very simple. The theme is simplicity. One comes and declares—he can even make this declaration privately before God —" 'There is no God but Allah and Mohammad is His Messenger.' " There is no need for a formal ritual. One who wishes to become a Muslim is welcome to come to prayer services and to become a member of this Foundation. All other formalities are a mere condescension to the modern spirit, but not obligatory in the traditional spirit of Islam. A person who claims that he has declared the oneness of God and the prophetship of Mohammad is recognized as a Muslim. In some countries he might encounter complicating regulations. However, according to Islamic law, such a person is a bona fide Muslim. This attitude is in keeping with Islamic insistence on a direct relationship between the believer and God, without the need for an intervening mediator or priest.

Q: What is the approximate number of Muslims in the United States today?

Dr. Shawarbi: About 1,000,000.

Q: Is there an increasing interest in Islam in this country?

Dr. Shawarbi: Yes, indeed. I can cite innumerable cases of inquiry from people who want to know about Islam.

Q: Do you sponsor an organized missionary program here and abroad in behalf of Islam?

Dr. Shawarbi: We are not interested in converting people to Islam. It does not concern us. We merely want to disseminate information about Islam so that we should not be looked down upon as heathens or as enemies of the other world religions. We would like to correct the slanted and incorrect views about us entertained by too many people. But conversion does not interest us at all. Our religion commands us to inform the world about Islam; no more. Our current task is directed more towards the organization and confederation of existing Muslim groups and the improvement of religious standards and practices of the individual Muslim.

Q: What about the Ahmadiya?

Dr. Shawarbi: They represent a sect, whose approach is not approved by everyone. Now, their activity is not so much in a missionary nature as an attempt to spread the knowledge of Islam.

Q: What about the Sunni and Shi'i?

Dr. Shawarbi: These are not 'sects' in the Christian sense of the term. We pray together and

believe together. What separates us are minor
traditions political in nature dealing with the
matter of succession to the Prophetic office.

Q: Are there any new trends in the Islamic
attitude to conversion?

Dr. Shawarbi: Our traditional views remain un-
changed. They are based on the Koranic statement "Let there be no compulsion in religion."
We permit a Muslim man to marry a non-Muslim
woman [4] and encourage her to remain true to her
faith. We do not want her to embrace Islam
unless she is prepared to do so from an inner
conviction. . . . We feel that all religion is from
God, but that it matured through successive
stages from Adam to Mohammad until it reached
perfection in Islam.

Q: What would you say to a person who came
to you with the statement that he wishes to become a Muslim?

Dr. Shawarbi: First, I would ask, "Why would
you like to become a Muslim?" Then I would
like to establish the genuineness of his convictions and give him literature to read.

In conclusion, becoming a Muslim is a very simple
and informal step, that is, devoid of all ritual. All one
needs to do is declare the oneness of God and
that Mohammed is his prophet. It is a very private
matter between man and God. Intermarriage is permitted in the case of a Muslim male; however, the
children must be raised as Muslims. Finally, a Muslim
is one who professes Islam, and his Muslim affiliation
is accepted on his word.

4. This applies only to a Muslim man. Islamic law forbids a
Muslim woman to marry a non-Muslim. And in the former case,
all children resulting from the union must be raised as Muslims.

Indian and
Far Eastern Religions

The Golden Temple of Amritsar, India, is sacred to the Sikhs

Introduction—Indian and Far Eastern Religions

S IMPLICITY AND INFORMALITY ARE the hallmarks of Eastern religions. Even the word "religion" seems too formal and narrow a designation to the Eastern mind. "Philosophy" often seems to be a more suitable term.

The Eastern approach to conversion is also philosophical. Eastern religions have no concept of conversion as it is understood in the West. Instead of formal procedures, rites, and ceremonies, one simply accepts the truths of the system and orders his life in consonance with them. In most cases, converts fulfill no formalities for conversion to the faith or acceptance into membership.

Indian and Far Eastern religions are syncretistic since they incorporate other religions and tend to preserve the old, side by side with the new. They generally show broad tolerance for other religions and approve of dual affiliations.

All Indian religions agree that the physical world is of secondary or transitory significance; the chief motive of these religions is "escape." In Jainism escape is from matter, and in Hinduism and Buddhism escape is from misleading appearances. In their rejection of the present, Indian religions could be called pessimistic. But this is inaccurate because they do seek the eternal and the ultimate with confidence and hope. And wherever hope resides with confidence there is no room for pessimism. Actually, the desired goals are in existence—somewhere beyond the physical.

Philosophical Hinduism rests on the belief that man's greatest error lies in his *thinking;* not in his living. Jainism, which stresses *behavior,* espouses an ascetic way of life designed to avoid contamination by contact with matter; early Buddhism found fault in man's *feeling* and sought to correct this by controlling desires.

Far Eastern religions, rather than assigning an illusory value to Nature, cultivated the aesthetic appreciation of it. Nature, though not the ultimate reality, is of immediate significance to man since it consists of real forms and forces. In Nature, one discovers beauty and sublime order. This may appear to the Western mind to be more of a system of aesthetics than of religion. However, this is the Oriental mystique in which even religion assumes the garb of the practical and the concrete. Moreover, an unobtrusive pantheism underlies the Oriental attitude that links man and Nature in an organic unit.

The major Eastern religions are the religions of India, including Hinduism, Jainism, Buddhism, Sikhism, and the Ramakrishna movement, and the religions of the Far East, including Confucianism, Taoism, and Shinto.

Some of these religions are still limited to the East. Others have become popular in other parts of the world, including the United States. Buddhism has attracted worldwide attention in recent years as a result of developments in South Vietnam, Burma, and other parts of Asia. The Ramakrishna movement has been popularized in the United States through extensive lectures and abundant literature available at its information centers.

Zoroastrianism, though technically a Near Eastern religion by origin, is included in this group because the majority of its adherents are Indian by nationality. Zoroastrianism, a small sect of 140,000 members, at one time vied with Christianity and Islam for world domination.

Todai-ji Temple at Nara, Japan, contains a colossal image of Buddha Vairocana

Ta Lung Tung Temple, Taipei, Taiwan, during a celebration of Teachers' Day, the anniversary of the birth of Confucius

23
Confucianism

THE CHINESE PHILOSOPHERS CONFUCIUS and Lao-tze or Lao-tzu) were contemporaries of Buddha who founded two great religions that are still practiced in the Orient. Confucianism was undoubtedly the greatest force for over 2,000 years of Chinese culture.

Confucianism is called a religion by some and a philosophy by others. The Chinese call it *Ju Chaio*, or the "scholar's teachings," referring to the teachings of Confucius and later tradition.

In essence, Confucius was not a creative philosopher. He limited himself to the formulation of moral guides for society. He edited some important Chinese classics, including *The Book of Poetry*, *The Book of Changes*, *The Book of History*, and *The Book of Rites*. After his death his students compiled his sayings and conversations in the *Analects*.

Confucius put little emphasis on the idea of God. He did not consider himself a prophet, but rather one who hands down the best of Chinese culture and ancient religion. Yet he himself eventually became an object of veneration. Early in the twentieth century Confucianism declined in the number of its followers, but today it is still a thriving religion.

Confucius taught a very rational and humanistic

religion. Its main principles are that man's nature is good, that he has freedom of choice, and that virtue is its own reward. Confucius' version of the Golden Rule, similar to that of Hillel of the Talmud, is: "What you do not wish done to yourself, do not do to others." He urged the cultivation of "the princely man" as the cornerstone of the "good society." The steps leading to this ideal personality are knowledge of final objective, purification of the heart, and sincerity of purpose.

Many followers of the teachings of Confucius are also adherents of Buddhism or Taoism. Such tolerance is characteristic of Oriental religions.

Statue of Confucius by the Japanese sculptor Seibo Kitamura

24
Taoism

TAOISM, "THE WAY," SUPPOSEDLY was founded by Lao-tze in the sixth century B.C. Today, 50,000,000 people are Taoists; many of them are also Buddhists or Confucianists. Popular Taoism is largely the religion of the uneducated masses. It bears little resemblance to philosophical Taoism based on the sublime teachings of its founder who spoke in the Judaeo-Christian tradition of peace, love, and human ennoblement. Lao-tze advocated regular periods of silence and called for the repayment of evil by good. He spoke of immortality and the supremacy of the spiritual world.

The chief literature of this faith, known by the name of *Tao Teh Ching* ("Classic of the Way and Virtue"), sought to penetrate the mysteries of the universe, leaving the problems of government, ethics, and virtue for other oriental religious philosophies to ponder. This scripture is popularly ascribed to Lao-Tze, but is of uncertain date and authorship. It teaches that the Great Tao—the powerful, irresistible, latent power of universal evolution—is the matrix of gods, spirits, and men, manifesting itself in the flux and flow of all existence. Tao is "The Way" of the universe from chaos to perfection, teaching that passive submission to this inexorable power, a yielding to the absolute, is the highest virtue.

25
Sikhism and Jainism

T HE INDIAN RELIGIONS, SIKHISM and Jainism, had their origins in the Hindu religion. Sikhism, a union of different faiths, has a following of 6,250,-000 people. Sikh mean "disciple" or "follower." It was founded by Nanok, a Hindu influenced by Islam, near the end of the fifteenth century. He taught that there is one immortal God and creator, and that salvation is attained by obedience to God. He forebade idols and denounced asceticism. Nanok regarded himself as a *guru*, Hindustani for "teacher," and was followed by a succession of *gurus*. In the nineteenth century the tenth *guru* led a conquering army of Sikhs into the Punjab in northern India and Pakistan, which became an area of Sikh settlement.

Jainism, a reform movement within Hinduism, was founded in the time of Buddha by Vardhamana Mahavira, who emphasized asceticism. Like Buddha, Mahavira preached the doctrine of *Karma*, the power behind rebirth. Today, 2,000,000 people follow Jainism. Jainism, like most Eastern religions, does not stress the concept of God. It teaches austere self-discipline and renunciation of worldly things. Early Jainism also denounced the caste system. The religion's three main principles are right knowledge, right faith, and right conduct.

The Jainists' sacred Scriptures are the *Agamas,* which equate "the good life" with monastic isolation. Jainists are pacifists and preach nonviolence to living beings. Because of this philosophy, the Jainists are vegetarians, and today in India they are usually engaged in commerce and finance, rather than in farming. Though small in number, the Jainists maintain a world mission and publish literature in English.

Shinto shrine on the sacred island of Itsukushima, Japan, was originally built in the seventh century

26
Shinto

SHINTO, KNOWN AS "THE WAY of the Kami" (*kami* means "superior" in Japanese and refers to the gods) is the national religion of Japan. Of the two wings of Shinto, the first is the original religion with its nature festivals, multiplicity of sects, and emphasis on mythology. The second is state Shinto, which is taught in the schools as a national system of ethics. It calls for religious patriotism and devotion to the emperor.

Shinto, with a membership of 60,000,000, is a religion of great tolerance, permitting concurrent membership in other religions. Many Shintoists are also Buddhists.

National defeat in World War II and the Emperor's abdication of the claim of divine descent caused the temporary decline of Shinto. The balm of time, however, had its effect, and the slump was followed by a reawakening and return. Today, interest in Shinto is again at a high level. Great emphasis is now placed on ethics.

Toshogu Shrine at Nikko, Japan, is one of Japan's many Shinto shrines

27
Buddhism

B UDDHISM, THE WORLD'S FOURTH-largest religion, has
150,000,000 followers. It was founded by the
Indian prince, Siddhartha Gautama, about 600
years before the advent of Christianity. Gautama, after
seeing the four facts of life for the first time (a sick
man, an old man, a dead man, and a holy man), fled
to the forest to seek enlightenment. He tried, and then
abandoned, the ways of the ascetic and the hermit.
After meditating under a sacred Bodhi tree for forty-
nine days he achieved *nirvana*, or enlightenment. Gautama became known as Buddha, the "Enlightened
One."

From then on, he wandered with his disciples
throughout India until his death at the age of eighty.
His final advice was "work out your salvation with
diligence." He did not emphasize God or divine
judgment.

Gautama's teachings may be summed up in the
Four Noble Truths:

1. Man suffers all his life, and continues to suffer
from one life to the next.
2. Craving for pleasure, possessions, and freedom
from pain are the source of man's suffering.
3. The practice of nonattachment to everything,

The Gold Buddha in Bangkok, Thailand, is said to be five
and a half tons of solid gold

including oneself, is the cure for craving.

4. Nonattachment is achieved by means of the "noble eightfold path": right views, right intentions, right speech, right conduct, right livelihood, right effort, right thought, and right meditation.

The *sangha* is the enormous group of monks and nuns who practice celibacy, vegetarianism, nonviolence, and poverty. Their only possessions, permitted by tradition, are robes, a begging bowl for food, prayer beads, a razor for shaving the head every two weeks, and a needle and a filter to remove bugs from drinking water (because of their attitude of nonviolence toward all beings).

The two great traditions in Buddhism are the *Hinayana,* or Lesser Vehicle, and the *Mahayana,* or Greater Vehicle. The former is more austere and limits *nirvana* to monks and nuns; the latter offers hope of *nirvana* to all. *Mahayana* also stresses compassionate concern for humanity; the *bodhisattva,* or the enlightened one capable of self-sacrifice for others, is its highest ideal.

Zen Buddhism, which will be examined later, is a subdivision of *Mahayana.* The Japanese imported it from China, as did many groups in Europe and the United States. Zen stresses prolonged meditation in combination with shock to achieve *satori,* or "enlightenment." Some specialists of religion consider Zen to be the purest type of spirituality in the Far East.

Representative of the literature distributed by American Buddhists is *Brief Introduction to Buddhism* by Takashi Tsuji, Director of the Bureau of Buddhist Education, Buddhist Churches of America Headquarters. [1]

1. Takashi Tsuji, *Brief Introduction to Buddhism.* National Young Buddhist Association, 1710 Octavia Street, San Francisco, California. Reprinted with permission.

Stone carving of Buddha in one of the caves at Ajanta, India, dating from the sixth century

Founder of Buddhism

Amid the vernal splendour of Lumbini Garden, Gautama, the Buddha, was born in 566 B.C., a son of a wealthy and powerful king, Suddhodana, the ruler of the Shakya clan, at Kapilavastu in the modern state of Nepal.

The Buddha was given the name of Siddhartha, which means "He who has attained his aim."

Rejoicing over the birth of the heir, the king made elaborate arrangements to see that nothing was lacking in the life of the prince. For his mental and physical education, sages, soldiers and athletes from all parts of the country were summoned to the castle. Whether it was knowledge requiring the highest of intellect or games taxing the utmost of his physical prowess, the young prince showed remarkable skill of mastery. At nineteen he was married to the fairest maiden of the land, Princess Yashodara who bore him a son, Rahula. The royal couple lived amidst inconceivable luxury.

In spite of this unsurpassed beauty and comfort that surrounded the prince at all times, he felt a deep despair. He wanted to go out to seek the Light of Truth. The faint stirring in his heart steadily grew stronger until at last he could not restrain himself from cutting the fetters that bound him to this existence. Leaving his sleeping son and wife, he went forth into the still Indian night, with great resolve to find salvation for himself and his fellow men. He was then twenty-nine years of age.

For six years he mingled with ascetics and hermits, practicing the difficult system of salvation they taught, subjecting his body to the severest of disciplines, but he realized that the extremes of asceticism like luxury led one no-where. The truest path to enlightenment, he found, lay in patient and systematic examination of all aspects of life, and discovering the solution to its sufferings.

As he quietly meditated under the Bodhi Tree, there developed in him a deep spiritual insight into the nature of existence. When the day ended and the first stars showed their lights in the sky above, Gautama attained Enlightenment, the highest wisdom man has yet reached. One by one, the heavy doubts of life and death, of sorrow, its cause and cure vanished—the great mystery had finally been solved. He became Buddha, the Fully Enlightened One.

He spent the remaining forty-five years of his life in a labor of love and compassion, spreading the Teachings the whole breadth and length of the country.

He passed away at the age of eighty, leaving the following message to his sorrowing disciples: "The Dharma which I have given you shall be your Teacher, when I am gone."

So great has been the influence of this Dharma, that today it is estimated that one-third of humanity pays homage to his Noble Teachings.

The Three Pitakas

The Three Pitakas or literally the Three Baskets are a collection of the sacred books of the Buddhists in which the Teachings of the Master have been preserved. The Pitakas are composed of three main divisions known as Sutra Pitaka, Vinaya Pitaka, and the Abhidharma Pitaka.

The Sutra Pitaka contains the discourses, addresses and sermons of the Buddha, dealing with the method of salvation for the laity.

The Vinaya Pitaka contains the moral standards to be observed by the priests, and various rules and conduct of the order.

The Abhidharma Pitaka contains the metaphysics and the philosophy of Buddhism.

The Tripitaka is a voluminous collection of Chinese texts, numbering 13,520 "scrolls" in 100 bound volumes of 1000 pages each. Included in this collection are three volumes, containing general catalogues of the Tripitaka.

These Pitakas were handed down to this day in various editions, the oldest being the Pali and Sanskrit editions. Other editions are the Chinese and Japanese editions. Some parts have been translated into English and other European languages.

The Doctrine

1. *Characteristics of the Buddha's Teachings*

When one studies the Teaching of the Buddha, he is surprised to find its closeness to the modern scientific spirit. Across the span of over two millenniums and a half, this scientific method links the sage of India to the foremost scientists of our day.

The Buddha constantly taught his disciples to accept nothing on hearsay, tradition or dogma. No statement was to be accepted because it had authority. Not even his own words were to be taken on trust. He urged his followers to investigate all principles he preached, and to test them out by every test of reason and by its application to ordinary life.

Truly, there is faith in Buddhism but it is not a belief in divine revelation. The Sanskrit word *Shraddha* means faith, but it "is based on an unfolding experience that is verifiable by

Temple at Buddh Gaya, India, where Buddha received
enlightenment, or Nirvana

both the self and others, and carries a sense of process and continuance. The Buddhist Faith is a cosmic process that goes on unfolding into aspiration, into knowledge, into realization of wisdom, into the self-giving of Bodhisattvas,[2] into Buddhahood."

2. *Buddhism and the Theory of God*

Buddhism does not deny the existence of God, but it interprets this complex concept in its own way. If by God we mean an ultimate reality, Buddhism affirms this. The Buddhist God is impersonal. We say that it is so great that it is beyond the comprehension of man. "We can neither define, describe nor usefully discuss the nature of that which is necessarily beyond the comprehension of our finite consciousness." Hence, it is sometimes called the Namelessness.

3. *The Four Noble Truths*

"This, O Bhikkhus, is the Noble Truth of Suffering: decay is suffering; illness is suffering; death is suffering. Presence of objects we hate is suffering; separation from objects we love is suffering; not to obtain what we desire is suffering."

This, O Bhikkhus, is the Noble Truth of the Cause of Suffering; Thirst that leads to Rebirth, accompanied by pleasure and lust, finding its delight here and there . . . thirst for pleasure, thirst for existence, thirst for prosperity.

This, O Bhikkhus, is the Noble Truth of the Cessation of Suffering; it is the complete cessation of this thirst—a cessation which consists in the absence of every passion—with the abandoning of this thirst, with the doing away with it,

2. Bodhisattvas are folowers of the Buddha who work for the salvation of mankind.

with the deliverance from it, with the destruction
of desire.

This, O Bhikkhus, is the Noble Truth of the
Path which leads to the cessation of suffering:
that holy Eightfold Path, that is to say, Right
Views, Right Aspirations, Right Speech, Right
Conduct, Right Livelihood, Right Effort, Right
Mindfulness, Right Meditation."

This was the first sermon that was preached
by the Buddha. A quick glance at this sermon
might lead one to conclude that the Buddha
was pessimistic in his view of life. However, if
one reads the above quotation carefully, he will
understand that the Buddha recognized the
values of life. "In fact the whole sting of tran-
siency is to be found in the very fact that these
passing things are good. That is why it is sad to
lose them." But he warns that the joys and
happiness are not final values for they are
transitory.

The supreme goal set before all Buddhists
is the escape from suffering, ignorance and illu-
sion and the attainment of the Truth and Enlightenment. Only in the pursuit of this lofty
ideal will man find the true meaning of Happiness and Joy.

"He who loves the Law lives happily, with
his mind at ease."

4. *The Eightfold Noble Path*

This is the fourth of the Noble Truths,
which leads to the cessation of suffering. The
Eightfold Path consists of:

Right Views . . . right understanding of the Bud-
    dha's Dharma (Law).

Right Speech . . . speaking of kind words.

Right Aspirations . . . high and noble aims.

Right Conduct . . . right behavior.

Right Livelihood . . . honest professional life.
Right Effort . . . perseverance in goodness.
Right Mindfulness . . . right use of the intellect.
Right Meditation . . . meditation on the Buddha
and the Dharma.

5. *The Nature of Existence:*

Anitya—Impermanence.
Duhkha—Suffering.
Anatman—Egolessness.

a. Anitya—This is a Sanskrit word meaning that nothing in this world is permanent. Everything that we see around us seems the same but is actually in a state of constant flux. The flowers that bloom today will wither tomorrow. Impermanence is a law of the universe which nothing can escape, from the mightiest of astronomical systems to the microscopic forms of life.

b. Duhkha—This word is rendered into English as suffering; sorrow, dissatisfaction. The first Noble Truth can be summed up in this one word. The cause of Duhkha as can be seen in the Second Noble Truth is Desire or the Clinging to pleasure, existence and prosperity. By the complete eradication of desire by man's own conscious efforts the Buddha taught that man can attain the realm of absolute Peace and Bliss, Nirvana. The Buddha taught the existence of suffering but He also taught the way of deliverance from suffering. He not only diagnosed the sickness but he prescribed a practical cure—the faithful following of the Eightfold Path. "This above all do I teach," He said, "Suffering and the Deliverance from Suffering."

c. Anatman—This is the doctrine that there is no permanent entity in man which separates

Buddhist monastery in the foothills of the Himalayas

him from others, the ego, self or soul. The self
or the "I" is made up of a number of attachment groups such as body, sensation, perception, will and consciousness. "Just as the word
'house' is but a mode of expression for wood
and other constituents of a house, surrounding
space in a certain relation, but in the absolute
sense there is no house . . . in exactly the
same way the word 'living entity' and 'Ego'
are but modes of expression for the five
attachment groups." The Buddha did not
teach the existence of an individual soul which
exists apart from the body and differentiates
each one from his neighbor. The "soul" in
Buddhism is not an individual, human, animate existence, but is the "spark" of the "Universal Flame" which unifies all animate and
inanimate objects. This is the philosophic basis
of the Buddhist doctrine of the Oneness of
Life.

6. *Karma:*

Karma is a Sanskrit word, taken from the
root "kri," to do or to make, meaning action.
On a physical plane karma acts as the law of
cause and effect and on a moral plane, it is
the "law of the conservation of moral energy."
It follows from this law, therefore, that the
seeds of good or evil planted by man must
necessarily be reaped by him.
"All that we are is the result of what we
have thought; it is founded on our thoughts
and made up of our thoughts. If a man
speaks or acts with a good thought, happiness
follows him like a shadow that never leaves
him."
Man is the sole creator and the builder of his
destiny. He is completely free to mold his

future from actions based on sound judgment.

7. *Nirvana*

Nirvana is the summum bonum or the Highest Good for all Buddhists. It is the supreme goal for those who tread the path to Buddahood.

Nirvana literally translated means the extinction of desire. Desire is the sinful grasping state of mind and heart which makes man desire this illusory world. When he extinguishes this fire of desire, he attains the peace of Nirvana.

Through ignorance of the Truth, he allows himself to cling to his passing, individual separate self as final, without realizing that he is a part of a greater whole. When the last fires of desire are put out, man loses his small self and is immersed into the Universal Self, just as "the dewdrop slips into the shining sea."

Nirvana is not a geographical location. It is the state of highest Consciousness.

8. *Bodhisattva*

The ideal man is the Bodhisattva—an aspirant to Buddhahood, who is ever willing to give up even his own salvation for the salvation of his fellow men. His service to his community is motivated by a deep faith in the Three Treasures—Buddha, Dharma, Sangha. The supreme purpose of his life is not the pursuit of wealth and pleasure but the increase of his own virtue and wisdom as well as that of his fellow men.

He, therefore, devotes himself to the practice of the Six Perfections—Giving, Morality, Endurance, Effort, Meditation, Wisdom.

28
Buddhist Churches of America

BUDDHIST CHURCHES OF AMERICA is an incorporated religious organization of Japanese Buddhists of Jodo Shin-shu faith in the United States.[1] Over fifty churches and numerous branches are spread throughout the country. About seventy ministers serve the spiritual needs of 60,000 Buddhists (of Shin-shu faith).

The Jodo Shin-shu movement began in San Francisco with the arrival in 1898 of two priests from the temple called the Hompa Hongwanji in Kyoto. They came to make preliminary surveys and to look into the possibility of establishing Buddhist congregations. As a result, the following year, Rev. Shuei Sonoda and Rev. Kakuryo Nishijima, both learned scholars, came to San Francisco as the first official ministers.

The founder of Jodo Shin-shu was Shinran Shonin who was born near Kyoto on May 21, 1174. He spent over fifty years of his life teaching an enlightened way of life through the "Wisdom and Compassion of Amida Buddha." Shinran Shonin was a humble man who claimed no disciples of his own. So influential, however, were his teachings that his followers organized the Hompa Hongwanji, the mother temple of thou-

1. The administrative offices of the national headquarters are at 1710 Octavia Street, San Francisco, California.

Seated Buddha in the Lahore Museum, Pakistan

sands of Jodo Shin-shu temples throughout Japan.

The Buddhist Churches of America is an autonomous organization, governed by Americans of Buddhist faith, that has spiritual ties with the Hongwanji in Japan. The Buddhist Churches of America is governed by its spiritual head and the members of the Board of Directors. The Buddhist Churches of America is divided into eight districts in the United States and Canada. Each district is represented by a minister, who is elected by the ministerial body in that district, and three lay members who are elected by the lay body.

Monthly Buddhist Churches of America dues assessed to each church provide the bulk of the operating expenses. To augment this income, an annual sustaining membership is solicited from volunteer subscribers. In addition, a Special Projects Fund drive is conducted each year to raise funds to promote the following programs: the training of future ministers with a scholarship program; the training of Sunday School teachers; the lay Buddhist training program; research and publications; Boy Scouts; and a retirement fund for the ministers. The Buddhist Churches of America Foundation, supported by individual and group contributions, was established many years ago to ensure the economic foundation of the Buddhist movement.

Lectures, preministerial training courses, lay leader training, research in music, and seminars are conducted at Buddhist Churches of America centers in the United States at the Buddhist Churches of America Study Center in Berkeley, California and the American Buddhist Academy in New York City.[2] Plans are under way

2. A calendar of events may be obtained by writing to the BCA Study Center, 2121 Channing Way, Berkeley, California, or the American Buddhist Academy, 331 Riverside Drive, New York, New York.

to develop these centers into accredited universities to train ministers and to offer university courses in Buddhism. At present, a candidate for the Buddhist ministry must take his courses at Ryukoku University in Kyoto or at other recognized universities.

The Sunday School Department guides and co-ordinates the activities of all Sunday schools in the Buddhist Churches of America. It operates the non-profit Material Department, which sells study guides, lessons, children's books, and other literature.[3]

The Bureau of Buddhist Education also conducts courses for adults, including seminars and lay Buddhist training courses. It operates the nonprofit Sales Department and distributes books on Buddhism and leadership training, and also sells Buddhist religious articles.[4]

The two official monthly publications are *Horin,* in Japanese, and the *American Buddhist,* in English.[5]

The Buddhist Churches of America sponsors a seminar on Buddhism at the Asilomar Conference Grounds in Pacific Grove, California, every summer. Extension seminars are also offered in various cities throughout the nation. Details may be obtained by writing to the Bureau of Buddhist Education in San Francisco.

---

3. Information regarding materials may be obtained by writing to the Sunday School Department at 1710 Octavia Street, San Francisco, California.

4. Catalogues may be obtained by writing to the Bureau at 1710 Octavia Street, San Francisco, California.

5. Published at 1710 Octavia Street, San Francisco, California. The subscription to the *American Buddhist* is $1.50 for twelve issues.

A Buddhist Creed

Buddhism teaches that truth and virtue must be realized through spiritual evolution, not by merely assenting to creeds or believing in doctrines. The following ideas, which are widely held among Buddhists, are offered solely as helpful signposts set up by those who have already traveled the Way. Buddhists believe that

1. Universes originate, develop, change, and perish through the operation of natural and inherent causes and that this series of cycles has neither beginning nor end.

2. Man is not a mixture of physical form and everlasting spiritual substance, but a complex of processes that persists as long as it functions, just as a fire lives only while its fuel lasts.

3. At death the vital forces cohere and, after an interval, precipitate again into a biological birth.

4. The unenlightened life is suffering, transitory, and empty, and they heartily desire to be free from it.

5. Sin in thought, speech, and action springs from wrong views and evil passions that obstruct compassion and insight.

6. Evil deeds are to be avoided and good deeds are to be done, not through fear of punishment or through desire for reward, but rather through understanding, compassion, and unselfish devotion to virtue.

7. The object of living is not the pursuit of wealth and pleasure, but the increase of virtue and wisdom.

Wat Arun, the Temple of the Dawn, one of the largest
Buddhist temples in Bangkok, Thailand

8. When the clouds of passion and ignorance are dispelled, the sun of insight will illuminate this world and will reveal that the world's true nature is Buddhahood.

9. Buddahood is perfect wisdom, perfect compassion, perfect power of accomplishing good, which is the underlying ground of all existing things, and the seed of enlightenment that lies within all living beings.

The Buddhist Way of Life

The natural, unreligious life is beset with sufferings—birth, old age, sickness and death, and all the complications and frustrations of daily existence. Buddhism gives insight into this life and teaches one not to flee from it, but to understand it. In the midst of suffering, the Buddhist is able to appreciate the real meaning of life. Through suffering he will rise to a higher life—the life of Nembutsu, or the life of faith. The properties of the life of Nembutsu are a high level of internal organization (meditation), a new vision and wider perspective of life (wisdom), and the establishment of a moral order (morality). The life of faith is a dynamic manifestation of inner gratitude to Amida's wisdom and compassion.

The principles of the Buddhist Way of Life are

1. A Buddhist affirms his faith in the Three Treasures of the Buddha, Dharma, and Sangha and then he joins the church.

2. A Buddhist devotes his time to self-study by reading the *sutras,* that is, Buddhist Scriptures, and Buddhist books.

3. A Buddhist constantly hears the teachings of

the Buddha by attending church regularly.

4. A Buddhist attends lectures and joins in discussions of the teachings with other members of the Church.

5. A Buddhist strives diligently to put into practice what he has learned by giving moral and financial support to his church and the Buddhist movement.

6. A Buddhist assists his minister and gives his time and effort to the propagation of the *dharma,* or highest truths, by availing himself of every opportunity to teach others.

7. A Buddhist deplores inequality, racial and religious prejudice, and injustice in society and strives to establish equality, understanding, and justice.

8. A Buddhist practices kindness to animals.

9. A Buddhist dedicates himself to the preservation of freedom and liberty and will sacrifice himself, if need be, for this noble cause.

10. A Buddhist supports the aims of the United Nations in the establishment of peace throughout the world.

A person who is determined to live the Buddhist Way of Life will follow the preceding principles to the best of his ability. As he follows the way, he will grow in a greater awareness of Amida's wisdom and compassion and will realize that the Buddhist Way of Life is a dynamic manifestation of his inner gratitude to Amida's Eternal Life and Light.

Conversion Procedure

Nelson Ying, Jr., a Buddhist preacher of New

York, summarized the process for "conversion" to Buddhism:

1. Our group could be divided into two separate classes. The first class consists of members who had taken a special oath—which I will describe later. The second class consists of members who come to the regular lectures to study Buddhism, to understand Buddhism, and to participate in Buddhist practices from an intellectual viewpoint. We have about twenty members in the first class and about twenty-five members in the second class.

2. To become a Buddhist, a person just has to believe that he is a Buddhist. Nothing else is necessary. But, to believe that he is a Buddhist, this person will have to live according to the teachings of Buddha. If the person lives thus, all that is necessary for him to do to join our religious body is to come and listen regularly to our lectures. This way he is considered a member.

   Once this person has sufficient understanding about Buddhism and starts to feel that he would like to be a Buddhist for the rest of his life, he can go to our chief priest and take an oath.

   The oath—roughly translated—is:

   I give myself to the Universal Spirit, Buddha. I wish, hope and will work in order that all living creatures in the universe will understand the great truth and will realize the feeling and the want to help others in their turn.

   I give myself to the Way and the Method. I wish, hope and will work in

Zenkoji Temple at Nagano is one of Japan's most famous Buddhist temples

order that all living creatures in the universe will study deeply into the sutras (Buddhist Bibles) so that their wisdom will be deeper than the deepest ocean. I give myself to those who are pure on earth—the priests. I wish, hope and will work in order that all living creatures in the universe will be able to assist or to rule-guard all the others in the universe so that nothing may stop their united seeking of truth.

3. Buddhism as religion does not go out and actively solicit membership. The theory behind the Buddhism conversion is that "he who realizes that the world is full of suffering and would like to find a definite method to end this suffering, is the person who is ready to be converted into Buddhism.

Buddhism is based upon the four Noble Truths which Buddha found after many years of search and meditation. They are as follows:

There is suffering in this world.

There is a definite cause for the suffering.

The suffering in the world could be ended.

There is a definite way to the ending of suffering.

Since Buddhism is based on the Four Noble Truths, therefore our objective is the discovery of the "Definite way to the ending of suffering." Buddhism tries to end the suffering on earth, thereby establishing a Heaven on Earth. (Buddhism is the only religion which said that heaven could be reached by the living.) Buddhism also tries to end the suffering forever; thereby we say that Heaven, where there are emotions, possessions, and the I-ego concept is not perfect, because the I-ego concept generates emotions, and when there are emotions, suffering is possible. (Buddhism is the only religion which said that Heaven is not the ultimate goal.)

Once a person finds Heaven on Earth and Ultimate Truth in Heaven, then that person becomes a Buddha. Such is the final goal of Buddhism.

On the subject of conversion to Buddhism, an informant from the United Nations Mission of the Republic of China said:

In Buddhism, we must draw a distinction between common believers and those who convert themselves into monks and nuns. There are no strict rules or regulations concerning the former. One can claim to be a Buddhist by reading a certain Buddhist script, by setting up a shrine of any of the Buddhas at home, or by making certain offerings at times, etc. There is even no particular temple to join. The Buddhist temple in China is open to everyone who wishes to go in and worship, regardless of whether or not he is a Buddhist. In other words, Buddhist believers do not go through the more rigid requirements as set forth by Christian churches such as the process of baptism, confirmation, and holy communion . . . Those who renounce the world and join the temple to become a monk or a nun have to be accepted first by the temple. Then they will have to go through the ceremony of "penitence" by having their hair shaved off, their scalps burned by incense, etc.

Ruth F. Sasaki, vice-president of the First Zen

Institute of America,[6] discusses Zen Buddhism:

Since Japan is a Buddhist country, no formal steps are necessary to become a member of that sect. In fact, there is no such thing as membership in the sense that it is used in religious groups in the West.

In Japan, since the beginning of the seventeenth century, almost all families have been connected with a temple belonging to some Buddhist sect. This means that they are expected to contribute to some extent at least to the support of this temple. In most cases, the family dead through the centuries have been buried in the cemetery of the temple. Today it is usual for at least part of the ashes of members of the family dying at a distance from the temple to be brought back for interment in the family plot. At that time the priest of the temple conducts the funeral rites. As far as belief is concerned, however, the members of the family may or may not believe in the tenets of the sect with which the temple is affiliated. A person who wishes to embrace the doctrines of the Zen sect has only to have the desire in his heart to follow in his daily life the Buddhist practices as they are set forth in the teachings of the Zen sect, and, through the practice of the Zen form of meditation known as *zazen,* to investigate and penetrate into his own inner nature. No formal ceremony is demanded, though such a person should recite to himself the Four Vows, or, if he prefers, may do so in the presence of a Zen priest. He usually affiliates himself thereafter with one of the groups of laymen who practice *zazen,* and goes from time to time to hear the sermons of one or more Zen teachers or *roshi.*

6. 113 East 30 Street, New York, New York, 10016.

Sokei-an Sasaki, the founder of the First Zen Institute of America, felt that it was advantageous for westerners to go through a simple ceremony when they embraced Zen Buddhism. It was his custom to require that a person come to hear his lectures and practice *zazen* in a group for several months. If after that he still wished to acknowledge the way of Zen as his way of belief and life, such a person took the Four Vows at a public meeting of the Institute before the officiating priest or *roshi*. This simple ceremony is held from time to time at the Institute.

For your interest, the Four Vows are as follows:

Sentient beings are numberless;
I take a vow to save them all.
Delusive passions are inexhaustible;
I take a vow to destroy them all.
The gates of Dharma are manifold;
I take a vow to enter them all.
The Buddha-way is supreme;
I take a vow to complete it.

Recent reports from Japan tell of the emergence of a new fast-growing Buddhist sect "Soka Gakkai" which is engaged in an intensive missionary program. It claims 100,000 convert families every month.

29
Hinduism

H INDUISM IS THE RELIGION of 340,000,000 people throughout the world. It uses the language of Sanskrit, which has no word for "religion." Yet, more than sixty Hindu sects worship a multiplicity of deities. Unlike most other religions, Hinduism cannot trace its origins to any one individual who could be called its founder. It is an evolutionary outgrowth of ancient Indian civilizations and archaic religions.

Hinduism has the world's oldest religious scriptures, the *Rig-Veda,* an extensive collection of hymns to the gods. These scriptures were followed by the *Upanishads,* writings which are on a more advanced spiritual plane and speak of a creative Universal Spirit, and are the basis of modern Hinduism.

Hinduism, in the course of time, cultivated many prophets and teachers. Many of them were regarded later as incarnations of divinity and became objects of veneration.

A major feature of Hinduism is Brahmanism, a religion with a triune deity (a trinity) consisting of Brahma, the source of life; Vishnu, the preserver; and Siva, the destroyer. The principal beliefs in Brahmanism are as follows:

1. *Kharma,* understood in terms of action or

works, currently interpreted as service to others
2. Transmigration of souls
3. The ascetic life stressed
4. The caste system.

Hindus are also known for their extreme reverence
for life—to the extent of not harming a fly or a beast
and not consuming a fertilized egg.

Yoga represents a discipline within the Hindu faith
that seeks illumination by means of uniting man's
spirit with the supreme creative spirit. This is done
through the complete control of bodily functions by
means of rigid breathing and posture exercises.

Vishnu has appeared in various forms to Hindu
worshippers. In the *Bhagavad-Gita,* one of the most
popular of Hindu scriptures, Krishna is the incarnation
of Vishnu, the preserver. In this manifestation the orthodox Hindu concept of salvation by works or knowledge gives way to the view more familiar to the
Western mind, that is, salvation by faith.

The caste system, a cornerstone of Hinduism, has
been the target of modern reform movements, including that of the late Mohandas K. Gandhi. Today, the
caste system is in violation of state law. Recently, an
attempt to reinterpret and reform the idea of the caste
system from within has gained ascendancy in Hindu
circles.

There is no organized Hindu priesthood, church,
or hierarchy. In addition to the many priests, there is
a large body of *sannyasins,* or "monks," many of whom
wander through the land as beggars.

Some of the many reform movements of Hinduism's long history have resulted in completely new
religions. Reform movements gave rise to Buddhism,
Jainism, and Sikhism. The Ramakrishna movement,

Rukshmani Hindu Temple at Kathiawar, India, was the temple of Lord Krishna's wife

which has a missionary attitude, has adherents all over the world. Ramakrishna Paramahamsa founded the movement in the last decade of the nineteenth century on the principle that all religions have a basic common heritage and a unity of ultimate goals. His principles were developed by a follower called Vivekananda. The Ramakrishna movement, called Vedanta Society in America, stresses a synthesis of Eastern mysticism and Western social action. There are 1,000 Vedanta Societies in the United States. Its social gospel has made this group active in public health, education, and other phases of public service.[1]

The Ramakrishna-Vivekananda Center of New York was founded in 1933 and was incorporated in the same year as a religious society under the laws of the State of New York. It is one of the many centers scattered throughout the United States, South America, and Asia that are affiliated with the Ramakrishna Order, an important monastic and philanthropic organization of India. Swami Nikhilananda, the leader of the New York center, is a monk of this Order.

The teachings of the Ramakrishna-Vivekananda Center are based on the ancient system of Vedanta philosophy, which has been made dynamic in modern times by Sri Ramakrishna and his disciple Swami Vivekananda.[2] Vedanta reveals the underlying harmony of all religions, philosophies, arts, and sciences, which are described as different approaches to one and the same reality. Its message is universal, rational, and nonsectarian. It proclaims the potential divinity of man, which is to be manifested through appropriate spiritual disciplines.

1. From a leaflet distributed by the Ramakrishna-Vivekananda Center of New York.
2. Romain Rolland has written of Swami Vivekananda in his *Prophets of the New India* (trans. Eugene Lohrke; New York: Boni, Inc., 1930).

The Center seeks to stimulate the growth of each man's innate spiritual powers. It lays down no inflexible rules of conduct. The disciplines it teaches are suited to individual needs and temperaments. It is not a religion of the occult, the mysterious, or the sensational. Its purpose is to dignify life by raising its meaning above the material and intellectual level.

The Center has no endowments. Neither the *swamis* (Hindu religious leaders) nor the officers receive a salary or other compensation. The work is entirely supported through the voluntary offerings of members, students, and friends.

Those who are in sympathy with the teachings of the Center are welcome to become members, regardless of their creed or religious affiliation. Application should be made to the Center's secretary, who will be glad to furnish additional information.

Translations of the Hindu scriptures, books on Vedanta and kindred subjects, the authorized life of Sri Ramakrishna, and the complete works of Swami Vivekananda may be purchased at the Center or ordered by mail. The Center's library is well stocked with books on Indian thought and culture, and also contains a large collection by Western authors. Everyone is welcome to read these books in the reading room, which is open an hour before each service. The privilege to withdraw books is extended only to members.

Services, with sermons on vital and practical religious and philosophical subjects, are conducted on Sundays at 11 A.M. On Tuesdays and Fridays at 8:30 P.M., classes are conducted for the study and interpretation of the Hindu scriptures, such as the *Upanishads,* the *Bhagavad-Gita,* and the "Aphorisms of Yoga," usually ascribed to the ancient Indian author, Patanjali. Those who attend the Friday class usually plan to

Gateway to a Hindu temple in India's Bengal Province

become members of the Center.

Students who want further explanation of religious or philosophical problems raised by the lectures or who desire assistance in their spiritual practice may arrange interviews with the *swamis*. The *swamis* do not ask remuneration, but they do expect that interviews be sought only by those whose interest is genuine.[3]

Conversion Procedure

Swami Nikhilananda[4] describes the Hindu attitude on the conversion of non-Hindus:

> . . . As a rule Hinduism is not a proselytizing religion. But about two thousand years ago many of the foreigners who came to India were converted. Since then orthodox Hinduism does not make converts. However, I know there are in India one or two small organizations within the Hindu fold who make converts.
>
> Our Center here in New York is a branch of the Ramakrishna Mission of India. We are orthodox Hindus. I do not convert people, but I instruct the members of our Center, both Christian and Jewish, in such spiritual disciplines as meditation and prayer. I do this without asking them to give up their religious traditions. We believe in the harmony of religions and accept all faiths as valid paths to the realization of truth or God. We also believe that a religion can be benefited by incorporating in its disciplines something of another.

3. Vedanta Centers are also located in Providence, Rhode Island; Boston, Massachusetts; Philadelphia, Pennsylvania; Chicago, Illinois; St. Louis, Missouri; Hollywood, San Francisco and Berkeley, California; Portland, Oregon; and Seattle, Washington.

4. Of the Ramakrishna-Vivekananda Center, 17 East 94 Street, New York, New York.

Another *swami* points out that within Hinduism many different procedures for the conversion of non-Hindus are practiced.

It is not a small demand you have been pleased to make on us, for to be in a position to properly and fully answer your enquiries, one will have to travel in various parts of India and study the whole issue under proper guidance, and that for a considerable time. As you would know, in India quite a few religions are professed and practised and they have their different methods of conversion. In Hinduism itself there are differing and different views and practices about conversion, though by and large Hinduism is not a proselytizing religion.

You will therefore kindly see how difficult it is for us to be of any real help to you except pointing out the complexities of your undertaking.

The Golden Lotus tank of Meenakshi Hindu Temple, Madura, India

30
Yoga

Y OGA, WHICH IN SANSKRIT means "union," is a mystical system within Hinduism. Its primary goal is the liberation of the individual from the illusory world of sense perception. This effort might take several lifetimes before it bears fruit. The ultimate goal of the pantheistic schools of Yoga is union with the universal soul, and the goal of the atheistic school is complete isolation from all other souls and absolute self-knowledge. Both wish to attain perfect "illumination." A rigorous system of physical, moral, and mental discipline is used to achieve this end.

Yoga has become very popular in many Western circles. Thousands hope to find relief from the distress of emotional and physical illness through the disciplined self-mastery it teaches.

The following is a statement by the Sivananda Yoga Vedanta Centre: [1]

WHAT IS YOGA?

Yoga is a Hindu science of bodily and mental control. It is one of the six classic philosophical systems of India. A disciple of this ancient teaching is called a Yogi. He is an adept

1. 5178 St. Lawrence Boulevard, Montreal, Canada.

who has attained spiritual illumination.

The traditional founder of Yoga is Patanjali, who is believed to have lived about the third century B.C., and whose "Yogasutra" is the oldest text in the literature. The name of this science is in the Sanskrit language and means union. Yoga aims at the union of the individual spirit with the Universal Spirit. In the West, this is sometimes spoken of as "cosmic consciousness." In Yoga it is known as "Samadhi." Samadhi is a state of profound meditation which cannot be described in words, but only experienced by the truly enlightened adept. The attainment of cosmic consciousness is the main object of Yoga, but it also has less exalted aims. It aims to free man from his own infirmities and wrong conduct.

The goal is accomplished in eight stages of which union with the Universal Soul is the culmination. The first two stages are concerned with self-control and self-culture. Yoga counsels the practice of moral virtues such as avoidance of injury to others, truthfulness, forgiveness, compassion, sincerity and so on. It also prescribes rules of inner control, such as contentment, charity, modesty and sacrifice. These are matters of conduct and character which are not unique to Yoga but to which other systems of physical and mental training and discipline also can lay claim.

What is unique to Yoga is the emphasis it places on postures (Asanas) combined with breath control for mental development. Though Yoga emphasizes the science of mental development, it has not neglected the basic science of health. The laws of health are the laws of nature on which the Yoga science is based. The following are needed for a healthy body: proper exercise through mobilization of various joints, relaxation, proper breathing, natural foods and lastly, control and discipline of the mind.

The postures, of which there are 84 main ones, are called Asanas. Among the most popular are Sirshasan or head-stand and Padmasan, the lotus pose. Others are mostly for the spine and other joints. Stiffness of the backbone brings symptoms of old age. This is due to the biological shortening of the ligaments and muscles. Many ailments can be removed by the practice of Yoga and regulation of diet.

Many persons who admire and practice Yoga do not have any religious interest in it, although some undoubtedly are interested in reaping some of its spiritual benefits such as peace of mind, relief from tension, etc. Whatever may be the aim of practising Yoga, everyone irrespective of his nationality and religion can practice Yoga as it never contradicts any form of religious belief.

THE SIVANANDA YOGA VEDANTA CENTRE HEADQUARTERS

The Sivananda Yoga Vedanta Centre propagates Yoga and Vedanta and the ethical and spiritual culture of India, promotes universal love, the unity of religions, the ideal of brotherhood and the spirit of service through regular classes on Yogic exercises, Yogic breathing, meditation and discourses under the guidance of the former Senior Professor of Hatha Yoga at the Yoga Vedanta Forest Academy founded by Swami Sivananda.

The Centre also aims to promote harmony between various religions and recognition of the Supreme Truth which underlies all the great religions of the world. The Centre gives regular classes on the Yoga physical culture, the oldest

Practice of Yoga includes special exercises

of all physical culture systems in the world. The classes are conducted for various groups, such as beginners, intermediate and advanced on diverse aspects of Hatha Yoga. There are meditation classes for serious students and Yoga exercise class for children. Regular Sunday prayer meetings and philosophical discussions are held which are open to all.

31
Zoroastrianism

Z OROASTRIANISM, ONCE A MIGHTY contender for worldwide spiritual supremacy, now has 1,000,-000 followers at most. The majority of them live in India. Its founder Zoroaster, or Zarathustra, was born, according to some scholars, in 660 B.C. in Persia near Afghanistan. He preached with an urgency born of his belief that the world was coming to an end.

Zoroaster's new religion, in an age when monotheism was becoming increasingly popular, taught an ethical dualism in which the individual plays a decisive role and carries a burden of responsibility to the universe on his shoulders. In Zoroaster's theology, the world has two antithetical forces that are in constant conflict—the power of good, represented by the Prince of Light called *Ahura Mazda* (or *Ormuzd*), and the power of evil, represented by the Prince of Darkness called *Ahriman* (but never completely spelled out in Zoroastrian scripture). It is man's duty to ally himself with the forces of good to fight evil. He is urged to cultivate a positive social attitude, work the land, take care of his family, and make the world a better place to live in.

With this concept of ethical dualism Zoroaster attempted to solve the perplexing riddle faced by monotheism: Why is there evil and suffering in the world?

The *Gathas* are poems containing the teachings of Zoroaster and the *Yasna* is the Zoroastrian prayer book. The *Zend Avesta* is the name of the body of Zoroastrian scripture. Some scholars maintain that Zoroastrianism shows many traces of Indian religious influence.

The *Dastur* or High Priest Khurshed S. Dabu of the H. B. Wadiaji Fire Temple in Bombay, India, explains the Zoroastrian's attitude on conversion:

> We the Parsis are descendants of those who voluntarily left Iran due to religious persecution by Arab invaders (Khalif Amar) who conquered the country about 1300 years ago. A few remained there. We (both groups) were in a hopeless minority. Both had to preserve *hereditary racial traits,* and so we have never admitted a total alien to our fold. A Parsi has *to be born* of a Parsi father. This is also the Legal Judicial decision in a contested claim for rights to participate in benefits of Parsi charities. The child of a Parsi father by alien mother duly admitted to Zoroastrianism can have such benefits. But neither in Iran nor in India is there any mode of conversion or proselytization. This is a measure *necessary for self preservation* of the race; and in Iran any attempt to receive an alien into our fold, would be causing fanatic murders by Mullas. In India most of our Trust funds have specified the beneficiaries as *Parsi Zoroastrians only.* Thus none can be a Parsi by merely professing Zoroastrianism.

Other Denominations, Beliefs, and Philosophies

Introduction—Other Denominations, Beliefs, and Philosophies

A BOOK OF THIS NATURE would be incomplete without a section on less well-known varieties of religious belief. The bypaths of religion are clustered with many small groups, including Shakers, Holy Rollers, the Church of the Living God and Pillar and Ground of Truth, the Ghost Dance Religion of the West Coast Indians, and the snake cults in remote mountain country.

The larger groups, however, which have earned for themselves a reputation by membership volume, uniqueness of message, and general significance as a factor in the religious economy of our country, are discussed in this section. These include the Unitarian Universalists, the Church of Latter-day Saints, or "Mormons," Jehovah's Witnesses, Christian Science, Religious Science, and the Ethical Culture Society.

The heterogeneous character of this collection of religious groups rules out the feasibility of a general introduction. The absence of any bond cementing them into some semblance of positive relationship compels the reader to rely solely on the brief prefatory remarks introducing each body.

32
Unitarian Universalist
Association

T HE UNITARIANS AND UNIVERSALISTS consolidated in
May, 1961, to become the Unitarian Universalist
Association. The merger was basically administrative rather than theological; the Unitarians are generally further from orthodox Christian views than are
the Universalists. Recent developments, however, may
bring about a closer unity in other areas in the future.
The Association has 165,000 members and 1,100
churches and fellowships.

Unitarian Universalism, a liberal church, is adverse to an intense program for winning converts. Yet,
this group does make itself known through notices in
magazines and the distribution of informational literature. Publicity is conducted by the Unitarian Laymen's
League. It has been reported that in a five-year period,
publicity resulted in 28,000 inquiries from interested
readers.

Unitarians usually avoid the term "conversion"
because of the certitude it implies. They do not claim
to have "all the answers," but rather to be committed
to an eternal search.

Conversion Procedure

The Unitarian Universalist Association has no formal system of conversion. It relies on the applicants to experience an inner conversion to the Unitarian way of thinking, free of external persuasion. Inner conversion is understood to be a gradual awakening "to new light and more meaningful truth," not a sudden emotional shock or experience. Unitarians believe in self-conversion.

In most Unitarian churches membership begins with the signing of the membership book. At a subsequent service the new members are officially received into the church in a simple service marked by readings and prayers.

The prerequisites and procedures of conversion all add up to an emphasis on simplicity, aversion to dogma, a striving for intellectual honesty, and the gradual spiritual growth of the individual toward the truths which are the bedrock of Unitarian Universalism.

Rev. Dale De Witt, executive secretary of the Unitarian Regional Headquarters in New York, emphasizes:

> We have no formal system of conversion. People come to our churches out of interest or through information about Unitarianism and either decide to become members of churches or not according to their wishes. Membership is entirely voluntary, and no aggressive effort is made to bring about conversion.

H. Talbot Pearson, executive director of the Laymen's League explains:

> Unitarians are averse from the idea of "conversion." We like to believe that our recruits

King's Chapel, Boston, Massachusetts, where trinitarian doctrines were removed from the liturgy in 1785

have converted themselves, have literally thought themselves into a theological position similar to ours—and have then discovered they are not unique and that fellowship and association awaits them in Unitarian Universalism.

We have, therefore, no procedures or techniques to report. As you know, we are fond of declaring that deeds are more than words and therefore the humanitarian work carried on by the Unitarian Service Committee on a completely non-sectarian basis is our best advertisement.

Turning to the local churches for information, this comment was obtained from Rev. Max F. Daskam, resident minister of the Unitarian Church of Germantown, in Philadelphia:

Conversion . . . is a word which is rarely used in this church, nor would I think it would be very meaningful in most Unitarian churches. Orthodox Christian churches, I believe, still use the term as a mark in time in which they accepted Jesus Christ as their God and Saviour. This is a language not familiar to our people unless they have at some time belonged to an Orthodox Christian Church.

Although we do not use the term, I am sure the experience itself is familiar to most of us. Growth would be more descriptive in our case. For most of us it is marked by no sudden revelation. It is a gradual awakening to new light and more meaningful truth. We make no effort by emotional shock or revival meetings to convert people to our faith. We are all searchers and we welcome those who would search with us.

The Community Church of New York is one of the most popular Unitarian churches in America. Rev.

Melvin C. de Workeen, one of its ministers, discusses the procedure for membership in the Community Church:

I

Membership in the Community Church is open to all those who share its purposes. Strictly speaking, there are no requirements or procedure for conversion to our religious persuasion. The matter of membership in the church is left entirely up to the individual. When a person decides to become a member of The Community Church, he then is encouraged to attend and participate in its many activities. Generally there is a lecture series for new members, which deals with the ideas, history, and the religious educational programs of the church. The Community Church of New York is a member of the Unitarian Universalist Association and participates in all of its programs and services.

II

Membership in the Community Church of New York is open to all who decide to sign the membership book. The statement in the membership book to which each person signing gives assent is:

> "We, the undersigned, accepting the stated Purpose of this church, do join ourselves together that we may help one another, may multiply the power of each through mutual fellowship, and may thereby promote most effectively the cause of truth, righteousness and love in the world."

This is the only thing anyone is asked to sign. There are no other steps to conversion. The new members are invited to an "at home" to meet with each other and the three ministers. There is a reception for new members twice during the year in December and in April. The new members meet the church leaders at the reception and hear about the various activities of the church. At the Sunday morning service following the reception the new members are welcomed into the membership by the congregation by the simple procedure of participating in a responsive reading.

During the year there are generally a series of three lectures by the ministers to acquaint the new members with the history, ideas, and the religious education program of the church. These orientation sessions are designed to inform and promote discussion. The new members are invited to participate; it does not have any effect on their status as members.

Beyond these practices there are no steps such as affirmation, confirmation, baptism (with or without flowers, water, etc.). We do have a simple Dedication service for children, which is a public recognition of the child, the parents' responsibility for the child, and the congregation's acceptance of the child as a member of the human family. Basically this is a naming service, or a service of recognition for a new member of the human race.

33
Church of Jesus Christ of
Latter-day Saints, or "Mormons"

BECAUSE THERE APPARENTLY STILL exists some misunderstanding about Mormon beliefs and practices, the author felt that a presentation best reflecting the actual beliefs and practices should come from a Mormon source. Accordingly, the following is reprinted from *About Mormonism*.[1]

Many persons have associated the Mormon Church almost exclusively with the practice of polygamy. The facts regarding this matter are as follows:

The Mormon Church is not a polygamous society. In the early days of the Church the doctrine of plural marriage was introduced through divine revelation. The practice of plural marriage has never been general in the Church, and at no time have more than 3 per cent of the families in the Church been polygamous. Plural marriage was considered by the Church to be a very sacred principle. Only those who were regarded as being worthy and exemplary

1. Stephen L. Richards, First Counselor in the First Presidency of the Church, *About Mormonism* (Salt Lake City, Utah: The Church of Jesus Christ of Latter-day Saints, 1959). Reprinted with permission.

in life and conduct and devotion to the Church were permitted to enter into it. It was surrounded by the Church with many limitations and safeguards which were calculated to invest it with lofty, idealistic attributes. Women who became plural wives were never subjected to any compulsion whatsoever—the arrangement was one of mutual understanding and consent of all parties concerned, including the Church itself. Many of the most prominent and able members of the Church and citizens of the communities in which the Church is established are the product of these family relationships.

The society of the Mormon Church is noted for its solidarity and homogeneity in thought and purpose. This has been brought about in large measure by adherence to certain controlling spiritual principles and ideals, by an almost universal deference and respect for Church leaders and their counsel, by uniformity and standardization of living practices and, to some extent at least, by the persecution and opposition which the people of the Church have encountered during much of their history. The unity of the people and responsiveness to their leadership have contributed to many of their achievements in colonization, in the perfection of their organization and in the promulgation of their faith throughout the world. . . .

Notwithstanding the many organizations and agencies maintained by the Church for the benefit of its members, the foundation of its society is the home. Parental obligations and authority are basic in Church philosophy and practice. Substantially every Church institution is regarded as an ally of the home and has for its ultimate objective the building and maintenance of finer and more effective home life. The place and importance of domestic relations in the sociology of

Temple Square in Salt Lake City, Utah, is the symbolic center of Mormonism

the Church will become clear when its doctrines are understood. . . .

. . . The Mormons believe in the Bible and accept the King James version as the standard translation. They have other volumes of scripture which they accredit with divine authenticity as they do the Bible, but these other scriptures do not, in any sense, contradict the Bible or detract from its authority and importance. The other volumes of scripture which they accept are: The Book of Mormon, which is an inspired translation of sacred plates, setting forth the history of prehistoric people who immigrated to and settled portions of the Americas, with an account of their religions, national and international experiences; the Doctrine and Covenants, which is a compilation of revelations on many subjects pertaining to the Church, divinely given to their prophet; and the Pearl of Great Price, containing the Book of Moses, the Book of Abraham and other inspired translations and writings of Joseph Smith. These four volumes— the Bible, the Book of Mormon, the Doctrine and Covenants, and the Pearl of Great Price—constitute what are called the standard works of the Church. These books amplify, but they do not contradict each other. In them are to be found authority and verification for substantially all of the theological and religious doctrines of the Church.

Some of the tenets of Mormon faith are not unlike those of other Christian churches. It believes in the Trinity, the Lordship and Atonement of Jesus Christ, resurrection from the dead and immortality of the soul. But the interpretation which it places on these and other commonly accepted doctrines and the contributions which it has made in new theological conceptions and principles have given it a very unique and distinctive place in the religious world. It asserts, however, that novel as some of its doctrines may appear to be, there is no principle or truth which it advocates which is not and has not always been part of the Gospel of the Lord Jesus Christ. . . .

The Church believes in faith, repentance, baptism by immersion, and the laying on of hands for the gift of the Holy Ghost. It believes that man must be called of God and ordained by those in authority to preach the Gospel and administer the ordinances thereof. It believes in the same organization and the same gifts of the Gospel as existed in the primitive Church of Christ. It believes in modern and continuing revelations from the Lord—that Zion will be built on the American continent and that Christ will reign personally upon the earth. It claims the privilege of worshipping Almighty God according to the dictates of conscience and allows honoring and sustaining the law. It believes in being subject to the civil authorities of all lands in which its members reside and in obeying, honoring and sustaining the law. It believes in pre-existence, mortal probation and eternal life hereafter with free agency or full freedom of choice in every man to select or determine the course of his life. It advocates no compulsion but only persuasion through kindness and love. It ascribes spirituality to all things, there having been a spiritual creation of the universe preceding the physical creation, with God as the Creator and Master Intelligence.

The human body is regarded as a tabernacle wherein is housed the spirit of man. There can be no pollution of the body by taking into it any unclean or unwholesome substance detrimental to health without injury to the spirit which inhabits it, so that contamination of the body has both religious and temporal significance. It is therefore against religious principles and practices to take into the body alcohol, tobacco, tea, coffee, and other stimulants, narcotics, and poisons which militate against organic efficiency. It is God's will to conserve health, intelligence, and spirituality. This doctrine is set forth in a revelation known as "The Word of Wisdom."

It is the belief of the Church that in the Fatherhood of God and the brotherhood of man it is the function of Christ's Church to endeavor to save the whole human family—that no one can be saved in ignorance of the Gospel plan and that the truth must be brought to all men before they can exercise intelligently the right of election. To this end the Church has devoted a very large portion of all its resources, energies, and power to the dissemination of its message. It takes the position that, through the spirit of the Lord which strives with all men, every person may know the truth when it is brought to him, if he will but receive it with open mind and heart and conform his life to its teachings.

Within these sacred temples, ordinances and ceremonies of an unusual character are performed for the living as well. By virtue of the Holy Priesthood, a man and woman may here be sealed to each other as husband and wife, not only for time but for all eternity. A marriage compact that shall endure forever is thus created, into which are born the children. The family is established as a sacred, religious institution, the perpetuation of which in righteousness and in the order of the Church constitutes the highest of blessings possible of attainment. Men cannot enter into such eternal relationships unless they hold the Priesthood of God and women must be faithful and worthy. The projection of such homes into eternity is no small part of the

Baptismal Room in the Mormon Temple at Ogden, Utah

Heaven which members of the Church envisage. This is called the principle of celestial marriage and is not to be confused with plural marriage.

It is a theological conception of the Church that God is the giver of all that men possess and that it is the duty of men to consecrate all that they have to the advancement of God's kingdom. In this consecration, it is not the practice of members of the Church to turn all property into the treasury of the Church, but it is their duty to contribute to the Church a tithe or one-tenth of all they earn in recognition of the Lord's goodness and to assist in the prosecution of His work. The remainder of their earnings and all their possessions they are expected wisely and reverently to devote to the maintenance of the home, the rearing and education of the children, and such other wise and useful purposes as will help in the establishment of our Father's Kingdom. Members of the Church are also expected to make contributions for the missionary service, for the care of the poor, for the construction and maintenance of places of worship and other Church purposes.

Conversion Procedure

The conversion procedure is very simple. After declaring his intention to join the Church, a candidate is required to engage in a series of logical discussions dealing with Mormon doctrines and practices. This is followed by a prebaptismal interview and baptism by immersion administered by a member of the priesthood. But the interest of the Church does not end at this point. Mark E. Peterson of the Council of the Twelve writes in *After Baptism What?* [2]

2. Mark E. Petersen, *After Baptism What?* (Unidentified, undated).

But after entering the Church, what are new members supposed to do? What are the next steps? Are they to become active participants in it or are they to remain passive in their worship of the Lord?

The Savior has given the answer. It is that each one shall labor in the kingdom with all his heart, might, mind and strength, and bring forth much fruit.

"I am the vine," said the Savior as he explained this principle. "Ye are the branches: He that abideth in me, and I in him, the same bringeth forth much fruit."

ALL WHO BECOME MEMBERS OF HIS TRUE CHURCH become part of that vine, actual branches, as the Lord explained. And all must produce "much fruit" to be acceptable to him.

The convert is urged to make definite postbaptism plans. He is urged to be active in the Church, whose program touches every righteous phase of one's life, including his personal habits, home, and relationship with people. This extends into business, local, and national activities.

The Mormon population is 1,700,000. They are distributed throughout the world in over 3,000 congregations. There are also several schismatic groups with doctrinal and historical differences, one of which, the Reorganized Church of Latter-day Saints of Independence, Missouri, has 160,000 members. The headquarters of the main body of Mormons is in Salt Lake City, Utah.

The Mormon religion is highly evangelistic; it has carried on a very vigorous missionary campaign for the past 130 years. Thousands of young Mormon missionaries over twenty years old carry the message of the "Restoration" to every corner of the globe. These missionaries, though ordained for their tour of duty, come from every walk of life. They go in pairs for periods of two years each, supported by stipends from their parents.

The Mormons have met with enormous success in Europe and in the South Pacific (the Fiji Islands, Samoa, and Toriga). In 1961 alone, the Church membership in England doubled to 40,000 and a more spectacular increase was predicted for the following year. In France, some 1,000 conversions were recorded. West Germany has also seen a remarkable increase recently in the number of conversions to Mormonism.

Giant vaults hewn out of solid granite near Salt Lake City, Utah, are used to store the Church's genealogical records

34
Christian Science Church

CHRISTIAN SCIENCE, WHICH IS essentially a synthesis of spiritual healing and a Hegelian[1] approach to the Bible, under the energetic leadership of its founder has become a very successful movement. Some 3,200 branches of the mother church in Boston are scattered all over the world. Membership statistics are not available due to the prohibition of census taking and reporting of statistics, according to *The Church Manual*. The Church publishes a variety of reading material as well as six daily, weekly, monthly, and quarterly periodicals, among them the highly esteemed *Christian Science Monitor*.

A brief historical extract describing the founding and the main tenets of the Christian Science Church, taken from official sources,[2] is given below:

> In the spring of 1879, a little band of earnest seekers after Truth went into deliberations to form a Church without creeds, to be called the *"Church of Christ, Scientist."* They were members of evangelical churches, and students of Mrs. Mary Baker Eddy in Christian

1. Christian Scientists believe that this view advanced by Francis Lieber was exploded by Conrad Henry Roehlman in *Ordeal by Concordance* (New York: Longmans Green, 1953).
2. Mary Baker Eddy, *The Church Manual* (Boston: The First Church of Christ, Scientist, 1936), pp. 17-19.

Mary Baker Eddy, founder of Christian Science

Science, and were known as "Christian Scientists."

At a meeting of the Christian Science Association, April 12, 1879, on motion of Mrs. Eddy, it was voted to organize a Church designed to commemorate the word and works of our Master, which should reinstate primitive Christianity and its lost element of healing.

Mrs. Eddy was appointed on the committee to draft the Tenets of the Mother Church—the chief cornerstone whereof is that Christian Science, as taught and demonstrated by our Master, casts out error, heals the sick, and restores the lost Israel, for "the stone which the builders rejected, the same is become the head of the corner."

The charter for the Church was obtained June, 1879 * and the same month the members, twenty-six in number, extended a call to Mary Baker Eddy to become their pastor. She accepted the call, and was ordained A.D. 1881. Although walking through deep waters, the little Church went steadily on, increasing in numbers, and at every epoch saying, "Hitherto hath the Lord helped us."

On the twenty-third day of September, 1892, at the request of Rev. Mary Baker Eddy, twelve of her students and Church members met and reorganized under her jurisdiction, the Christian Science Church and named it *The First Church of Christ, Scientist.*

At this meeting twenty others of Mrs. Eddy's students and members of her former Church were elected members of this Church—those with others that have since been elected were known as "First Members." The Church Tenets, Rules

* Steps were taken to promote the Church of Christ, Scientist, in April, May, and June; formal organization was accomplished and the charter obtained in August, 1879.

and By-laws, as prepared by Mrs. Eddy, were adopted. A By-law adopted March 17, 1903, changed the title of "First Members" to "Executive Members." (On July 8, 1908, the By-laws pertaining to "Executive Members" were repealed.)

The First Church of Christ, Scientist, in Boston, Mass., is designed to be built on the Rock Christ; even the understanding and demonstration of divine Truth, Life, and Love, healing and saving the world from sin and death; thus to reflect in some degree the Church Universal and Triumphant.

Tenets of the Mother Church, the First Church of Christ, Scientist

(to be signed by those uniting with The First Church of Christ, Scientist, in Boston, Mass.)

1. As adherents of Truth, we take the inspired Word of the Bible as our sufficient guide to eternal Life.
2. We acknowledge and adore one supreme and infinite God. We acknowledge His Son, one Christ; the Holy Ghost or divine Comforter; and man in God's image and likeness.
3. We acknowledge God's forgiveness of sin in the destruction of sin and the spiritual understanding that casts out evil as unreal. But the belief in sin is punished so long as the belief lasts.
4. We acknowledge Jesus' atonement as the evidence of divine, efficacious Love, unfolding man's unity with God through Christ Jesus the Way-shower; and we acknowledge that man is saved through Christ, through Truth, Life, and Love as demonstrated by the Galilean Prophet in healing the sick and overcoming sin and death.

5. We acknowledge that the crucifixion of Jesus and his resurrection served to uplift faith to understand eternal Life, even the allness of Soul, Spirit, and the nothingness of matter.

6. And we solemnly promise to watch, and pray for that Mind to be in us which was also in Christ Jesus; to do unto others as we would have them do unto us; and to be merciful, just, and pure.

Mary Baker Eddy.

Conversion Procedure

Qualifications for membership in the Mother Church as spelled out in Article IV of *The Church Manual* include belief in the doctrines of Christian Science in keeping with the teachings contained in *Science and Health, with Key to the Scriptures,* the official textbook of the Church authored by Mrs. Eddy. The applicant must also renounce membership in any other church or denomination. A child of twelve years is eligible for membership when his applications are countersigned by the designated students or officers of the Church.

Candidates for membership require the approval of students of Christian Science who are loyal to the teachings of the Church's official textbook. The various categories of applicants include those coming from the Christian Science College [3] and pupils of Christian Science students. Details are given in Article V of *The Church Manual.*

Articles VI and VII give the details pertaining to the recommendation and election of members and to probationary membership.

3. At present there are no living students of Mrs. Eddy's Massachusetts Metaphysical College.

The First Church of Christ, Scientist, Mother Church of
Christian Science in Boston

For membership in local branches, a prospective convert indicates his interest in Christian Science by attending regularly the Christian Science church services in his neighborhood. He then formally applies for membership according to the means established by the branch church.

The prospective convert submits his application blank to the clerk of the church. The executive board in turn informs him when he is to appear before the examining committee. If he meets the requirements of the examining committee, his name is then presented to the membership at a regular business meeting for a vote on his membership in the church.

A qualification for membership is abstinence from the use of tobacco and alcoholic beverages.

Documents

APPLICATION
I
PROPERLY SIGNED AND ENDORSED, ACCORDING TO ARTICLE V, SECT. 2

If you have been taught by a loyal student who has taken a degree at the Massachusetts Metaphysical College, or by one who has passed an examination by the Board of Education, fill this blank.

FORM 1.

The First Church of Christ, Scientist, in Boston, Mass., is designed to be built on the rock of Christ—Truth and Life—and to reflect the Church Triumphant.

One who is not a member of any church, excepting a branch church of Christ, Scientist, who loves Christian Science, and reads understandingly the Bible, and SCIENCE AND HEALTH WITH KEY TO THE SCRIPTURES, by Reverend Mary Baker Eddy, and other works by this author, and who is Christianly qualified and can enter into full fellowship with the Tenets and Rules of The First Church of Christ, Scientist, in Boston, Mass., is eligible to membership.

To The First Church of Christ, Scientist, in Boston, Mass.

............................, *Clerk.*

I hereby make application for membership, and subscribe to the Tenets and the By-Laws of the Church.

My teacher in Christian Science is

...., *C.S.D.*............

I am not a member of any church.

APPLICATION

PROPERLY SIGNED AND ENDORSED, ACCORDING TO ARTICLE V, SECT. 2

I was formerly a member of the ....

.... denomination, but have definitely severed my connection therewith.

Name ....

Street and Number ....

Town or City ....

State ....

Date ....

I cordially approve the applicant.

(*a*) ...., *C.S.D.* ....

Countersigned by ....

TO THE APPLICANT:

Please fill out the following for the use of the Treasurer of the Church:

Name ....

Street and Number ....

Town or City ....

State ....

35
Liberal Catholic Church

THE LIBERAL CATHOLIC CHURCH was organized in England in 1916 as an independent religious body. Its bishops derive their orders from the mother see of the Old Catholic movement, which is the archiepiscopal see of Utrecht in the Netherlands. The Liberal Catholic Church synthesizes the ancient form of sacramental worship, and episcopal succession with liberal thought and the use of a vernacular liturgy.[1] The layman has complete freedom of interpretation of creed, scriptures, and liturgy, but the clergymen have a great measure of discipline.[2] This body has a membership of 4,000 in the United States.[3]

Conversion Procedure

The Liberal Catholic Church welcomes to its membership all who are seeking truth, and does not require acceptance of a specific body

1. Cf. *The Liberal Catholic Church* (Statement of Principles and Table of the Apostolic Succession) (Los Angeles: The Liberal Catholic Church, 1956).
2. Cf. the Most Reverend Edward M. Mathews, *Freedom of Thought* (Los Angeles: The Liberal Catholic Church, 1959).
3. Headquarters are at 2041 N. Argyle Avenue, Los Angeles 28, California.

of doctrine. The distinctive contribution of the Liberal Catholic Church to Christian thought is this wide freedom, together with the traditional sacraments it administers.[4]

Terms of Communion

. . . The Liberal Catholic Church welcomes to its altars all who reverently and sincerely approach them. It looks upon the Christian Church as a great brotherhood of all who turn to Jesus Christ—their Master and their Friend—as the inspirer of their spiritual life. It offers the Blessed Sacrament of His love to any member of the brotherhood who reverently desires it.

Candidates are admitted to the Liberal Catholic Church by Baptism, or (if that has been duly performed) by Confirmation. If the candidate has received both Baptism and Confirmation in complete form, a simple form of admission is used, in which a blessing is invoked on the religious aspirations of the person.

The essentials of its baptismal rite are the use of water and the usual Trinitarian formula, together with the application of the Oil of Catechumens and Chrism; and those of the Confirmation rite are the imposition of the Bishop's hand with the proper formula, and the use of Chrism. When persons who wish to join the Liberal Catholic Church have received these Sacraments in a less complete form, it is usual to repeat them "conditionally." . . .

The Liberal Catholic Church is not a new sect. It is a constituent part of the One, Holy, Catholic and Apostolic Church: that historical Church which is truly One, despite its many outward divisions both in East and West, because

4. *The Liberal Catholic Church*, p. 11.

the One Life of Christ animates and sustains it through the Sacraments He instituted. The Liberal Catholic Church has preserved these Sacraments in their integrity and plenitude and believes its doctrine to be in conformity with the teachings of Christ and freed from the corruption of later ages.

It regards Christ's Church as consisting of "the blessed company of all faithful people." The different churches, whether historical or new, receive His blessings in proportion to the earnestness of their members and the extent to which they retain the Sacraments of His grace and reflect His teachings.

The Liberal Catholic Church, therefore, seeks to work in amity with all other Christian denominations. It has no wish to proselytize and welcomes all to regular and full participation in its services, without asking or expecting them to leave their own church. On the other hand, if members of other churches are attracted by the distinctive features of its work, they are welcomed. Its chief appeal is to the thousands who stand outside the existing church organizations and religious societies, and are bereft of the help they might otherwise receive. . . .

36
Jehovah's Witnesses

BASICALLY, THE WITNESSES ADHERE to no creed, but follow the Bible as a practical guide for our times. They derive their name from Isaiah 43:12, "Ye are My *Witnesses* saith *Jehovah,* and I am God." They are not an incorporated body; the incorporated Watchtower Bible and Tract Society is used for governing purposes. Witnesses accept the Virgin Birth but reject the Holy Trinity. They refuse to salute the flag of any earthly nation and, on conscientious grounds, object to participation in war or military training. This attitude has brought persecution to many of their members in different parts of the world.

Witnesses believe in baptism by immersion. They permit youths to preach. Their clergy work as volunteers, with many of them supplementing their meager stipends with secular work. These workers bring the message of the movement into the homes of people, as did Paul, teaching "publicly from house to house."

Jehovah's Witnesses reject all other religions, claiming theirs to be the only true one. This view is set forth in a leaflet entitled, *Which Is the True Religion?* [1]

1. *Which Is the True Religion?* (New York: Watchtower, undated).

Jehovah's Witnesses filled New York City's Yankee Stadium at the opening of the Divine Will International Assembly of Jehovah's Witnesses in 1958

The purpose of religion is to show man the way of salvation. Today in the United States, where "the scandal of sectarianism is at its worst," there are more than 250 religious denominations. Since all are different, not all can be right. Which one is?

Many hold it does not matter what your religion is, that the various religions are just different roads all leading to heaven or salvation. Is that view correct? How could it be when the Bible says there is just "one faith, one baptism?" —Ephesians 4:5.

In fact, the frequent contention that any religion is all right so long as one is sincere in his belief is a subtle snare, for the Bible warns: "There is a way which seemeth right unto a man; but the end thereof are the ways of death."—Proverbs 14:12.

The God of the Bible states: "Is there a God besides me? yea, there is no Rock; I know not any."—Isaiah 44:8. And Jesus said of himself: "I am the way and the truth and the life. No one comes to the Father except through me." And referring to the name of Jesus, Peter said: "There is not another name under heaven that has been given among men by which we must get saved."—John 14:6; Acts 4:12. So according to the Bible the right religion recognizes only Jehovah God and Christ Jesus.

Since many claim to worship the God of the Bible and to accept Jesus how can we determine which is the right religion? By comparing their teachings and actions with those of Christ and the apostles. "By their fruits you will recognize those men."—Matthew 7:20.

The leaflet goes on to show how the practices and doctrines of the popular religions are inconsistent with the teachings of Scripture. Held up for special criticism are mutual rivalry and enmity of the popular churches, as well as their concern about financial matters. The leaflet concludes:

> From the foregoing it is evident that the popular organized religions of Christendom have been weighed in the balances and have been found wanting. But God has not left mankind without the right religion. Today there is a body of Christians, known as Jehovah's Witnesses, who teach and practice it. First of all, they adhere strictly to the Bible and discard all tradition and worldly knowledge that conflicts with God's Word.—Isaiah 8:20; Acts 17:11.
>
> These keep on seeking first the Kingdom by obeying Jesus' command to preach the good news of the Kingdom in all the earth, doing so in more than 130 lands and isles of the sea and in upward of 100 languages, and that by every possible means, from house to house, on the streets, publicly, by use of radio and printing press.—Matthew 24:14.
>
> They keep separate from political campaigns and commercial enterprises, and because of their obedience to God's commands they are persecuted in every land. They support no man-made disgusting substitute for God's kingdom.—Matthew 24:15, 16.
>
> They show real love for one another, making no distinction because of nationality, race, social position, etc. They put God's law above man's law and so refuse to kill one another at the behest of worldly governments. Instead they are ready to die for one another. They love Jehovah with their whole heart, mind, soul and strength and their neighbor as themselves.—Acts 5:29; Mark 12:30, 31.

After considering the foregoing facts, now, honestly, which religion bears the fruits that identify it as the one right religion? Rather than its being one of the many popular, respected orthodox religions of Christendom, do not the facts say it is Jehovah's Witnesses?

Conversion Procedure

Vincent M. Ross, presiding minister of the Germantown Congregation (Philadelphia Company) of Jehovah's Witnesses,[2] discusses conversion:

The procedure of admission into our faith is outlined in both the Hebrew and Christian Greek Scriptures. You undoubtedly are familiar with the Divine procedure which brought the early nation of Israel into a covenant relationship with God. According to the Inspired scriptures at Exodus the nineteenth chapter and the seventh and eighth verses, Moses read the law after which the people upon hearing agreed to do all the things which Moses had spoken as God's mouthpiece or channel of communication.

In agreeing to perform these things they willfully dedicated their lives to from henceforth do the will of Jehovah. The account in Exodus further reveals at Exodus 24:7, 8 that after Moses read the book of the law covenant inaugurated at Sinai to the people and they agreed to perform them they entered into a covenant relationship with Jehovah. First they had to hear the words of Jehovah through his chosen channel, then they had to agree to endeavor to perform these things wholeheartedly and without reserve.

We today adhere closely to that Divine

2. Kingdom Hall, 419 Locust Avenue, Philadelphia, Pennsylvania.

precedent. Therefore before one enters into a dedicated position or covenant relationship with God he must first hear the words of God by being orally instructed, and gain an accurate knowledge of God's Will and purposes. After understanding what is required of him or her, such a one who desires to perform God's revealed will makes a personal dedication within himself to do the will of God unreservedly and unconditionally. Such a decision is a vow to God to be obedient and faithful, and it must be faithfully carried out as all vows should. Therefore it is not made hastily based on emotion or as a result of coercion. It is a decision made by the individual due to an intelligent appreciation of the responsibilities involved. See Ecclesiastes 5:2, 4–6.

After such a prayerful, sincere dedication is made it is followed by water baptism. The word baptism is from the Greek Word baptisma, meaning "to dip," "submerge, immerse." This baptism is to be performed as the meaning of the word suggests therefor. In the Christian scriptures it is associated with large bodies of water (see Matthew 3:16, Mark 1:10, John 3:23, Acts 8:36, 38, 39.) Because it is to be performed by a complete Immersion of the body under water it is likened to a burial in the Christian scriptures. (Rom. 6:4, Col. 2.12.)

This burial of the body in water is submitted to by the scripturally enlightened and dedicated individual who has come to recognize that his former course of conduct was not fully in accord with God's Will. This condition of inactivity from God's standpoint kept the individual alienated from God and from the manner of life God would have men live. Christian water baptism is an outward symbol, as a testimony before witnesses, of the dedicated one's complete, unreserved and unconditional dedication and agreement to do the will of Jehovah God, the Universal Sovereign, through his greater Moses Christ Jesus. It means his past course is buried and he is demonstrating his desire to henceforth do only God's Will.

Before the actual baptism is performed a discourse is given on the subject of dedication and baptism summarizing the significance of the occasion, the responsibilities to be thereafter borne and the proper attitude to have. After the candidates for baptism answer the questions propounded to them in the affirmative they are encouraged to be immediately baptized symbolizing their dedication before others.

The entire nation of Israel gave evidence of their dedication to God by going through the Red Sea under the cloud of the Divine presence. Because they were surrounded by water (the sea on both sides and the cloud above) this is likened to a baptism in the Christian Greek Scriptures (see 1 Corinthians 10:1, 2). This baptism was evidence of their dedication to follow the leadership of Moses.

Baptism as a symbol of one's dedication to God has its roots not only in the Christian Greek Scriptures but also in the equally inspired Hebrew text. Baptism is therefore an elementary step in the Christian's life as exemplified by Christ Jesus the founder of our faith. He also directed baptism and commanded continuance of it.

This simple yet most significant occasion is what fully admits one into brotherly association with other dedicated and ordained Ministers of our faith.

37
Spiritualist Churches

THERE ARE THREE MAJOR Spiritualist bodies in the United States: the International General Assembly of Spiritualists, organized in 1936 for the purpose of chartering Spiritualist Churches; the National Spiritual Alliance of the U.S.A., organized in 1913 with a creed of faith in the supernormal, personal, and impersonal manifestations and in intercommuniction between inhabitants of different worlds; the National Spiritualist Association of Churches, teaching Spiritualism as a science, philosophy, and religion, based upon scientifically proved communication between the worlds of the living and the dead. Total United States membership is 175,000.

Martha Feldstein, secretary of the United Spiritualists' Church [1] in New York City, affiliated with the General Assembly of Spiritualists, explains:

> Spiritualism is a Religion, Science and Philosophy. Spirit Manifestations have been experienced by all the Prophets, also by many persons on this earth plane who have had these experiences. . . . Definite personal proof is the key that opens the door for further knowledge.

1. 213 West 53rd Street, New York, N. Y. 10019.

Each one is on the path for soul progression.
Its teachings are Spiritual Natural Law—How
one can use them for one's spiritual growth and
to help humanity. . . .

Conversion Procedure

An invitation to membership distributed by this
Church lists the teachings of the Church and the
creed of Spiritualism to which Spiritualists subscribe: [2]

This Church is maintained to teach and demon-
strate the religion of Spiritualism, and to make
available the opportunity for spiritual guidance
and consolation.

If you become a member of the United Spiritualists' Church you will have the opportunity to
enjoy the understanding companionship of others
who have learned the truth of spirit communication and who are trying to live in the illumination
of Christian truth that is gained through the
clearer insight of those who have passed beyond
the limitations of this physical plane.

You will have an opportunity to share in the
development of an enterprise that will insure
continued availability of finest mediumship for
the people of New York City and of the whole
country when they visit here. In common with
other Spiritualist Churches affiliated with the
General Assembly of Spiritualists, we subscribe
to the principles as set forth by that body as
follows:

We believe in Infinite Intelligence.
We believe that the phenomena of nature,
    both physical and spiritual, are the ex-

2. United Spiritualists' Church, Rev. Edward Lester Thorne,
Pastor, 213 West 53rd Street, New York, N. Y. 10019.

pression of Infinite Intelligence.

We affirm that a correct understanding of such expression, and living in accordance therewith, constitute true religion.

We affirm that the existence and personal identity of the individual continue after the change called death.

We affirm that communication with the so-called dead is a fact scientifically proven by the phenomena of Spiritualism.

We believe that the highest morality is contained in the Golden Rule: "Whatsoever ye would that others should do unto you, do ye even so unto them."

We affirm the moral responsibility of the individual, and that he makes his own happiness or unhappiness as he obeys or disobeys nature's physical and spiritual laws.

We affirm that the doorway to reformation is never closed against any human soul, here or hereafter.

If you find it in your heart to become one of us, we ask you to subscribe to the following statement:

United Spiritualists' Church
213 West 53rd St.
New York 19, N.Y.

I hereby accept obligations of membership in the United Spiritualists' Church.

I accept substantially the foregoing statement of principles as adopted by the General Assembly of Spiritualists.

I agree to give my loyal support to the United

Spiritualists' Church in extending its value to my
fellow members and to the community.

Name ....

Address ....

....

Telephone ....

While there is no "membership fee," this Church
like all other Churches, has financial obligations
which must be met. It is supported by donations
and love offerings. Members are expected to contribute accordingly.

All Spiritualist churches are uniform in their acceptance of the basic tenets or principles as they
appear in the letter. However, each church is free
to enact its own by-laws regulating the admission of
new members. Members accept the tenets by signing
the membership form.

Rev. Edward L. Thorne, minister of the United
Spiritualists' Church, presents the quintessence of
Spiritualism in the preface to his booklet, *Development
of Mediumship:*

> We have but to open our Bible to find the
> teaching that though the body may wither and
> die, the spirit of the individual lives on forever-
> more. This beautiful truth is the basis of true
> Spiritualism.[3]

3. Rev. Edward L. Thorne, *Development of Mediumship*
(Cooksburg, N. Y.: Silvernoon Press, 1960).

38
Baha'i Faith

THE BAHA'I MOVEMENT BEGAN in Shiraz, Persia, now Iran, on May 23, 1844, with a young Persian merchant, an Islamic heretic known as the Bab ed-Din or Gate. He announced that he was the long-awaited, inspired spokesman expected by members of the Sunis, a Moslem sect, and foretold the appearance of a great world teacher who would call into being a world of peace for all mankind. Thirteen years after the martyrdom of the Bab, Baha Ullah announced his own revelation in Baghdad, now the capital of Iraq. He became the founder of a new faith; his followers were called Baha'i, or "followers of Baha Ullah."

The basic tenet of this faith is progressive revelation. It preaches that the Word of God, which once came to the religious teachers and prophets of old, was not hushed by time, but was also revealed to the Bab and Baha Ullah, who were greater than their precursors.

The Baha'i have no official ministry. Their number is estimated at 2,000,000 throughout the world. Baha'i headquarters are located in Haifa, Israel, on a majestic site on Mount Carmel overlooking the calm, blue waters of the Mediterranean. Here 504 leaders of the

Shrine of the Bab and the Archives Building, world center of the Baha'i Faith in Haifa, Israel

faithful gathered in 1964 to elect, by secret ballot, nine of their members to comprise a Universal House of Justice, which has infallible powers to legislate for the sect.

The Baha'i faith is eclectic, welcoming the basic teachings of all the great religions. Baha'is believe that no religion has a monopoly on the truth. Consequently at their simple services they read with equal devotion from the Bible, Koran, and the *Bhagavad-Gita*.

In summary, Baha'i teaches progressive revelation, the oneness of mankind under "the one God in Whom all believe," and the dawn of a new world order.

Baha'i, despite its Moslem origins, denies that it is an Oriental religion. It has members in about 250 countries, and its literature has been translated into 190 languages, giving it claim to universal status.

Baha'i Answers [1] lists the new truths that Baha'is accept in addition to the prophecies of old:

    a. Each man must investigate truth for himself without depending upon the interpretations of others.

    b. Religion must be the cause of unity and harmony.

    c. Education for youth of both sexes is compulsory and includes training for a useful art, trade or profession.

    d. National, racial and religious prejudices are specifically forbidden. Mankind is proclaimed to be one family.

    e. Peace in this age will be attained in two stages—first, through a world federation; and second, through the unity of religion.

    f. The solution of the economic problem is spiritual in nature. Since complete equality

1. *Baha'i Answers* (Wilmette, Ill.: Baha'i Publishing Trust).

is impossible, the voluntary sharing of wealth is deemed highly meritorious. The Baha'i teaching asserts that only a world economy can be effective in this age.

g. The equality of man and woman is proclaimed for the first time in religious scriptures.

h. The Baha'i Faith rests on a Covenant written by its Founder, linking this new Revelation with the Gospel and other Holy Books, provides for interpretation of Baha'i Scriptures and insures the Faith against schisms. The principles of the administrative order are set forth in the Writings of Baha Ullah Himself. They were further developed by His son, Abdul Baha (known as the Exemplar of His teachings), and enunciated in His Will and Testament. They are presently being implemented through the guidance of the first Guardian of the Baha'i Faith who resides at the World Center in Haifa, Israel.

The nine-sided Baha'i Temple in Willmette, Illinois, with the ubiquitous nine inscribed in every aspect of architecture and landscaping was built to symoblize the unity of God, His Prophets, and mankind.

The Baha'is bring the message of their faith to all by means of free literature distributed widely and by the use of other types of modern media. Since one of the basic principles of the Baha'i faith is the independent quest for truth, proselytizing is forbidden.

Conversion Procedure

Sophia A. Rieger, secretary of the Spiritual Assembly of the Baha'is of Philadelphia, Pennsylvania, dis-

Baha'i Temple, Wilmette, Illinois, center of the Baha'i
Faith in the United States

cusses the requirements of conversion to the Baha'i faith:

> We have no conversion to the Baha'i World Faith. Anyone wishing to inform themselves of the teachings of the Baha'i Faith must independently investigate the Teachings for himself and really know what the Faith requires of him, as it is not only a privilege but a responsibility to become a member of the Baha'i World Community.

Baha'i Answers has this to say:

> When a seeker is convinced that Baha Ullah is a true Revealer of God's Will, is willing to abide by His laws in his personal life and in the Baha'i community, and knows the essential teachings of the Faith and the nature of its administrative order, he informs the local Assembly of his desire to become a Baha'i. When convinced that he is sincere, the Assembly welcomes him into the world-wide Baha'i community. Youths between the ages of fifteen and twenty also may enroll. At the age of twenty-one membership includes voting rights.[2]

---

2. Further information about this faith may be secured from the National Baha'i Administrative Headquarters, 536 Sheridan Road, Wilmette, Illinois.

39
Peace Mission Movement

UNITED STATES SOIL IS fertile for the growth of sects and cults. This is especially evident in the Negro community. These sects, as that of Daddy Grace and the countless Holiness Churches presided over by male and female bishops, form in response to a deep emotional need felt by American Negroes. One such sect, the Peace Mission Movement, founded by Father Divine, has emerged and grown despite early persecution and derision. It is a successful and highly respected organization. Everyone agrees that its followers are among the most honest and scrupulous people in the community.

Conversion Procedure

Father Divine defines his teachings and outlines his position on conversion:

> . . . In reference to a conversion to MY Faith—the Christian Faith, as I hold true Judaism synonymous with Christianity, even with true Buddhism—all one needs do is to live the precepts

of his faith, and the spirit of harmonization and of sincerity within him will reveal the mystery of the WORD, and of the WORD made Flesh among men in this Fatherhood Dispensation.

The Peace Mission Movement is international, interracial, and interdenominational. It is founded on Christ's Sermon on the Mount as given in the 5th, 6th and 7th Chapters of St. Matthew in the King James Version of the Holy Bible; for this cause we are known as the Christian Religion. Nevertheless it is given: "For the law was given by Moses, but grace and truth came by Jesus Christ." (St. John 1:17)

The Gospel of St. John brings in a higher order of truth, as compared with the Synoptic Gospels, for the birth of Jesus by the Holy Ghost reveals man's true heritage in GOD. It is not after the order of mortal heritage, for He did not bear record of Himself after the flesh, but He paved out the way for all mankind to gain their mental and spiritual rebirth of consciousness in the Divine Mind.

This is it that the major prophet Isaiah declared:

> "For my thoughts are not your thoughts, neither are your ways my ways, saith the LORD."
>
> (Isaiah 55:8)

Moses also declared it saying:

> ". . . that man doth not live by bread only, but by every word that proceedeth out of the mouth of the LORD doth man live."
> (Deut. 8:3)

I do not proselyte, for I hold true that which the Word declares: "Hear, O Israel: the LORD our God is one LORD." (Deut. 6:4) The conversion I AM interested in is to convert mankind

from sin; to lift him up from the preconceptions
of the adamic consciousness that may no longer
live in lacks, wants, sickness and death, but that,
through the Mind of GOD, he may live—eternally, even in his physical body.

For this cause I AM resurrecting the consciousness of humanity, as Jesus said to Nico-
demus: "Ye must be born again." I AM giving
man that new birth of understanding—that new
birth of spiritual awakening, making the TRUTH
practical and real in his life, for even the law,
and the spirit of the law summed up in the WORD
is impractical excepting it be made tangible,
practical and personified among men.

MY Messages in The NEW DAY [1] will give
you, not merely the interpretation of the scriptures, but the fulfilling of them in this Dispensation of GOD tabernacling among men, for this is
the prophecy of Ezekiel through the Word:

> A new heart also will I give you, and a new
> spirit will I put within you: and I will take
> away the stony heart out of your flesh, and
> I will give you an heart of flesh.
> And I will put my spirit within you, and
> cause you to walk in my statutes, and ye
> shall keep my judgments, and do them.
> And ye shall dwell in the land that I gave
> to your fathers; and ye shall be my people,
> and I will be your God.
> (Ezekiel 36:26–28)

1. Father Divine's messages in *The New Day,* published in
Philadelphia, have the status of Holy Scriptures.

40
Armenian Church

THE UNITED STATES BRANCH of the Ancient Church of Armenia, established here in 1889, includes some fifty-four churches with an inclusive membership of 130,000. Local churches are under the jurisdiction of the Holy See of Etchmiadzin, Armenia, in the Soviet Union. The Armenian Church was not included in the chapter on the Eastern Orthodox Church because it rejects both the doctrine of the two natures, divine and human, of Jesus, and the decisions of the early councils of the Church. The saints and the Virgin Mary are venerated, but the Immaculate Conception is not accepted. Church doctrine is derived from the historic writings and declarations of the early Church fathers.

In considering the Armenian Church, it is worth noting that Armenia looks upon itself as the oldest Christian nation; Christianity was adopted as the state religion in the year 301.

Conversion Procedure

Rev. Garen Gdanian, pastor of St. Gregory the Illuminator Church of Armenia in New York City, discusses conversion in his Church:

. . . Conversion is simple.

a. Seek proof of the sincerity of the person to be converted by learning about his character and thoughts.

b. Teach him the fundamentals of the Christian Doctrine; and finally

c. Baptize, Confirm and give Communion to the converted person.[1]

1. More information is available at the Public Relations Department of The Armenian Church, 630 Second Avenue, New York, N. Y.

41
Ethical Culture Movement

ETHICAL CULTURE, FOUNDED BY Felix Adler in 1876, is a religious fellowship "to admit new and ever larger classes of society into inalienable bonds of right and fellowship." The unity of the fellowship is based on the conviction that ethical values are more important than creedal and doctrinal details. Members of the Ethical Societies strive for the realization of the noblest religious and moral potentialities of man in his relationship to his fellow man and to the universe. Ethical Culture teaches respect for individual differences "and for the integrity of the individual in exercising his own intellectual, moral and religious powers." Felix Adler, founder of the movement, epitomized its purpose when he declared: "Our ethical religion has its basis in the effort to improve the world and ourselves morally." The movement has a membership of 7,000.

The American Ethical Union, the national federation of Ethical Societies, in New York City,[1] published a definition of an Ethical Culture Society, a part of which is quoted below:

> Ethical Culture Societies—groups of people seeking to define, practice and extend a good life for themselves and others—are dedicated to the cultivation of ethical values in human relations.
>
> To this end they conduct Sunday Meetings for adults and Sunday Schools for children. They sponsor a wide range of educational programs, public meetings, and community projects dealing with specific problems.

1. 2 West 64th Street, New York, N. Y.

The Ethical Society occupies the place of a church or synagogue in the lives of most of its members. It differs from traditional religious bodies in that ethical concern rather than theological doctrine constitutes the basis of fellowship. Members may hold to whatever philosophical and religious views impress them as true or reasonable, so long as they recognize the Society's central concern with human relationships: a positive and constructive faith in the values and potentialities of human life in the natural universe.

The Sunday Meeting consists of readings, music and an address by a Leader or guest speaker. Addresses of a general philosophical nature are heard as well as subjects of a more specialized and concrete content, such as human relations, political ethics, civic and global affairs, war and peace, etc.

Ethical Societies engage in a wide range of community service and public affairs programs. While these activities will vary with the size, resources and interests of the local groups, even the smallest societies concern themselves with ethical issues in the life of the community, nation and world.

Conversion Procedure

Dr. Morris Wolf, director of the Philadelphia Ethical Society, points out his group's attitude on membership:

. . . We have no formal conversion procedure. Those who wish to join an Ethical Society request membership and are accepted when recommended by the Leader who previously interviews them and assures himself that they understand our Ethical fellowship and what joining it requires. . . .

42
Rosicrucian Order

T HE ROSICRUCIANS, WHO CLAIM to be "Traditionally The World's Oldest Fraternity," trace their descent from the secret mystery schools of ancient Egypt. In Rosicrucian teachings are to be found traces of wisdom from many civilizations and various philosophical schools. One can discern survivals of ancient Greek religions as well as the more recent teachings of Theosophy.

The Rosicrucians were first introduced to the United States in 1694 when a small group of members, led by Johann Kelpus, landed in Philadelphia in search of freedom of thought and organized their first colony in Philadelphia. Their descendants founded the colony of Ephrata in Pennsylvania.

Rosicrucian publications are emphatic in their claim that the Order is

> . . . kept free of religious sectarianism and affiliations, desiring rather that each member follow the dictates of his own conscience in religious matters.[1]

1. *Mastery of Life* (San Jose, Cal.: Rosicrucian Park, 1953), p. 18.

Like other religions and philosophies, Rosicrucianism deals with life and death, mystical powers, a way of life, the hereafter, and many other matters.

The Rosicrucian Order promotes a program of education in esoteric lore for self-improvement. Monographs or lessons are provided for all participants in their System of Guidance, which is conducted as a home study course. Several titles from the course of study are: "Perfecting the Physical Body"; "Intuition through Cosmic Attunement"; "How to Operate the Powers of Mind at Will"; "The Mysteries of Time and Space"; "The Development of the Inner Self"; "The Principles of the Mystical Laws"; "Rosicrucian Mystics and the Creative Power of Mind"; "Discourse on Experiments in Creating Life out of Nonliving Matter."

Members will become familiar with the setting aside of an evening of study, or "A Lodge At Home," demonstrations and simple experiments, "signs of recognition," *The Rosicrucian Digest,* a monthly magazine, and other features.

Invitations to inquiry and membership are published in numerous newspapers and periodicals throughout the country. All inquiries are followed up with letters, descriptive literature, and book lists. There is a registration fee and regular "monthly dues to be paid by members only so long as they are active members of the Order, sharing in all its manifold benefits."

Conversion Procedure

The formal steps leading to membership begin with the signing of the acceptance of invitation, statement of motive, and completed application blank forwarded with the registration fee to the supreme secretary in California.[2]

Application for
Rosicrucian Membership

The Rosicrucians invite you to unite with them in their fascinating researches, investigations, and studies of the universal laws of nature and the mysteries of life in every branch of human improvement and development.

THEREFORE . . .

You are cordially requested to submit this Questionnaire, with your personal answers, so that the Dean of Students and the Directors of Instruction may take the proper steps to admit you to Student Membership and prepare The Way for your proper place in the Rosicrucian System of personal progress and attainments.

▽

THE MEMBERSHIP COMMITTEE
of
AMORC

ACCEPTANCE OF THIS INVITATION

Please Read Very Carefully

To the Recording Secretary of the Grand Lodge of AMORC
International Jurisdiction of North, Central, and South America
British Commonwealth and Empire, France, Switzerland, Sweden, Africa
AMORC Temple, San Jose, California, U. S. A.

2. AMORC, Rosicrucian Order, Rosicrucian Park, San Jose, California.

Respected Sir:

I hereby accept your cordial invitation to unite with the Rosicrucians in their researches, studies, and individual experiments, as outlined in your literature. If I am found worthy of receiving the First Principles and private studies, I will abide by the traditional pledge made by all Neophytes, to wit:

> *"I will keep confidential all reading matter, lessons, and discourses sent to me, and will carefully examine them to determine each step I am to take in being prepared for a more practical and masterful position in Life."*

43
Religious Science Churches

T HE INTERNATIONAL ASSOCIATION of Religious Science Churches was organized in 1948 by Dr. Ernest Holmes, the founder of the movement. The present organization of the Church dates from 1954. Religious Science, as defined by Dr. Holmes,

> . . . is a correlation of the laws of Science, the opinions of Philosophy and the revelations of Religion, applied to human needs and aspirations.

Religious Science is similar to Christian Science in some ways. Like Christian Science it maintains a healing ministry with trained practitioners. It also sponsors a "Treatment Department" offering "scientific spiritual treatment, which is affirmative prayer" and similar services. It differs from Christian Science in that it permits the use of orthodox medical means in conjunction with spiritual efforts. The First Church of Religious Science in New York City maintains a twenty-four-hour-a-day Treatment Service offering "Telephone Treatments" and a full program of preaching, services, and church activities.

Conversion Procedure

Reginald C. Armor, RSc.D., general secretary of the Church, states that the membership application form is as close as they come to

> . . . requiring prospective members to state that they will adhere to what are usually designated as tenets or creeds.
>
> . . . We do have the basic teaching of Religious Science as expounded in our textbook, "The Science of Mind," and other literature and, of course, a prospective member must be familiar with this teaching. To this end an indoctrinational procedure is usually conducted embodying definite sessions of teaching the rudiments of the ideas involved in the textbook.
>
> I may say also that the affiliated churches in our organizational structure are more or less autonomous with certain binding declarations necessary for the granting of a charter. The membership indoctrination and admission differs somewhat in cases of the individual churches, but most of them follow the above described procedure.
>
> The actual admission ceremonies usually take place during a Sunday service and are conducted by the minister with the assistance of the President of the Board of Trustees, or one of the executive officers of the church taking part. . . .
>
> . . . Dual membership is permitted except in cases in connection with any of our ecclesiastical workers, such as practitioners, teachers or ministers. In these cases, only membership in our organization is permitted, either as a member of Headquarters Church or an affiliated church in the field.

Documents

APPLICATION FOR MEMBERSHIP

In The

FIRST CHURCH OF RELIGIOUS SCIENCE

New York, N.Y.

I believe that Jesus taught a way of thinking and living that is essential to man's well being, and to the creation of a society of justice and goodwill for all. Recognizing that this church of Religious Science is teaching this message of happy, healthful and successful living, I desire to become a member, and thus encourage group action toward these ideals.

Name ....

Street ....

City .... Zone ....

This Church is a duly chartered and authorized ministry of the International Association of Religious Science Churches, Inc. of Los Angeles, California.

44
Scientology

S CIENTOLOGY IS THE SUCCESSOR to Dianetics, which
became briefly popular in the United States during the 1940's. The Dissemination Secretary of
The Hubbard Association of Scientologists, founded in
1952, gives the following information about the beliefs
of the group.

The Church of Scientology Creed

We of the Church believe:
That all men of whatever race, color or
creed were created with equal rights.
That all men have inalienable rights to their
own religious practices and their performance.
That all men have inalienable rights to their
own lives.
That all men have inalienable rights to their
sanity.
That all men have inalienable rights to their
own defence.
That all men have inalienable rights to con-
ceive, choose, assist and support their own organizations, churches and governments.
That all men have inalienable rights to think
freely, to talk freely, to write freely their own
opinions and to counter or utter or write upon
the opinions of others.

That all men have inalienable rights to the creation of their own kind.

That the souls of men have the rights of men.

That the study of the mind and the healing of mentally caused ills should not be alienated from religion or condoned in non-religious fields.

And that no agency less than God has the power to suspend or set aside these rights, overtly or covertly.

And we of the Church believe:

That man is basically good.

That he is seeking to survive.

That his survival depends upon himself and upon his fellows and his attainment of brotherhood with the Universe.

And we of the Church believe that the laws of God forbid Man:

To destroy his own kind.

To destroy the sanity of another.

To destroy or enslave another's soul.

To destroy or reduce the survival of one's companions or one's group.

And we of the Church believe:

That the spirit can be saved and

That the spirit alone may save or heal the body.

Conversion Procedure

On the procedure for becoming a member of the Church of Scientology, the following information is given by the Secretary.

The term "Conversion" is not a useful or very accurate term in regard to Scientology as this implies one must reject their own native religious practice or faith or worship in order to become a Scientologist. This is not the case and some would be distressed at this idea. In order to more accurately describe what one might term conversion in Scientology we should be understood to mean that we are talking about the conversion of the materialist to an understanding of the existence and fact of their spiritual nature and the abandonment by the materialist of his belief that Man is an animal sprung from Mud. This is the only conversion which is of interest to the Scientologist or to the Church of Scientology.

The Scientology Minister seeks to bring the spiritually poor or spiritually unaware from this depth to a rich plane of awareness of his own basic goodness and immortality, through the introduction of the convert to religious experiences attainable with these exact technologies of Scientology, exactly applied.

This is a broad goal and strengthens the individual's belief in his ability to support his religious faith and practices and better understand them. It is the aim of the Scientology Missionary to return the "spiritually bankrupt" Man to his faith and belief in his own spiritual abilities. It seeks to strengthen his striving to survive as a member of a religious body. So it enhances, in its successful application, other religions.

It would be better, in the case of Scientology, to speak of Dissemination than conversion, as the communist or materialist generally neglects Scientology as an alien thing and makes himself an enemy. Dissemination of the understandings of Scientology is accomplished through

the means of encouraging all men of good will
and ability to attend Scientology functions in
ethical ways, so as to give them the experience
of applied Scientology Technology, and through
them to gain eventually the cooperation of all
men.

These may take the form of "Personal Efficiency Courses" or "Communications Courses."
They may take the form of "Co-Audits" or other
Scientology functions. These also take the form
of the usual services of the Church in the society
such as marrying, christening and performing
funeral services for those who do not have a
religious practice other than that they encounter
in Scientology.

The basic mission of Scientology is to give
Man wisdom and freedom. It is a civilizing mission, but it is also one of Individual Freedom.
Men are prisoners of themselves and only truth
can set them free. If all men were sane then
Society would be sane. It is impossible to combat
this mission and so Scientologists seldom con-
front the opposition or take it seriously. The
opposition deals with days where Scientologists
deal with eternity. No organization which can
achieve individual immortality ever worries
much about momentary hostility or racial prejudice or fleeting social problems such as these,
and Individual immortality is not only in our
grasp but is now being achieved.

Glossary

Judaism

AMIDAH—A group of nineteen benedictions (originally eighteen) in use since earliest times. This most important part of the liturgy, after the confession of faith, or the *sh'ma,* is recited three times a day, during each of the three services. The *Amidah,* traditionally called by that name among Jews adhering to the *Sephardic* rite, is popularly known as the *shmone esrai,* or "eighteen" (benedictions).

BETH DIN—A Jewish religious court of law, which is composed of a rabbi and at least two assistants who have a jurisdiction concerning Jewish law.

GER—A proselyte. The term used to apply to an alien who lived in Hebrew territory and was protected by early Hebrew law. Eventually came to refer only to converts.

GER ZEDEK—A righteous proselyte.

HALACHAH—Literally means "the going." A body of Jewish laws that govern the Jewish way of life.

KABBALAT HAMITZVOT—Acceptance of the (binding nature of the) Commandments, one of the required steps in the traditional conversion ritual.

KOHEN or COHEN—A priest. A member of a nonprofessional priesthood tracing its descent from the biblical high priest Aaron.

MIKVAH—A pool of waters used for ritual immersion and spiritual purification in accordance with Jewish law.

MINYAN—A quorum of ten adult (over the age of thirteen) males traditionally required for public worship.

MI SHEBERACH—Literally, "May He Who blessed . . . ," the opening words of the series of benedictions recited as part of the Torah reading service on Sabbaths, festivals, Mondays, and Thursdays.

MITZVAH—A commandment, precept, or good deed. The plural form is *mitzvoth.*

MOHEL—A religiously qualified person authorized to perform circumcisions in accordance with Jewish ritual.

TALMUD—The "Oral Torah." It refers to the vast range of

rabbinic literature composed and developed during the first five centuries of this era.

TORAH—"The Guide." It is the name for Hebrew Scripture. It designates in its narrower connotation the Pentateuch, or Five Books of Moses.

Roman Catholicism, Eastern Orthodox Church, Protestantism

ABJURATION—A recanting or renunciation of former heretical or erroneous beliefs required by the Roman Catholic Church of certain categories of converts.

ABSOLUTION—A Roman Catholic sacramental act performed by a priest or duly delegated cleric in the sacrament of Penance affecting a remission of sins, or releasing a sinner from censures such as excommunication. The formula "I absolve thee" is invoked. Variants of this rite are found in several other religions too.

APOSTOLIC SUCCESSION—The acceptance by the Roman Catholic, Eastern Churches, and many churches of the Anglican communion as fact and necessary for valid administration of the sacraments, of the doctrine of uninterrupted succession of bishops by successive ordinations from the Apostles.

ARMINIAN—One who adheres to the doctrines of James Arminius (1560-1609), a Dutch Protestant clergyman, consisting of five basic articles of faith:

1. Conditional election and reprobation, in contradistinction to Calvin's doctrine of absolute predestination.
2. Universal redemption (i.e., that the Atonement, the benefits of which are reserved only for believers, was made for all mankind).

3. Man must be regenerated or renewed by the Holy Spirit, which is the gift of God, in order to exercise true faith.

4. Man may resist divine grace.

5. It is possible for a recipient of divine grace to relapse, as opposed to Calvin's doctrine of the "perseverance of the saints."

Arminianism was condemned by the Synod of Dort in 1619, but it has become part of the theology of a large segment of Protestantism, notably that of the Methodists.

BANNS—The official proclamation in church of a forthcoming marriage, allowing anyone who wishes to object to the union on valid grounds, to do so.

BAPTISM—A religious ceremony of sacramental initiation in which water is applied either by means of immersion, sprinkling, or pouring. The manner of administering baptism depends on the doctrinal views of the various churches and denominations. There is also a *"conditional baptism,"* administered to a convert who has undergone a questionable form of baptism; *"baptism by desire,"* which is validated by the wish of one who earnestly desired baptism but died before it could be administered; *"baptism of blood,"* associated with martyrs who did not receive the prescribed rite.

CATECHISM—A book of instruction in the basic principles, doctrines, and practices of the Church, arranged in question and answer form used by several Church bodies (e.g. Lutherans, Anglicans, Dutch Reformed, Presbyterians, Roman Catholics) at present or during some time in the history of the Church.

CONFESSION—The act of disclosing sins to a priest (as part of the Roman Catholic sacrament of Penance) or minister (as also practiced in some churches of the Anglican Communion, and observed as a purely voluntary act among Lutherans) in order to receive sacramental absolution.

CREED—A formula or confession of religious faith which represents an authoritative summary of the essential articles of faith (e.g., The Nicene Creed, The Apostles'

Creed, the Athanasian Creed, etc.). An unqualified reference to *The Creed* usually refers to the Apostles' Creed.

DIOCESE—The district over which a bishop's jurisdiction or authority extends.

DISPENSATION—Authoritative exemption from ecclesiastical law, vows, oaths, marriage and other impediments conferred by the Church on deserving individuals at the discretion of the Church.

DOGMA—A formally proclaimed and duly authorized tenet, opinion, or doctrine of the Church.

DUNKERS—("Dippers" or Baptists). German Baptist Brethren, a denomination founded in 1708 in Germany by Alexander Mack. Many of them subsequently immigrated to the United States, settling in Pennsylvania before moving westward. Generally, the Dunkers consider nonconformity to the world as a basic principle, adhering closely to Scriptural teaching and the primitive simplicity of the Church. There are four branches of Dunkers:

1. Conservative
2. Old Order
3. Progressive
4. Seventh-day German Baptists.

EUCHARIST—The solemn ceremony of commemorating Jesus' death with the appointed emblems of bread and wine in the sacrament of the Lord's Supper.

GLOSSALALIA (or "Gift of Tongues")—This term, from a Latin root meaning "tongue" refers to the experience of the worshipper who, in a state of religious ecstasy, utters words in an exotic language which he does not understand.

GRACE—Divine favor, mercy, love, or pardon bestowed upon man. It is distinguished from Justice in that it is free and unmerited.

HERESY—A religious view, especially of one who is a member of the Church, which is opposed to the authorized doctrinal standards of that Church, and which tends to create a schism. One who entertains such a view is called a *heretic* or a *schismatic*.

HIGH CHURCH—One of two parties in the Church of England, which emphasizes the doctrine of apostolic succession and generally subscribes to a sacramental presence of Christ in the Eucharist, baptismal regeneration, and the sole validity of episcopal ordination. The layman usually identifies the High Church by its emphasis on symbols and ceremonies.

HOLY COMMUNION—The Sacrament of the Eucharist, etc.

LOW CHURCH—The second party in the Anglican Church which attaches less importance to or completely rejects the special tenets and ceremonials of the High Church.

MASS—The service or liturgy of the Eucharist; the Sacrament of the Lord's Supper; the celebration of the Holy Communion.

MILLENARIANISM (or Millenialism)—The doctrine of those who believe in the "thousand years" mentioned in Revelations XX during which holiness will reign supreme in all the world. Some believe that at that time Jesus will sit enthroned in the company of His saints.

PARISH—A local ecclesiastical unit determined by territorial boundaries, voluntary association, or the ethnic background of its members. Some or all of these factors apply to a number of religious communions including the Roman Catholic Church.

PIETISM—A religious movement in seventeenth-century Germany which sought to instill a more sincere and emotional religious feeling into a somewhat intellectualized Protestantism. (The term is sometimes used disparagingly in connection with people who are ostentatious with their religious feelings.)

RECTOR—In the Church of England a Rector is the clergyman in charge of a parish, with jurisdiction over the tithes. In the Protestant Episcopal Communion, he is a clergyman elected by the members of a parish, with permanent tenure as official head of the parish and its affiliate organizations. A Rector in the Roman Catholic Church is the head or superior officer of a religious institution, such as a convent (among the Jesuits he is the head of an educational institution).

SACRAMENT—A solemn religious ordinance or ceremony re-

quired by the Church as an outward and visible sign of
an inward and spiritual grace. The number of sacraments and the significance attached to them varies from
one Church to another.

SALVATION—Redemption or deliverance from sin and eternal death.

SCHISM—A division in the Church.

Islam

FATIHA—A basic Moslem prayer, which is the first sura
of the Koran.

HADITH—Oral traditions about the sayings and customs of
the prophet Mohammed and his followers.

HAJJ—The pilgrimage to Mecca that all Moslems are obligated to make at least once in their lifetime.

HEGIRA—The flight of Mohammed from Mecca in 622 A.D.
It marks the beginning of the Moslem calendar. (From
the Arabic *hejirah,* "flight.")

IMAM—One who leads the prayers in a mosque.

KAABA—The principal shrine of Islam in Mecca. It houses
a sacred black stone. (From the Arabic *ka'bah,* "square
building.")

KORAN ALSO: QURAN, QORAN—The Moslem bible written
by Mohammed from revelations by Allah. (From the
Arabic *qara'a,* "to read.")

MUEZZIN—A Moslem crier who, from the minaret of the
mosque, calls the faithful to worship.

MUFTI—An Islamic religious judge who interprets Islamic
law.

RAMADAN—A fast observed from sunrise to sunset during
the Moslems' sacred month.

SALAT—A ritual prayer that Moslems make five times a day.

SCHOOLS OF MOSLEM JURISPRUDENCE: HANAFI, SHAF'I,
HANBALI, MALIKI—Different schools for the interpretation
of Islamic laws arose within Islam. The major "Sunna"
schools are four. They are: the *Hanafi, Shafi'a, Hanbali,*
and *Maliki* schools. Their differences, however, are not

theological, and they cannot be considered religious "sects."

SHAHADA—The Moslem profession of faith. "There is no god but God; Mohammed is the prophet of God." (From the Arabic *shāhada,* "to see.")

SUFI—The *Sufi,* or Moslem mystics, do not form an Islamic "sect." A Sufi wants to remain in the world and serve humanity while being above worldliness. Some Sufis believe that, through contemplation, ecstasy, and sublimation of human instincts, they may reach a sort of union with God. The Moslem Sufi literature is a very rich one. Some of the Sufis, writing in Persian, Arabic, and Urdu, have contributed some of the world's masterpieces of literature.

SUNNI AND SHI'A—In the early days of Islam, the problem of succession to Mohammed as a secular leader in the community centered around the issue of whether succession should be elective or hereditary. Those who favored elective succession were called the *Sunni,* or the "traditionalists"; those who favored hereditary succession, through his daughter Fatima, were called partisans, or *Shi'a.* This political division was complicated later, but it is the origin of the two major branches, sometimes called *sects,* in Islam today. The Shi'a are now dominant in Iran; the Sunni, in almost all other Moslem countries.

SURA—A chapter or section of the Koran. (From the Arabic *surah,* "row.")

ZAKAT—A yearly alms tax expected of Moslems as a religious duty. It is used for charitable causes.

Indian and Far Eastern Religions

AGAMAS—The Sacred Scriptures of Jainism.

AHRIMAN—The Zoroastrian "Prince of Darkness" and spirit

of evil who is the implacable opponent of *Ahura Mazda*.

AHURA MAZDA (*or Mazd*)—The "Prince of Light," the supreme deity, power of good, creator of the world, and guardian of mankind which he created to aid him in his ceaseless war against evil (*Ahriman*), in the dualistic theology of Zoroastrianism.

BHAGAVAD GITA—"The Song of the Exalted One." A popular Hindu scriptural treatise, dating from about the second or third centuries of this era, which is a valuable source of Indian pantheistic philosophy. It supports the Karma Yoga doctrine of action (as opposed to the passive doctrine of Patanjali Yoga), which seeks emancipation from the world by means of intellectual insight into the illusory character of things and actions holding "doing" and "refraining from doing" as being equally harmless.

BODHISATTVA (also *Bodhisat or Bodhisattwa*)—Buddist term for highest degree of saintship reached by "the enlightened one." This person, who is capable of self-sacrifice for others, will, in the next incarnation, emerge as a Buddha—a savior of the world.

BRAHMANISM—A later development of the primitive Vedic religion of India's Aryan invaders, noted for pantheistic conceptions and the view that extinction of desire is a means to blessedness. It was also responsible for the caste system, now almost extinct. A triune godhead consisting of Brahma, Vishnu, and Siva is the object of Brahman veneration.

    a. Brahma: The Source of Life
    b. Vishnu: The Preserver
    c. Siva: The Destroyer
    d. Krishna: The incarnation of Vishnu as presented in the Bhagavad Gita.

DASTUR—The title of a Zoroastrian priest.

GATHAS—Poems containing instructions of Zoroaster, the founder of the religion bearing his name.

HINAYANA—Sanskrit for "little or lesser vehicle," referring to the Buddhism of southern India, the essential distinguishing characteristic of which is the reservation of salvation for a select minority. The schism between this group and the Mahayana (see below) dates from the Council of Jullundur called by Kanishka in the year 40 of our era.

KAMI—Shinto gods who are the spirits of the dead elected to rule the world. "The Way of the Kami" is a popular Japanese description of Shintoism.

KARMA (or *Kharma*)—Buddhism's doctrine of moral causal sequence resulting from the continuous action of every word, thought, or deed throughout eternity. It represents the entire ethical consequence of a person's deeds as a projection of one's lot in his future existence. It is currently interpreted in Hinduism in terms of social service.

MAHAYANA—Sanskrit for "Greater Vehicle," the Buddhism of northern India which maintains that salvation is open to all.

NIRVANA—Key Buddhist concept relating to the ultimate emancipation of the soul from transmigration, introducing a beatific freedom from worldly evils through annihilation or by absorption into the divine.

SANGHA—A large body of Buddhist monks and nuns practicing celibacy, nonviolence, and poverty.

SANNYASINS—Large groups of Hindu monks dedicated to a mendicant life.

SATORI—Japanese Zen Buddhist term for "enlightenment," similar to *Nirvana.*

SWAMI—A Hindu religious leader.

UPANISHADS—Hindu religious treatises, part of the Vedic literature, the earliest of which dates from the sixth century, B.C. Hinduism derives much of its philosophy from them. These writings examine the nature of man and the universe from a pantheistic viewpoint. They accept the doctrines of transmigration and the emanation of creation from the "world soul" comprising in its essence all individual souls.

VEDA—The most ancient Hindu religious scriptures, comprising over one hundred books, subdivided into four groupings: *Rig-Veda* (the oldest and most important class), the *Yajur-Veda,* the *Sama-Veda,* and the *Atharva-Veda.*

VEDANTA—A Hindu school of pantheistic philosophy, deriving its name from its emphasis on the investigation of the latter part of the *Vedas* to which was eventually ascribed the ultimate aim of the *Vedas.*

YASNA—The Zoroastrian Prayer Book.

ZEND AVESTA—The sacred writings of Zoroastrianism.

Other Denominations, Beliefs, and Philosophies

BAHA'I—Followers of Baha Ullah, founder of the movement by that name, with headquarters in Haifa, Israel.

CHRISTIAN SCIENCE—The system of healing of body and mind, founded by Rev. Mary Baker Eddy, based on the belief that all cause and effect is mental, and that a full understanding of the Divine Principles of Jesus' teaching and healing will destroy sin, sickness, and death.

DIANETICS (or *Dianoetic*)—Logic related with the reasoning or conceptual faculties, and associated with the name of Sir William Hamilton.

ECLECTIC—Choosing opinions and doctrines from many sources or systems.

HUMANISM—A system or attitude of thought and action centering on human interests and ideals in contradistinction to naturalistic as well as religious interests.

MEDIUM—A person who claims to be the recipient of messages from the spirit world.

PROGRESSIVE REVELATION—The doctrine holding that divine revelation is continuous and did not end with one particular prophet or in one specific era.

SPIRITUALISM—The belief that departed spirits communicate with mortals by means of physical phenomena (e.g. rapping) during special mental states, as in trances, commonly manifested through a medium.

THEOSOPHY—A system of philosophy or mysticism which seeks to obtain a direct, as distinguished from a revealed, knowledge of God, by means of extraordinary illumination. Traces of theosophical views are to be found in several of the Indian and oriental religions.

UNITARIANISM—Denial of the doctrine of the Trinity, belief that God exists only in one person, and affirmation of the right of private judgment in theological matters.

Index

Index